REVISION WORKBOOK

Succession:
THE LAW OF WILLS AND ESTATES

Third Edition

EDITOR: VEENA KANDA ROVATI
LLB, MA (Business Law), Barrister

OLD BAILEY PRESS

OLD BAILEY PRESS
at Holborn College, Woolwich Road,
Charlton, London, SE7 8LN

First published 1997
Third edition 2002

ISBN 1 85836 469 8

British Library Cataloguing-in-Publication.

A CIP Catalogue record for this book is available from the British
Library.

Printed and bound in Great Britain.

Acknowledgement

Some questions used are taken or adapted from past University of London LLB (External) Degree examination papers and our thanks are extended to the University of London for their kind permission to use and publish the questions.

Caveat

The answers given are not approved or sanctioned by the University of London and are entirely our responsibility.

They are not intended as 'Model Answers', but rather as Suggested Solutions.

The answers have two fundamental purposes, namely:

a) to provide a detailed example of a suggested solution to an examination question; and

b) to assist students with their research into the subject and to further their understanding and appreciation of the subject.

Introduction

This Revision WorkBook has been designed specifically for those studying succession law to undergraduate level. Its coverage is not confined to any one syllabus, but embraces all the major succession law topics to be found in university examinations.

Each chapter contains a brief introduction explaining the scope and overall content of the topic covered in that chapter. There follows, in each case, a list of key points which will assist the student in studying and memorising essential material with which the student should be familiar in order to fully understand the topic.

Additionally in each chapter there is a key cases and statutes section which lists the most relevant cases and statutory provisions applicable to the topic in question. These are intended as an aid to revision, providing the student with a concise list of materials from which to begin revision.

Each chapter ends with several typical examination questions, together with general comments, skeleton solutions and suggested solutions. Wherever possible, the questions are drawn from University of London external succession law papers, with recent questions being included where possible. However, it is inevitable that, in compiling a list of questions by topic order rather than chronologically, not only do the same questions crop up over and over again in different guises, but there are gaps where questions have never been set at all.

Undoubtedly, the main feature of this Revision WorkBook is the inclusion of as many past examination questions as possible. While the use of past questions as a revision aid is certainly not new, it is hoped that the combination of actual past questions from the University of London LLB external course and specially written questions, where there are gaps in examination coverage, will be of assistance to students in achieving a thorough and systematic revision of the subject.

Careful use of the Revision WorkBook should enhance the student's understanding of succession law and, hopefully, enable you to deal with as wide a range of subject matter as anyone might find in a succession law examination, while at the same time allowing you to practise examination techniques while working through the book.

Studying Succession Law

Memorising

Some students will find that statutes need not be memorised as they may be taken into the examination, while the less fortunate will have to commit some statutory provisions to memory. Other course material must be learnt thoroughly. You should be familiar with the following statutory provisions, not all of which will be in the statutory material permitted in the examination.

Rules 20 and 22 NCPR 1987 for priority for obtaining a grant of letters of administration;

Section 46 AEA 1925 for priority of interests on intestacy;

Section 34(3) and Part II First Schedule to AEA 1925 for the order of payment of debts in a solvent estate;

Insolvency Act 1980 and AIEDP Order 51 No 1999 for order of payment of debts in an insolvent estate.

Problem questions

Every fact in a problem is relevant and should be discussed with reference to the law pertaining to it. Very occasionally a fact which has a bearing on an answer will be omitted, and this should be commented upon. Practice at answering problems is vital. Reading past examination papers and suggested solutions will give a good idea as to technique.

Essay questions

A good essay technique and fluency on paper are required. As to the former, the student should plan his answer carefully and use the course material to answer the question. This will rarely ask him to write all he knows about a topic. It is more likely to ask him to discuss a statement or critically examine a topic. As to the latter, reading suggested solutions and practising writing answers will help. If English is not the student's first language, he should aim to read novels and a quality newspaper on a daily basis.

Cases

Names of cases should be memorised. They should not be listed but quoted as authority for a point of law. If the law is unclear because cases conflict, the student should say so. In these circumstances, the status of the case should be stated, and whether it has been approved or disapproved by a later decision.

For a list of cases relevant to succession law, see the Table of Cases.

Statutes

The student must be thoroughly appraised of the contents and citations of all relevant statutes. Take, for instance, s9 Wills Act 1837 in Chapter 1: The Formal Requirements for Making a Will. The student will not need to write out the whole section in the examination in a question on this topic. However, he will need to know that the formal requirements for making a will are laid down by s9 and say so; and he must know exactly what the formal requirements are, and discuss them.

Where the law has been changed by the Administration of Justice Act 1982 and the Law Reform (Succession) Act 1995, it is important to know the law as it was before the Act as well as the new law.

For a list of statutes relevant to succession law, see the Table of Statutes.

Revision and Examination Technique

Revision Technique

Planning a revision timetable

In planning your revision timetable make sure you do not finish the syllabus too early. You should avoid leaving revision so late that you have to 'cram' – but constant revision of the same topic leads to stagnation.

Plan ahead, however, and try to make your plans increasingly detailed as you approach the examination date.

Allocate enough time for each topic to be studied. But note that it is better to devise a realistic timetable, to which you have a reasonable chance of keeping, rather than a wildly optimistic schedule which you will probably abandon at the first opportunity!

The syllabus and its topics

One of your first tasks when you began your course was to ensure that you thoroughly understood your syllabus. Check now to see if you can write down the topics it comprises from memory. You will see that the chapters of this WorkBook are each devoted to a syllabus topic. This will help you decide which are the key chapters relative to your revision programme, though you should allow some time for glancing through the other chapters.

The topic and its key points

Again working from memory, analyse what you consider to be the key points of any topic that you have selected for particular revision. Seeing what you can recall, unaided, will help you to understand and firmly memorise the concepts involved.

Using the WorkBook

Relevant questions are provided for each topic in this book. Naturally, as typical examples of examination questions, they do not normally relate to one topic only. But the questions in each chapter will relate to the subject matter of the chapter to a degree. You can choose your method of consulting the questions and solutions, but here are some suggestions (strategies 1–3). Each of them pre-supposes that you have read through the author's notes on key points and key cases and statutes, and any other preliminary matter, at the beginning of the chapter. Once again, you now need to practise working from memory, for that is the challenge you are preparing yourself for. As a rule of procedure constantly test yourself once revision starts, both orally and in writing.

Strategy 1

Strategy 1 is planned for the purpose of quick revision. First read your chosen question carefully and then jot down in abbreviated notes what you consider to be the main points at issue. Similarly, note the cases and statutes that occur to you as being relevant for citation purposes. Allow yourself sufficient time to cover what you feel to be relevant. Then study the author's skeleton solution and skim-read the suggested solution to see how they compare with your notes. When comparing consider carefully what the author has included (and concluded) and see whether that agrees with what you have written. Consider the points of variation also. Have you recognised the key issues? How relevant have you been? It is possible, of course, that you have referred to a recent case that is relevant, but which had not been reported when the WorkBook was prepared.

Strategy 2

Strategy 2 requires a nucleus of three hours in which to practise writing a set of examination answers in a limited time-span.

Select a number of questions (as many as are normally set in your subject in the examination you are studying for), each from a different chapter in the WorkBook, without consulting the solutions. Find a place to write where you will not be disturbed and try to arrange not to be interrupted for three hours. Write your solutions in the time allowed, noting any time needed to make up if you are interrupted.

After a rest, compare your answers with the suggested solutions in the WorkBook. There will be considerable variation in style, of course, but the bare facts should not be too dissimilar. Evaluate your answer critically. Be 'searching', but develop a positive approach to deciding how you would tackle each question on another occasion.

Strategy 3

You are unlikely to be able to do more than one three hour examination, but occasionally set yourself a single question. Vary the 'time allowed' by imagining it to be one of the questions that you must answer in three hours and allow yourself a limited preparation and writing time. Try one question that you feel to be difficult and an easier question on another occasion, for example.

Misuse of suggested solutions

Don't try to learn by rote. In particular, don't try to reproduce the suggested solutions by heart. Learn to express the basic concepts in your own words.

Keeping up-to-date

Keep up-to-date. While examiners do not require familiarity with changes in the law during the three months prior to the examination, it obviously creates a good impression if you can show you are acquainted with any recent changes. Make a habit of looking through one of the leading journals – *Modern Law Review*, *Law Quarterly Review* or the *New Law Journal*, for example – and cumulative indices to law reports, such as the *All England Law Reports* or *Weekly Law Reports*, or indeed the daily law reports in *The Times*. The *Law Society's Gazette* and the *Legal Executive Journal* are helpful sources, plus any specialist journal(s) for the subject you are studying.

Examination Skills

Examiners are human too!

The process of answering an examination question involves a communication between you and the person who set it. If you were speaking face to face with the person, you would choose your verbal points and arguments carefully in your reply. When writing, it is all too easy to forget the human being who is awaiting the reply and simply write out what one knows in the area of the subject! Bear in mind it is a person whose question you are responding to, throughout your essay. This will help you to avoid being irrelevant or long-winded.

The essay question

Candidates are sometimes tempted to choose to answer essay questions because they 'seem' easier. But the examiner is looking for thoughtful work and will not give good marks for superficial answers.

The essay-type of question may be either purely factual, in asking you to explain the meaning of a certain doctrine or principle, or it may ask you to discuss a certain proposition, usually derived from a quotation. In either case, the approach to the answer is the same. A clear programme must be devised to give the examiner the meaning or significance of the doctrine, principle or proposition and its origin in common law, equity or statute, and cases which illustrate its application to the branch of law concerned. Essay questions offer a good way to obtain marks if you have thought carefully about a topic, since it is up to you to impose the structure (unlike the problem questions where the problem imposes its own structure). You are then free to speculate and show imagination.

The problem question

The problem-type question requires a different approach. You may well be asked to advise a client or merely discuss the problems raised in the question. In either case, the most important factor is to take great care in reading the question. By its nature, the question will be longer than the essay-type question and you will have a number of facts to digest. Time spent in analysing the question may well save time later, when you are endeavouring to impress on the examiner the considerable extent of your basic legal knowledge. The quantity of knowledge is itself a trap and you must always keep within the boundaries of the question in hand. It is very tempting to show the examiner the extent of your knowledge of your subject, but if this is outside the question, it is time lost and no marks earned. It is inevitable that some areas which you have studied and revised will not be the subject of questions, but under no circumstances attempt to adapt a question to a stronger area of knowledge at the expense of relevance.

When you are satisfied that you have grasped the full significance of the problem-type question, set out the fundamental principles involved.

You will then go on to identify the fundamental problem (or problems) posed by the question. This should be followed by a consideration of the law which is relevant to the problem. The source of the law, together with the cases which will be of assistance in solving the problem, must then be considered in detail.

Very good problem questions are quite likely to have alternative answers, and in advising a party you should be aware that alternative arguments may be available. Each stage of your answer, in this case, will be based on the argument or arguments considered in the previous stage, forming a conditional sequence.

If, however, you only identify one fundamental problem, do not waste time worrying that you cannot think of an alternative – there may very well be only that one answer.

The examiner will then wish to see how you use your legal knowledge to formulate a case and how you apply that formula to the problem which is the subject of the question. It is this positive approach which can make answering a problem question a high mark earner for the student who has fully understood the question and clearly argued their case on the established law.

Examination checklist

a) Read the instructions at the head of the examination carefully. While last-minute changes are unlikely – such as the introduction of a compulsory question or an increase in the number of questions asked – it has been known to happen.

b) Read the questions carefully. Analyse problem questions – work out what the examiner wants.

c) Plan your answer before you start to write.

d) Check that you understand the rubric before you start to write. Do not 'discuss', for example, if you are specifically asked to 'compare and contrast'.

e) Answer the correct number of questions. If you fail to answer one out of four questions set you lose 25 per cent of your marks!

Style and structure

Try to be clear and concise. Fundamentally this amounts to using paragraphs to denote the sections of your essay, and writing simple, straightforward sentences as much as possible. The sentence you have just read has 22 words – when a sentence reaches 50 words it becomes difficult for a reader to follow.

Do not be inhibited by the word 'structure' (traditionally defined as giving an essay a beginning, a middle and an end). A good structure will be the natural consequence of setting out your arguments and the supporting evidence in a logical order. Set the scene briefly in your opening paragraph. Provide a clear conclusion in your final paragraph.

Table of Cases

Table of Statutes

Chapter 1

The Formal Requirements for Making a Will

1.1   Introduction

1.2   Key points

1.3   Key cases and statute

1.4   Questions and suggested solutions

1.1 Introduction

It is essential that this chapter be mastered thoroughly. Section 9 of the Wills Act 1837 specifies all the formalities necessary for the execution of a valid will. This chapter is not very complex but errors are often made in the examination on the very basic rules. A wide range of cases must be studied.

1.2 Key points

a) Section 9 Wills Act 1837.

b) The will must be in writing: includes typing, printing in any language/code (see, eg, *Re Berger* [1990] Ch 118), on any material, but preferably on material which can be photocopied.

c) Must be signed by testator or someone in his presence and at his direction.

   i)   The 'signature' need not literally be the testator's signature, so long as it is some mark which the testator intends to be his signature: *In the Estate of Finn* (1935) 52 TLR 153.

   ii)   Half signature is sufficient where the testator is too ill to do more: *In the Goods of Chalcraft* [1948] P 222.

   iii) The testator need not even sign his name: *In the Estate of Cook* [1960] 1 All ER 689.

d) Must appear that testator intended by his signature to give effect to the will – signature need not be at end of will, or precede writing of substantive provisions if writing and signing all one operation: *Wood & Another* v *Smith & Another* [1992] 3 All ER 556; see also *Weatherhill* v *Pearce* [1995] 2 All ER 492 and Chapter 4: Animus Testandi.

e) Signature must be made or acknowledged by testator in presence of two or more witnesses present at the same time: *Re Colling* [1922] 1 WLR 1440.

   i) If the testator signs the will, the witnesses must see the act of signing: *Brown* v *Skirrow* [1902] P 3; *Smith* v *Smith* (1866) LR 1 P & D 143.

   ii) If the testator acknowledged his signature, the witnesses must see or have the opportunity to see his signature: *Re Groffman* [1969] 1 WLR 733.

   iii) Acknowledgement may be expressed or implied: *Daintree* v *Butcher* (1888) 13 PD 102 (CA).

f) Each witness must either attest and sign the will or acknowledge his signature in the presence of the testator, and testator must be able to see witnesses sign: *Casson* v *Dade* (1781) 1 Bro 99; 28 ER 1010.

   i) Witnesses must sign or acknowledge their signature in the testator's physical and mental presence: *In the Goods of Chalcraft* [1948] P 222; see also *Couser* v *Couser* [1996] 3 All ER 256.

   ii) But not necessarily be in each other's presence: *In b Webb* (1855) Dea & Sw 1.

g) No form of attestation is necessary, but desirable as raises presumption of due execution.

h) Note also cases on the issue of professional negligence: *White* v *Jones* [1995] 1 All ER 691 (HL); *Smith* v *Claremont Haynes & Co* (1991) The Times 3 September; *Kecskemeti* v *Rubens Rabin* (1992) The Times 31 December; *Welby and Another* v *Caswell* (1995) The Times 18 April; *Worby and Others* v *Rosser* (1999) The Times 9 June; *Horsfall and Another* v *Haywards (A Firm)* [1999] 1 FLR 1182.

i) Section 7 of the 1837 Act – testator must not be under 18 – but see Chapter 2: Privileged and Mutual Wills.

j) Section 15 of the 1837 Act – where a beneficiary or the spouse of a beneficiary, signs the will as a witness, any gift to the beneficiary under the will is void. Section 1 of the Wills Act 1968 now provides that s15 does not apply where there are at least two supernumerary witnesses.

1.3 Key cases and statute

* *Brown* v *Skirrow* [1902] P 3
  Witnesses must be mentally and physically present when the testator signs the will

* *Clarke, In b* (1839) 2 Curt 339
  A person who signs on behalf of the testator can sign either the testator's name or his own

- *Couser* v *Couser* [1996] 3 All ER 256
  The witnesses must sign or acknowledge their signatures in the mental and physical presence of the testator

- *Daintree* v *Butcher* (1888) 13 PD 102
  The acknowledgement of the signature may be expressed or by gesture

- *Flinn, In b* [1935] LJP 36
  A thumbprint was considered sufficient signature

- *Fulton* v *Kee* [1961] NI 1
  The testator's hand may be guided in signing if he is ill or blind

- *Glover, In b* (1847) 11 Jur 1022
  The testator may sign an assumed name

- *Groffman, Re* [1969] 1 WLR 733
  The will must be signed or acknowledged in the presence of both witnesses present at the same time and they must see, or have the opportunity to see, the signature

- *Kell* v *Charmer* (1856) 23 Beav 195
  Bequests written in code are also admissible

- *Savory, In b* (1851) 15 Jur 1042
  The testator may sign using his initials

- *Weatherhill* v *Pearce* [1995] 2 All ER 492
  The name of the testatrix written by her in the body of the attestation clause was held to be sufficient signature

- *Whiting* v *Turner* (1903) 89 LT 71
  A will may be written in any language

- *Wood* v *Smith* [1992] 3 All ER 556
  The position of the testator's signature is immaterial so long as he intends to give effect to the will – a signature at the beginning of the will was valid as the testator had been found to have written the will as part of one single operation

- Wills Act 1837 (as amended by the Administration of Justice Act 1982) – s9 provides the formalities necessary for the proper execution of the will

1.4 Questions and suggested solutions

QUESTION ONE

Ian and Jenny have lived together for many years but have never married. They have a daughter, Karen, aged 15. Ian decides to make a will in which he leaves all of his property to Jenny. When he has written it out, he signs it 'Dad' at the bottom of the will (he is often called 'Dad' by Jenny and Karen). He shows the will to Karen and asks her to sign it. When she has done so he asks his neighbour, Len, to come round.

When Len arrives Karen shows him the will in Ian's presence, points to her signature and says, 'look, I have signed it'. Ian then states that it is his will and that he would like Len to sign it. Len does so. Karen and Ian are present throughout.

A few weeks later Ian and Jenny get married. At the reception following the wedding Ian produces his will, alters it by making a small cash gift to Karen, and writes at the bottom 'At last Jenny is Ian's wife'. All this is witnessed by two wedding guests, Louise and Mark, who add their signatures to the will at Ian's request.

Ian has recently died leaving a large estate.

Advise Jenny and Karen.

University of London LLB Examination
(for External Students) Succession June 1998 Q4

General Comment

This question is deceptively short but actually requires a discussion of various areas of law. Most students would have missed the fact that one of the witnesses is only aged 15. Another important point students should note is the chronological sequence of events highlighted in *Couser* v *Couser*.

Skeleton Solution

Section 9 formalities – capacity of witness – revocation – alteration – revival – s15 Wills Act 1837.

Suggested Solution

Jenny and Karen would wish to know whether Ian's will is valid, and if so, whether they are entitled under it.

For a will to be valid, s9 of the Wills Act 1837 must have been complied with. Section 9(a) states that the will must be in writing (which it is) and signed by the testator. The attitude of the courts has been somewhat relaxed in that any mark intended by the testator as his signature is sufficient. Ian had signed the word 'Dad'. Following *Re Cook* [1960] 1 WLR 138, so long as the word 'Dad' was meant to represent Ian's signature, it will be accepted as such. Ian must intend the word to represent his signature as he is referred to as 'Dad' by both Jenny and Karen.

The facts indicate that Ian intends his signature to give effect to the will: s9(b).

According to ss9(c) and (d), the testator must sign or acknowledge their signature in the presence of at least two witnesses and the witnesses must then sign or acknowledge their signatures in the presence of the testator.

In showing the will to Karen, Ian has acknowledged his signature. Witnesses must be mentally and physically present during acknowledgment, and they must either see or have had the opportunity to see the signature: *Daintree* v *Butcher* (1888) 13 PD 102.

However, the acknowledgment is invalid at this stage as it was only carried out in front of one witness.

Karen signed the will before the second witness, Len, arrived. However, Ian did state that it is his will in front of both witnesses present at the same time and Karen is allowed to acknowledge her signature to the testator under s9(d) (as amended by the Administration of Justice Act 1982), which she did by her words accompanied by her pointing to her signature. Len signed his name after all this.

In essence ss9(c) and (d) have been complied with but the will may still be invalid as the chronological order of ss9(c) and (d) have not been followed: *Couser* v *Couser* [1996] 3 All ER 256. Karen appeared to have acknowledged her signature to Ian before Ian acknowledged his signature to both witnesses.

Assuming the will is valid, the next issue is whether Karen, who is aged 15, is a capable witness. There is no minimum age to be a witness and so long as Karen is aware of her actions and the effect of the will, she qualifies as a witness. According to *Hudson* v *Parker* (1844) 1 Rob Ecc 14, witnesses should see and be conscious of the act done and be able to prove it by their own evidence.

Ian's marriage to Jenny would automatically revoke his will according to s18(1) of the Wills Act 1837. However, at the reception, Ian made an alteration to the will which was validly executed following s21 of the 1837 Act.

On the other hand, as the will was revoked by the marriage, it may be more accurate to say that Ian had attempted to revive the will at the reception via re-execution of the revoked will. The effect is that the will is deemed to have been made at the time of the revival: s34 of the Wills Act 1837.

Karen was made a beneficiary under the revived will. Section 15 of the Wills Act 1837 does not apply here and she would not lose her gift as she was a witness to the revoked will, not the revived one.

QUESTION TWO

Explain the purpose of s9 of the Wills Act 1837 (ie as amended by s17 Administration of Justice Act 1982). To what extent do you consider that s9 needs amendment?

University of London LLB Examination
(for External Students) Succession June 1993 Q1

General Comment

This type of reform question often appears and is rarely attempted by students. If prepared in advance, it is an excellent question to attempt, with very defined issues to be discussed.

Skeleton Solution

The original reasons for s9 – what was the original section? – the first amendment – cases on the continuing injustices – the Administration of Justice Act 1982 – still problems – a new court discretion to dispense with formality when it has broken down – critical view of today's procedure.

Suggested Solution

The purpose of s9 of the Wills Act 1837 was to establish uniform requirements for all wills, and to provide formalities for wills to prevent false wills, forgeries and fraud, thus rendering titles certain and secure. Only the documents intended to have dispositive effect would be admitted to probate, and thus loose statements or draft documents would not be considered as a will. The strict requirements of s9 would ensure that there was strong and reliable evidence as to the testator's wishes. It was also thought that the section would cut down the scope for undue influence on the testator, and ensure that he had knowledge and approval of the contents of the will. Thus, knowledge and approval of the will is not presumed in cases where the will is in the handwriting of another who benefits by that will, as such a situation is described in law as 'suspicious circumstances'. Neither is it presumed where the testator is blind or illiterate. It was also considered that such a document so drawn up and executed in accordance with the formalities of the section would invariably be treated as a testamentary document and not as an inter vivos disposition of property.

Originally the section provided that the written document should be signed at the foot or end in the presence of at least two witnesses present at the same time and who would attest the will in the presence of the testator.

Because of the extremely strict interpretation by the courts of what was the 'foot or end' of the will the law was amended by the Wills Act Amendment Act 1852 so as to allow a certain leeway to the courts in deciding what the testator intended to be the 'foot or end'.

An example of this is *In the Goods of Hornby* [1946] P 171 where the testator ruled an oblong box half way down the page before he commenced writing the will, and this was held, when he executed the will by signing in the box, to be the 'end' of the will according to his intention.

This case should be contrasted with *Re Stalman* (1931) 145 LT 339 where the testator wrote his will on a single page which was filled with writing to the bottom, so that there was no room for the signature, so he signed it in the top right-hand corner. The Court of Appeal refused to admit the will to probate, relying on s1 of the Wills Act Amendment Act 1852 and Lord Hanworth said in his judgment 'Although the section gives a wide geographical liberty as to where the signature should be placed, the liberty does not go so far as to say that the signature could be placed at the beginning'. He further pointed out that there was in the section a prohibition that words following the signature cannot be operative.

There were a number of cases under the old law where a testator's intentions were defeated on a technicality and in 1982 s17 of the Administration of Justice Act amended the section by replacing it with one which was substantially the same save for two major innovations. The first provided that instead of having to sign at the 'foot or end' of the will it satisfied the requirements in this respect if 'it appears that the testator intended by his signature to give effect to the will'. Furthermore a witness 'may, either attest and sign the will or acknowledge his signature in the presence of the testator but not necessarily in the presence of any other witness'. So, for the first time acknowledgment by a witness was permitted. This had been permitted previously, of course, in the case of testators but not witnesses. This has been upheld by recent case law in *Couser* v *Couser* [1996] 3 All ER 256.

Although this change is a definite improvement, the signing and alteration of a will is still a technical matter and the non-lawyer can easily be caught out, so that his intentions are defeated, beneficiaries may be disappointed and an injustice done. So the question of further amendment presents itself.

One possibility is to retain the present formalities but to provide machinery whereby an application can be made to the Probate Court of the Family Division or county court where the estate is within the jurisdiction, for leave to grant probate notwithstanding that the formalities have not been strictly observed, where the court is satisfied that the testator intended the document to be his will. It should not be overlooked that in the case of privileged wills the court already has a discretion.

In support of this suggestion one can look critically at the original reasons given for s9 Wills Act 1837 including those of the Real Property Commissioners in their Fourth Report in 1833 which led to the passing of the Act in the first place.

It could be argued that if someone is prepared to forge a testator's signature, are they not equally likely to forge the signatures of two witnesses?

Because of the law relating to undue influence in succession cases, as opposed to that in trust law, there are very few cases on this ground anyway, and as for coercion, the will could be revoked immediately on the cessation thereof.

Most of the contested cases depend on evidence of the background situation and the cases involving pure formalities arise by way of accident. That is, failing to follow precisely the procedure laid down in the Act by some inadvertance or non-observance of detail.

It is therefore contended that to give a court a discretion to dispense with procedure in cases where a patent injustice would occur would be a further amendment that could obviate much of the problem which still arises in this area.

QUESTION THREE

Fred, aged 80, is blind and suffering from a terminal illness. He is being cared for in a

nursing home. He tells Erica, his favourite nurse, that he would like to make a will, and asks for her assistance. She says that she will write down his wishes and find out how to execute the will. Fred dictates a list of bequests which she reads back to him when he has finished. He confirms the list and writes his signature at the top, guided by Erica's hand (as he cannot see). Erica takes the will to her nephew, a law student, to find out how it should be executed.

She returns next day and tells Fred that his signature must be witnessed by two witnesses. She offers to be one of them and suggests that Arthur, a patient in the adjoining bed, should be the other. Arthur agrees, although he says that he cannot see properly because of the stroke that he suffered recently.

While Erica is showing Arthur the will, Fred shouts out, 'That's my will, Arthur. There's something in it for you.' Arthur adds his own signature to the will. Erica then takes the will to her desk at the end of the ward in order to sign it. She is delayed by another patient en route, and it is some ten minutes before she is able to sign the will. She returns to Fred with the will only to discover that he has just died. Among Fred's bequests there is a gift to Erica's sister, whom Fred knew well, and to Arthur.

Discuss.

University of London LLB Examination
(for External Students) Succession June 1995 Q4

General Comment

Candidates were invited to discuss the circumstances of an aged testator who had terminal illness and was blind. The answers turned largely upon issues of formal validity and testamentary competence. The technical problem would have arisen for the student who discovered very early that Fred's will was invalid because it was not executed in the presence of two witnesses. Does the student terminate all further discussion and anticipate a high mark? Therein lies the problem of not leaving all possibilities open.

Skeleton Solution

Requirements of mental capacity – burden of proof – when competence judged – evidential requirement with blindness – formal validity for will – position of testator and witnesses – concept of 'presence' – is there testacy or intestacy?

Suggested Solution

This question involves a number of issues of testamentary capacity and due execution of a will.

A testator must be of sound mind, memory and understanding, appreciate the extent and nature of his property and the moral claims to which he ought to give effect: *Banks v Goodfellow* (1870) LR 5 QB 549. The fact that Fred is aged 80 and is suffering from a terminal illness may suggest that the required conditions for his testamentary competence are not present, aside from any issues raised by his blindness.

If the will is rational on the face of it then an assumption would be made that it is not vitiated by lack of testamentary competence. It would have been better had a doctor witnessed the will, or left a note that he considered the testator to be of sufficient testamentary competence at the time of execution of the will: see *Re Simpson* (1977) 121 SJ 224. Competence at the time of giving instructions for the drawing-up of the will would be sufficient where competence at the time of execution of the will cannot be established: *Parker* v *Felgate* (1883) 32 WR 872.

Fred's blindness will mean that the propounder of the will (Fred's executors, if any) would have to establish that he had knowledge of its contents: r13 Non-Contentious Probate Rules 1987. This requirement would be satisfied if the will was read over and explained to a testator prior to execution; this could be established by a suitable attestation clause at the end of the will, reciting the facts. Erica has read back a list of bequests he has dictated to her but we do not know if the will *as a whole* has been read back to Fred. If it has not been, and the will otherwise satisfies the requirements of formal validity, the burden of proof will lie with the propounder to establish Fred had knowledge of its contents.

The requirements of formal validity, as set down in s9 Wills Act 1837, as substituted by s17 Administration of Justice Act 1982, are that the will must be in writing, signed by the testator or by some other person in the presence of the testator and by his direction, and that it must appear that by the signature the testator intended to give effect to the will. Further, the will must be signed (or the signature must be acknowledged) in the presence of two or more witnesses who are present at the same time; and each witness must either attest and sign the will, or acknowledge his signature in the presence of the testator.

Fred's signature, guided by Erica's hand, will be sufficient provided the signature is intended to give effect to the will. The fact that the signature is at the top of the page is now immaterial (it used to be the case until 1983 that the signature had to be 'at the foot or end thereof').

The difficulty here is that it does not appear that Fred has signed in the presence of two witnesses. After Fred has signed Erica consults her nephew, a law student, and it is only then that the formal validity requirements come to be understood!

The will, in principle, would then have to be signed by both witnesses who must be competent in appreciating the nature of their act, that of witnessing a signature (rather than witnessing a will). The witnesses must sign in the presence of the testator, Fred, although not necessarily in the presence of each other.

Again, there is a difficulty. Arthur appears not to have the requisite competence to witness Fred's signature. He cannot see properly because of a stroke. In *Re Gibson* [1949] P 183 Pearce J considered that witnessing is exclusively a visual act. Thus a person such as Arthur, with impaired vision, could hardly be a competent witness. However, Fred's shouting out: 'That's my will, Arthur ...' might allow for an interpretation that Arthur could acknowledge his own signature, if this were pointed out to him, in accordance with s9 Wills Act 1837.

Erica's position is that she clearly has competence to be a witness but it may be argued that by taking the will to her desk at the end of the ward she is not 'present' for the purposes of the statute; and, further, that the delay of ten minutes in Erica's signing of the will destroys the essence of a single, uninterrupted action of attestation envisaged in formal validity.

It is established that the witnesses need not see the testator sign, nor need he see them sign: *Carter* v *Seaton* (1901) 85 LT 76. The test is whether the person in whose presence the signature is made *could* have seen the other signing had he wished to do so: *Shires* v *Glascock* (1685) 2 Salk 688. Given that Fred is in bed and Erica is at the end of the ward this becomes a question of fact.

The essential issue is whether or not Fred has died testate. There seems little doubt that the requirements of formal validity for Fred's will have not been complied with. At the very minimum he would have had to acknowledge his signature in the presence of Arthur and Erica before his death. This he has not done. Accordingly, Fred's bequests do not take effect and he dies intestate. If the will had been valid, and Arthur adjudged to be a competent witness, he would have lost the benefit under s15 Wills Act 1837, because a witness to a will cannot take under it. If the will had been valid and there had been another competent witness then by virtue of s1 Wills Act 1968 Arthur would have been entitled to retain the bequest.

See also Chapter 2, Question 3.

QUESTION FOUR

Discuss whether the wills in the following cases satisfy the requirements of s9 of the Wills Act 1837:

a) Tom, who wants to make a will, takes a blank sheet of paper and writes his name in capitals at the top of the sheet. He then writes the provisions of his will on the same side of the sheet of paper. When he has finished he shows the will to his wife, Janet, and his daughter, Sarah, aged 15, and asks them to sign at the bottom of the sheet. After they have done so, Janet says, 'But where is your signature?' Tom replies that he has read somewhere that he need not sign as long as he puts his name at the top to identify the author of the will. Janet expresses surprise at this, so Tom adds his initials below the signatures of the witnesses.

b) John has been injured in a recent motor cycle race. He has broken his hand (the one he writes with) and is suffering from mild concussion. He decides to make a will before his next race. As he cannot write because of his broken hand, he asks his friend Leo to come to John's house and sign the will on John's behalf. Just as Leo starts signing, John's huge Newfoundland dog, 'Woofy', bounds into the room between John and Leo, jumps onto John and sends him sprawling.

When John has recovered, he takes the will to his neighbours Frank and Lucy, but finds that Frank is out. John shows Lucy the will and asks Lucy to sign it as a witness. Lucy does so. Frank arrives a few minites later. Lucy, pointing to her signature, tells Frank what she has done. John then asks Frank to sign, whereupon Frank adds his signature.

University of London LLB Examination
(for External Students) Succession June 2000 Q6

General Comment

This is a fairly straightforward question on formalities. It is important to focus on what the question asks. In this instance although there may be an issue on capacity in part (b), the question requires discussion whether s9 requirements have been satisfied. As such s9 must be discussed in full before embarking on the possible capacity issue.

Skeleton Solution

a) Is the signature by the testator valid? – intention of the testator – was chronological order of events as required by s9 satisfied? – can a minor be a valid witness?

b) Did Leo sign in John's presence? – what is the effect of Lucy's actions? – testamentary capacity.

Suggested Solution

a) This is a problem concerned with the formalities required by s9 and the qualifications for witnesses. Section 9 requires that the testator sign his will. There is no longer a requirement that the will be signed at the foot or end of the will. Instead, the signature may appear on any part of the will so long as the testator intended to give effect to the will by it. In *Wood v Smith* [1992] 3 All ER 556 the Court of Appeal was prepared to accept a signature at the top of the will as valid where the will was written in one single operation. The Court was also prepared to allow extrinsic evidence to prove the intention of the testator. In the case at hand, Tom appears to have written his name at the top of the will and the conversation he has with Janet indicates that he may not have intended that to be his signature, but only a means of identifying that it was his will. If this is the case, then the signature at the top of the will would not be valid and it is necessary to consider the initials used at the end of the will and of course if the correct chronology of events as required by s9 has occurred.

As far as the use of initials is concerned, there is considerable case law to suggest that this is perfectly acceptable. Section 9 does not require the testator to sign his will in his name or indeed by his usual signature. The courts have interpreted the requirement for signature in a broad fashion and any mark placed on the will by the testator which is intended to be his signature will suffice. This is amply demonstrated by cases such as *In b Savory* (1851) 15 Jur 1042 and *In b Glover* (1847) 11 Jur 1022. If a court is prepared to accept that Tom's act of initialling his will in the circumstances was indeed intended by him to be his signature, the next issue is if the order of events as prescribed by s9 has been complied with.

It would appear that Tom has signed after the witnesses and as such s9 was not complied with and the will is invalid. The only way in which the will could have been valid, would be if Tom had acknowledged the initials as his signature to both witnesses and if they had then acknowledged their signatures thereafter: *Couser* v *Couser* [1996] 3 All ER 256.

One further issue remains to be considered and that is the capacity of a person to be a witness. In this case, one of the witnesses is Tom's daughter, aged 15. Whilst there are no conditions imposed on the capacity of a person to be a witness to a will, it is advisable to choose an adult of sound intelligence. When dealing with minors the courts have indicated that minors may be acceptable witnesses where they are not too young and are able to understand the nature and importance of the transaction. In *Smith* v *Thompson* (1931) 146 LT 14, a will witnesses by a 16-year-old was considered valid.

b) Section 9 allows a testator to direct some one else to sign his will on his behalf. For this type of signature to be valid, the person signing must do so in the presence of the testator. The person who signs on behalf of the testator can either sign the testator's name or his own name: *In b Clarke* (1839) 2 Curt 339. Thus there is little difficulty in allowing Leo's signature on behalf of John. However, the requirement that the person signing does so in the presence of the testator may cause some difficulty in this case. 'Presence' in this context must be regarded in the same way as elsewhere in the Act, thus it is necessary that John is aware of what was going on at the time as per *Brown* v *Skirrow* [1902] P 3 in relation to witnesses. In the circumstances, although his dog jumps on him, he is aware of what was going on as Leo had started to sign the will.

As for the witnessing of the will, s9 requires the signature to be signed or acknowledged in the presence of two witnesses present at the same time. In this case, John appears to acknowledge his signature to Lucy alone, after which she signs the will; this is followed by Lucy acknowledging her signature to Frank, after which John asks him to sign the will. The order of events as described above do not comply with s9 as Lucy should not have been the first to acknowledge her signature. In fact John should have acknowledged his signature first – to both Lucy and Frank – after which Lucy should have acknowledged her signature, followed by Frank's signing.

Having established the proper execution of the will, the next stage is to ensure that the testator has sufficient testamentary capacity. The onus of proving capacity rests on the propounder of the will. In this case there is evidence that at the time of execution of the will John was suffering from mild concussion. There is no evidence however, to suggest that this affected his mental capacity to make a will. What is required is proof that John was of sound mind, memory and understanding. It is worth bearing in mind the presumption that the testator who had the requisite testamentary capacity before he executed the will will be presumed to have continued to have the ability to make a will until the contrary is proven: *Chambers and Yatman* v *The Queen's Proctor* (1840) 2 Curt 514.

Chapter 2
Privileged and Mutual Wills

2.1   Introduction

2.2   Key points

2.3   Key cases and statutes

2.4   Questions and suggested solutions

2.1 Introduction

Privilege is a fairly popular topic in examinations and can easily be mixed with other areas. It is therefore wise to study this area thoroughly. You must deal with both the statutory provisions as well as the case law. Some thought should be given to the extent of privilege and the effect of a privileged will on other testamentary documents made either before or after the privileged status.

This chapter also covers the topic of mutual wills. It is vital to learn the requirements necessary for the execution of a mutual will, as well as the effect of the trust on the freedom of the survivor.

2.2 Key points

a) Section 11 Wills Act 1837 and the Wills (Soldiers and Sailors) Act 1918

   i) Formal requirements for a will do not apply to privileged testators.

   ii) Privileged: any soldier in actual military service or mariner or seaman at sea.

b) Soldier in actual military service

   i) 'Soldier' broadly interpreted: see especially s5(2) of the 1918 Act (RAF members).

   ii) For 'actual military service' see *Re Wingham* [1949] P 187 and *Re Jones* [1981] 1 All ER 1.

c) Mariner or seaman at sea

   i) Broad interpretation: includes typist, barman on a liner: see *In b Sarah Hale* [1915] IR 362. See also s2 of the 1918 Act.

   ii) Sufficient if will made while under orders to sail or while ashore in the middle of voyage.

d) Must intend wishes to take effect upon death: *In the Estate of Knibbs* [1962] 1 WLR 852.

e) Privileged will does not have to comply with s9 Wills Act

   i) May be oral; needs no witnesses.

   ii) A minor may make a privileged will.

   iii) Section 15 Wills Act does not apply.

   iv) A privileged will remains valid even after testator ceases to be privileged.

f) Mutual wills are wills with almost identical terms made by two or more persons: *Re Dale* [1994] Ch 31.

g) Conditions for a valid mutual will

   i) made pursuant to an agreement;

   ii) agreement for survivor to be bound by terms of will;

   iii) occurrence of binding event, ie death of one party.

   See *Goodchild* v *Goodchild* [1997] 3 All ER 63 and *Re Hobley (Deceased)* (1997) The Times 16 June.

2.3 Key cases and statutes

Privileged wills

- *Booth, Re* [1926] P 118
  A privileged will can only be revoked according to the formalities in the Wills Act 1837 once the privileged status has ended

- *Gossage, In the Estate of* [1921] P 194
  Revocation of a formal will could take place in an informal manner if the testator is privileged at the time

- *Hale (Sarah), In b* (1915) 2 IR 362
  Privilege extends to every person employed in any branch of the Royal Navy

- *Jones, Re* [1981] 1 All ER 1
  The test of actual military service is that nature of the activities of the deceased

- *Knibbs, In the Estate of* [1962] 1 WLR 852
  Although no formalities are required, a privileged will must have been made with animus testandi

- *Lay, In b* (1840) 2 Curt 375
  At sea interpreted as 'on a voyage'

- *Wingham, Re* [1949] P 187
  Defines the meaning of 'soldier in actual military service'

- Wills Act 1837, s11 – general rule

- Wills (Soldiers and Sailors) Act 1918, s2 – extends privilege to the naval and marine forces

- Wills (Soldiers and Sailors) Act 1918, s3(1) – allows disposal of real property by a privileged will

- Wills (Soldiers and Sailors) Act 1918, s5(1) – soldier includes a member of the Air Force

Mutual wills

- *Dufour* v *Pereira* (1769) 1 Dick 419
  Evidence of an agreement not to revoke is an essential element of a mutual will – a constructive trust is imposed on the survivor from the moment of death of one of the parties to the mutual will

- *Goodchild* v *Goodchild* [1997] 3 All ER 63
  There should be a clear contract between the parties that the will be irrevocable after the death of the first party

- *Green, Re* [1951] Ch 148
  The scope and extent of the trust

- *Hobley (Deceased), Re* (1997) The Times 16 June
  Alteration of the mutual will by one party releases the survivor from the obligations of the mutual will

2.4 Questions and suggested solutions

QUESTION ONE

Last year George, a merchant seaman, on a cargo boat which had been ordered to the Falklands, wrote from Southampton to his sister Jill: 'if anything happens to me while I am in the Falklands, I want you to have all my property.' Whilst at sea on his way home George wrote again to his sister. 'Destroy the letter about my property; I am going to make a proper will.'

Jill kept the original letter. George returned to England, and left the merchant navy to work in a bar in an hotel. At the end of last year George wrote out a document in the form of a will in the presence of his friend, Tim, giving all his estate to his only relatives, his three sisters, Jill, Shirley and Hilary, in equal shares. George signed the document and then Tim wrote his name beneath that of George. Bert was then called into the room and George said, 'I want you to witness my signature to this document.' Bert then wrote his name below that of Tim's and they both went out.

George died this year. Advise on the distribution of the estate.

University of London LLB Examination
(for External Students) Succession June 1984 Q2(a)

General Comment

This is a fairly typical question on privilege. It examines both the rules on privilege as well as the formalities under s9 Wills Act 1837. The only real complication is the manner of revocation of a privileged will.

Skeleton Solution

First letter privileged? – s11 Wills Act 1837, seaman at sea, animus testandi – second letter privileged?: status; s20 Wills Act 1837; *In the Estate of Gossage* – s9 Wills Act.

Suggested Solution

There are two documents in this case, which express George's testamentary wishes at various stages in his lifetime. In order to decide which, if either, can be admitted to probate it is necessary to see if the formal requirements, if any, are satisfied by each to ensure revocation has not subsequently occurred.

The letter which George wrote to his sister Jill, from Southampton last year, when his boat was ordered to the Falklands, was a privileged will within s11 of the Wills Act 1837. This provision permits inter alia, a 'seaman being at sea' to make a will without following the formalities of s9. All that is necessary is animus testandi, see *In the Estate of Knibbs* [1962] 1 WLR 852. In this case there is no reason to doubt animus testandi. Although George does not appear to have left port at the time he wrote the letter this does not matter because the term 'seaman being at sea' includes sailors who are under orders to sail. See *In b Sarah Hale* [1915] IR 362 and *In b Newland* [1952] P 71. In the latter case Havers J held it was sufficient if the document was executed in contemplation of a fresh voyage at a time when the testator was under orders to rejoin his ship. It appears from the facts that George wrote the letter after receiving his orders so he would be regarded as entitled to the privilege.

On his homeward journey George wrote another letter to his sister asking her to destroy the letter as he intended to make a proper will. As George was still at sea when he wrote this letter he was within the privilege accorded by s11. The fact that he was no longer in danger from the Falklands conflict is irrelevant since the privilege of s11 applies to sailors at sea regardless of the reason for their being at sea. However, one problem which arises is whether s11 extends to revocation of a will and permits a privileged testator to revoke his will informally. *In the Estate of Gossage* [1921] P 194 the majority if the Court of Appeal treated s20 of the Wills Act as applicable to privileged testators and treated a letter from a soldier to his sister instructing her to burn his will as 'writing declaring an intention to revoke' within s20, but added that s11 did not require this writing to be executed with the formalities required by s9. On this authority the letter telling his sister to revoke the will had the effect of revocation. Even on the minority view (of Younger LJ) in the *Gossage* case this letter would amount to revocation since his view was that s20 did not apply to a privileged testator and he could revoke the will without any formality. The instructions which George gave were absolute and unqualified and there is, in my view, no room to argue that this is a case of conditional revocation: see *Re Jones* [1976] Ch 200.

George wrote out a document in the form of a will at the end of last year. At the time this document was executed it clearly did not satisfy s9 of the Wills Act because at that time s9 required both witnesses to attest the will in the presence of the testator after the operative signature or acknowledgement by the testator and this was not done in the present case. When George signed the will in the presence of Tim, this was ineffective as there was only one witness, it was his acknowledgement which was operative for the purposes of s9 as it was in the presence of both Tim and Bert. However under the then s9 it was necessary for Tim and Bert to attest the will after the operative acknowledgement even if one of them had signed already as this was ineffective: see *Re Colling* [1972] 1 WLR 1440; *Wyatt* v *Berry* [1893] P 5. However these provisions will not affect the present case since George died this year and his will is therefore subject to the provisions of the 'new' s9 substituted by s17 of the Administration of Justice Act 1982. This provision applies to all wills which come into operation on or after 1 January 1983. See s73(b) AJA 1982. Under the new s9(c) the testator must sign or acknowledge his signature in the presence of two witnesses as was required under the old provision. However, the new s9(d) now permits a witness to either 'attest' the will or acknowledge his signature if already on the will, to the testator. The decisions in *Re Colling* and *Wyatt* v *Berry* are no longer good law. On the facts of the present case these changes are unlikely to save the will. This is because Tim does not seem to have acknowledged his signature after George's operative acknowledgement but was content to leave his signature as it was. The reform brought in by s9(d) was only intended to permit acknowledgement of a signature by a witness and not to alter the steps in making a will. The steps are that the testator must sign or acknowledge his signature first and then the witnesses attest or acknowledge their signatures. As only Bert appears to have signed after George's acknowledgement the will must be regarded as improperly executed.

The proper conclusion in this case would appear to be that George died without leaving an effective will and therefore his property will be distributed according to the intestacy rules. As his only relatives are his three sisters, they will take all his estate in equal shares as his next of kin. This result happily coincides with George's wishes under the ineffective formal will.

QUESTION TWO

James, a captain in the British Army, was about to embark on a troopship for Belfast when he fell into conversation with another officer. 'It's going to be rather dodgy over there by all accounts', James said. 'If anything happens to me, I expect my sister Moira to get all my bits and pieces.' They went on to talk of other matters.

A month after his arrival in Northern Ireland, James was injured in a booby trap while searching an abandoned house for explosives. He suffered serious brain damage which left him muddled and incoherent for much of the time, although at other times he was able to think quite rationally and express himself clearly. He was invalided out of the army and set up house with his former batman, Hector, a dominating person on whom James increasingly depended and on whose advice he tended to rely.

Eighteen months after his discharge from the army, James died. A will was found among his possessions; it had been executed a few days before his death and left the whole of his estate (worth about £200,000) 'to my devoted friend Hector absolutely'. The will was not drawn up by James' usual solicitor but by another solicitor who had never met James and who received his instructions for the will over the telephone.

Moira, James' only living relative, seeks your advice as to her entitlement, if any, to her brother's estate.

University of London LLB Examination
(for External Students) Succession June 1990 Q7

General Comment

An interesting question that combines privilege with animus testandi. Students should not consider leaving privilege out of their revision as it is increasingly mixed in with other favourite topics.

Skeleton Solution

Status of James – in active service? – capacity – knowledge and approval? – suspicious circumstances.

Suggested Solution

Maria's entitlement to her brother's estate, I should advise, depends upon her establishing one of two things:

a) that James made a valid privileged will in her favour, which was not revoked by the later will, the later instrument being invalid; or alternatively

b) on the footing that there was no privileged will, the will in favour of Hector is invalid and that Moira should take on James' intestacy.

Normally, a will should fulfil the formal criteria specified by s9 of the Wills Act (WA) 1837, but these are relaxed in relation to so-called privileged testators. Provided James was a soldier in actual military service at the time, he may dispose of his property without complying with any formalities: WA 1837 s11, as amended. The word 'soldier' has been broadly construed, and James undoubtedly qualifies. More controversy has arisen over the precise connotation of 'actual military service'. Originally, the phrase was construed as requiring the person concerned to be so circumstanced that he could be regarded as being on a military campaign or expedition (*Drummond* v *Parish* (1843)

3 Curt 522, per Sir J H Fust), but this test was emphatically rejected by Denning LJ in *Re Wingham* [1949] P 187 as being unduly narrow. His Lordship favoured a more relaxed approach, and formulated a test that requires the testator to be actually serving with the armed forces in connection with military operations which have either taken place, or are doing so currently, or are believed to be imminent. Imminent embarkation on a troopship to Belfast must be covered: see *Gattward v Knee* [1902] P 99. The fact that the operation is mainly one of internal security, and the adversaries not afforded military status, does not detract from the military nature of the activity: *Re Jones* [1981] 1 All ER 1. If it is accepted that James' utterances were made under privileged conditions, then they may be regarded as constituting a will. The fact that they were purely oral is no bar to this; privileged wills can be nuncupative: see *In the Estate of Yates* [1919] P 93. The major stumbling block for Moira (who presumably will be the propounder of the will) is that the statements must have been made with testamentary intent. The words must consist of a specific communication of the deceased's wishes as to the disposition of his property after his death. It must also be clear that the statements were made in the desire and expectation that they would be acted upon. If they were made in the course of a casual conversation, merely by way of information, the requisite intent will be held to be absent: see *In the Estate of Knibbs* [1962] 1 WLR 852. It may be questioned whether James had a true testamentary intent when he had the conversation with the other officer, but if he did, the other officer's testimony would establish the contents of the will.

Even if the privileged will proves to be nothing of the kind Moira may still be able to claim James' estate on a total intestacy. This will depend upon her managing to prove that the will in favour of Hector is invalid. If not, the later testamentary instrument will be admissible to probate. Even if the earlier privileged will is allowed to stand, it would be either expressly revoked by the later testamentary instrument, or impliedly revoked to the extent that the later will is inconsistent with the terms of the earlier. (A privileged will, incidentally, must be revoked in accordance with ss18 and 20 of the WA 1837, once the priviliged conditions have ceased to obtain: *Re Wardrop* [1917] P 54.)

For the will to be admissible to probate it must not merely satisfy the formal requirements, the testator must also satisfy the mental element. The general rule is that the document in question must be the definitive representation of the last wishes of a capable testator, and the onus of proof is on the propounder of the will (presumably Hector): see *Barry v Butlin* (1838) 2 Moo PC 480. It must be proven that: (a) the testator had the mental capacity to make a will; (b) the testator intended to make a will; and (c) the testator exercised genuine freedom of choice in so doing. On the issue of capacity James must have been possessed of a sound and disposing mind and memory: *Banks v Goodfellow* (1870) LR 5 QB 549. It can, of course, be argued by Moira that James' brain damage precluded him from being of sound mind at the time of execution. Normally, Hector could rely on the principle that if a will appears rational on its face, capacity is presumed (*Barry v Butlin*), but the presumption is reversed if the testator has a history of mental disability – this is deemed to continue: *Banks v Goodfellow*. The burden of proof would then shift onto the propounder to establish that the will was made during a lucid interval (see *Cartwright* v *Cartwright* (1793) 1 Phill 90), although it is not necessary to show final recovery: *Chambers and Yatman* v *The Queen's Proctor* (1840) 2 Curt 514.

It must be shown that James had the mental capacity at the time of execution. Apparently, there was a lapse of time between the giving of instructions and the execution of the will. This would not be fatal to the will's validity, provided that James gave instructions at a time when he was in possession of his mental faculties, and that at the time of execution, he both appreciated that he had given instructions for a will to be prepared, and believed that the will he was executing was the one prepared in accordance with those instructions: *Parker* v *Felgate* (1883) 32 WR 186. Even so, the court would be circumspect in applying the rule in the circumstances outlined, given that a solicitor having no prior acquaintance with James prepared the will, acting on instructions received over the telephone. There is no mention of any independent verification of either the accuracy or the authenticity of those instructions: cf *Battan Singh* v *Armirchand* [1948] AC 161.

The testator must have intended to make a will, and he must have exercised genuine and unfettered discretion when he did so. Such intention could not have been present if the testator had been pressured in some way into signing the will in question, for he will have been a victim of undue influence. There must be some element of coercion, though. A testator may be led, although he cannot be driven: *Wingrove* v *Wingrove* (1885) 11 PD 81. Undoubtedly, Hector was in a position to persuade James, but this in itself is not improper conduct: *Hall* v *Hall* (1868) 1 P & D 481. The normal evidentiary rule 'He who alleges must prove' applies, and Moira would have to lead evidence of undue influence. There is no testamentary presumption of undue influence comparable to the doctrine that prevails in the law of contract: *Parfitt* v *Lawless* (1872) LR 2 P & D 462. The facts might also suggest a fraud by Hector, in the sense of some form of deception practised by him (see *Wilkinson* v *Joughin* (1866) LR 2 Eq 319), but the onus of proof would again be on Moira, and it is a notoriously difficult burden to discharge.

Moira might get more 'mileage' from the knowledge and approval criterion. As well as having capacity, the testator must know and approve the contents of the will: *Guardhouse* v *Blackburn* (1866) LR 1 P & D 109. This is customarily presumed from the fact of execution, but the presumption does not operate where, inter alia, suspicious circumstances are present. The suspicion lies in the fact that the will exclusively benefits Hector, and that instructions for the same were not delivered by the testator personally. The will is not admissible to probate unless the suspicion can be removed (*Tyrell* v *Painton* [1894] P 151), and the burden of proof is on the propounder. This is advantageous to Moira, who can content herself with making the allegation, and oblige Hector to refute it. The weight of evidence necessary to dispel the suspicion varies with its gravity (*Wintle* v *Nye* [1959] 1 WLR 284), and here the suspicion is quite strong.

To recapitulate, I should advise Moira that unless she can successfully challenge the will on one of the above-mentioned grounds, she will not benefit either under the earlier privileged will (assuming it is valid) or, alternatively, on intestacy.

QUESTION THREE

a) John, an elderly bachelor, is very nervous about travelling on public transport. He is known to wear crash helmets when he travels on buses. He wins a competition entitling him to a free flight to Florida, USA. Rather boldly he decides to take up the offer, despite being extremely worried about the flight. Just before boarding the flight he says to his friend, Alec, who has taken him to the airport, 'Look, I am really scared about flying. You had better take the keys to my house. Keep it if anything happens to me.' He hands Alec some keys. John is killed a little later when his plane crashes on take-off. When Alec enters the house he discovers several other keys to the front door.

Advise Alec, who has just heard that the Crown is claiming the whole of John's estate as John died intestate and was not survived by any relatives.

b) Dan works on an off-shore oil rig in the North Sea. Normally he is transported to the rig by helicopter but sometimes a boat is used for this purpose by Dan's company. Dan has even been known to swim to the rig when feeling in the mood for some exercise. Last year Dan made a properly executed will in which he left all his estate to his mother, his only relative. However, earlier this year, while Dan was being flown to the rig, he told the helicopter pilot, Joe, with whom he had become very friendly, 'I made a will last year in favour of my mother but I do not want her to take after all. You may as well have all my property when I die'. Dan was killed last week as the result of an explosion on the rig.

Advise Joe.

University of London LLB Examination
(for External Students) Succession June 1995 Q3

General Comment

This was a two-part question, the first part of which involved a full discussion of a donatio mortis causa requiring the candidate to display a detailed knowledge of the subject area. The second part of the question was, in the event, extremely simple. The facts presented required nothing further than a discussion of how a valid will might be revoked and a realisation that an oral statement could not have this effect. A one-page answer would have been sufficient to score a high mark.

Skeleton Solution

a) Effect of a total intestacy where no relatives – elements required for a valid donatio mortis causa – case law discussion of conditions – whether realty can pass by donatio mortis causa.

b) Valid will in favour of mother – methods of revocation of a will – not satisfied on these facts – oral revocation, in absence of privilege, insufficient.

Suggested Solution

a) This first part of the question involves a consideration as to whether the assets of an intestate, John, without relatives, which would normally devolve as bona vacantia to the Crown, may be subject to an effective lifetime disposition made conditional upon death in favour of Alec.

Where there is no one within the category of entitlement under s46 Administration of Estates Act 1925 to inherit the intestate's estate the estate passes to the Crown, or Duchy of Lancaster or Duchy of Cornwall, as bona vacantia. The Crown may at its discretion provide for persons who were dependent upon the intestate whether related or not and for such other persons for whom the intestate may have been expected to provide: s46(1)(iv) AEA 1925.

John's statement to Alec may suggest that he has created a donatio mortis causa (dmc), a gift which is neither entirely inter vivos nor testamentary whereby the donee is to have absolute title to the subject of the gift, not at once but if the donor dies. It may be defined, therefore, as a gift made by a person during lifetime with the intention that it should take effect only on death. The gift is conditional upon death, but once the condition is satisfied it takes effect retrospectively from the date the gift was made. The donor must have intended that the gift should be absolute on the condition being fulfilled: *Re Beaumont* [1902] 1 Ch 889.

Apart from the requirement of the condition being satisfied the other requirements for a valid donatio mortis causa are as set down in *Cain v Moon* [1896] 2 QB 283 by Lord Russell of Killowen, as follows:

i) the gift must have been made in contemplation, although not necessarily in expectation, of death;

ii) there must have been delivery to the donee of the subject matter of the gift or the means of obtaining that subject matter, such as keys.

Here, clearly, John contemplates death from an aeroplane accident because of fear, however unlikely that may become reality. In *Re Lillingston* [1952] 2 All ER 184 a donor expressed a feeling that he was 'done for': that was held to carry the necessary contemplation of death for a dmc; and in *Re Miller* (1961) 105 SJ 207 it was held that a woman about to fly from London to Geneva was capable of making a dmc, even though flying is statistically safer than driving a motor car.

It is established that delivery of a means of access to the subject matter suffices. In *Re Craven's Estate (No 1)* [1937] Ch 423 delivery of the *only* set of keys to a box containing the subject matter was held to be sufficient.

The difficulties for Alec in seeking to set up a valid dmc are threefold: first, there must be some considerable doubt that in passing the keys to Alec, John intended to pass the title of the property to him; second, there are several other keys to the front door so that the delivery of one set of keys was not the unique means of obtaining dominion; third, if the words 'keep it if anything happens to me' is a reference to the house the question arises as to whether realty can be the subject matter of a valid dmc. Until *Sen v Headley* [1991] 2 All ER 636, it was accepted that only personalty could pass in this way. In that case the Court of Appeal held that the delivery of title deeds to a house could constitute a valid dmc of the house. But here it is not title deeds but keys, an entirely different evidential factor, and one not suggesting transmission of ownership rights, however imperfect.

For the reasons and principles stated above Alec is unlikely to be able to set up a valid dmc against John's administrators.

b) In advising Joe, it needs to be pointed out that there are only limited circumstances in which a properly executed will, as that in which Dan has left all his estate to his mother, can be revoked by:

i) a later will executed with the requisite formalities of s9 Wills Act 1837, as substituted by s17 Administration of Justice Act 1982;

ii) a burning, tearing or otherwise destroying of the will with the intention of revoking the same – s20 Wills Act 1837 (the words 'otherwise destroying' construed eiusdem generis with burning or tearing and therefore could not cover an oral declaration);

iii) the subsequent marriage of the testator, unless the will is made in contemplation of marriage: s18 Wills Act 1837.

There is no suggestion that Dan has privileged status, as a soldier in actual military service or a sailor at sea, in which case an informal revocation might be effective.

Dan's death last week as the result of an explosion on the rig will mean that he has died testate and his executors will administer his estate in favour of his mother. There is nothing in the facts of the question to warrant discussion of a donatio mortis causa in favour of Joe, or that Joe has any family provision claim.

QUESTION FOUR

Tom, Dick and Harry were three friends living in London. Tom was in the Army, Dick and Harry were civilians. Two years ago, Tom was told that he was to be posted to Northern Ireland. The night before he was due to leave for Northern Ireland, Tom went out for a drink with Dick and Harry. When they were talking about their families, Tom said to Dick and Harry, 'If anything were to happen to me, Sally will get all my stuff.' Sally was Tom's sister. He had no other brothers or sisters but his mother was still alive and he had an illegitimate child by his girlfriend, Gretel. He was trying to avoid paying maintenance for this child at the time. The next day Tom was killed in a car accident. There is no indication that he ever executed a formal will.

After Tom's funeral, Dick and his wife Kate discussed the need to make wills and they both decided to make a will. They saw a solicitor and each made a will leaving everything to the other but, if the other were dead, to their three children in equal shares absolutely. Not long afterwards, Dick died of a sudden heart attack. Kate remarried almost at once and then made another will in favour of her new husband, Gilbert.

Harry was now very depressed. He believed that fate intended him to die soon. One day he handed his brother, Bob, a packet with a key in it and said 'this is for when I'm gone'. The key was the key to a safe deposit box in which were the deeds of his flat, some share certificates and some bank deposit books. Harry fell under a train a few days later – it was thought to be suicide. He was survived by his wife Marilyn. He left no will.

Discuss.

University of London LLB Examination
(for External Students) Succession June 1997 Q4

General Comment

This is actually a three-part question with each part covering a different area of law. The issues raised are straightforward.

Skeleton Solution

Privileged will – mutual wills – donatio mortis causa.

Suggested Solution

The first issue is whether Tom's statement to Dick and Harry could amount to a valid will. Generally, s9 of the Wills Act formalities must be complied with in order to make a valid will. However, s11 of the Wills Act 1837 states that a soldier being in actual military service may make a privileged will, ie a will which need not be executed according to the formalities.

Tom was clearly a soldier as he was in the Army. The courts have always given a wide definition to the word 'soldier' and it generally includes anyone serving with the forces: *Re Wingham* [1949] P 187.

As for whether Tom was in actual military service when he made the statement, the term according to Denning LJ in *Re Wingham* (above) applies not only to military service directly concerned with the operations in a war which is in progress or is imminent but also include cases during peacetime when a soldier is in or is about to be sent to a disturbed area.

This was later applied in *Re Jones* [1981] 1 All ER 1 where privilege was extended to a soldier serving in Northern Ireland. Applying these principles to Tom, who had received orders to go to Northern Ireland, it seems clear that he was entitled to make a privileged will.

The next thing to decide is whether the statement made was an expression of his wishes to be carried on his death; ie whether Tom had animus testandi. In *Re Knibbs* [1962] 1 WLR 852, it was held that the deceased's words could not amount to a privileged will as it was spoken as an exchange of family gossip without animus testandi.

In this case, the phrase '... Sally will get all my stuff' seems to imply that he had already made a will in which Sally is the sole beneficiary. This is also supported by the fact that he was trying to avoid paying child maintenance.

The conclusion is that although Tom was capable of making a privileged will, he had not made one due to the lack of animus testandi on his part. Tom had therefore died intestate.

The next issue is whether Dick and Kate had made valid mutual wills. Mutual wills are wills in similar terms made by two or more persons containing an agreement that the survivor is to be bound by those terms. Mutual wills may but need not confer reciprocal benefits: *Re Dale* [1994] Ch 31. The doctrine of mutual wills ensures that on the death of the first to die, the survivor becomes bound by a constructive trust to dispose of his estate in the manner agreed upon: *Dufour v Pereira* (1769) 1 Dick 419.

For this doctrine to apply, the mutual wills must have been made pursuant to an agreement that the survivor is bound and the binding event must have happened: the binding event being the death of the first of the mutual will testator who dies without having revoked his will.

The agreement not to revoke may either appear on the face of the will (*Re Hagger* [1930] 2 Ch 190) or be proved by extrinsic evidence. The question does not state that such an agreement is on the face of the wills of Dick and Kate but it may be that the solicitor who prepared the wills could adduce evidence of such an agreement.

However, in the absence of any such evidence, the mere fact that both Dick and Kate had made wills at the same time containing almost the same terms is insufficient evidence of mutual wills: *Re Oldham* [1925] Ch 75.

If there is no evidence of an agreement between Dick and Kate, then Kate is free to leave her estate to Gilbert.

On the other hand, if the doctrine of mutual wills applies, then on Dick's death a constructive trust will arise to cover the property agreed upon. Kate's remarriage would automatically revoke her will following s18(1) of the Wills Act 1837 and her new will is effective but only so far as the terms do not go against the constructive trust: *Re Green* [1951] Ch 148. This means that on her death, her estate will be distributed according to the terms of her second will subject to the constructive trust.

The problem is whether Kate is allowed to deal with the property she inherited as her own. According to the court in *Birmingham v Renfrew* (1937) 57 CLR 666, Kate may deal with the property as absolute owner but equity will not allow her to deal with it inconsistently with the agreements in the mutual wills.

Finally, it must be decided whether Harry's flat, his shares and savings will go to his brother Bob as donatio mortis causa or will be distributed according to intestacy principles. Donatio mortis causa is where a donor passes possession of certain gifts to a donee on the condition that it will only belong to the donee absolutely after the donor's death.

Firstly, the gift must have been made in contemplation of death. Harry must have been considering death in the near future. The facts suggest that he was, although if the death contemplated was suicide, the donatio mortis causa is invalid: *Re Dudman* [1925] Ch 553.

However, it is no longer a crime to commit suicide following the Suicide Act 1961, so the decision in *Re Dudman* may no longer be followed. In *Mills v Shields* [1948] Ir R 367 it was held that a donatio mortis causa is valid where a donor who killed himself had earlier made a gift in contemplation of death other than by suicide.

Secondly, the gift must have been intended to be conditional on death. Harry's words to Bob clearly show that.

Thirdly, there must have been delivery of the subject matter of the gift. This means actual delivery of the property, the means of obtaining it (*Re Lillingston* [1952] 2 All ER 184) or the essential indicia of title: *Birch v Treasury Solicitor* [1951] CLY 4312. Harry must intend to part with dominion over the property. In this case, provided the key given to Bob was the only key to the safe deposit box, the third condition is satisfied: *Reddel v Dobree* (1834) 10 Sim 244.

Finally, it must be decided whether the property in question is capable of being the subject matter of a donatio mortis causa. According to the Court of Appeal in *Sen v Headley* [1991] 2 All ER 636, land can be the subject matter of a donation mortis causa; the title deeds being the essential indicia of title. The share certificates and the savings are likewise capable, the bank deposit books being the essential indicia of title: *Birch v Treasury Solicitor* (above).

As all the conditions to a valid donatio mortis causa have been satisfied, Bob is entitled to the flat, the shares and the savings.

QUESTION FIVE

a) Norma and Oswald, a married couple, are anxious to make mutual wills in favour of each other, with a gift over to their daughter, Polly, aged four, in case of the other's predecease. They wish to know (if they make mutual wills) what their position will be prior to either of them dying, ie during their joint lives.

Advise them.

b) Paula is a helicopter pilot serving with the British Army in Northern Ireland. One day the helicopter crashes due to mechanical failure while engaged in routine surveillance operations. Paula survives the crash but is very badly injured. On the way to being taken to hospital she cries out, 'Mum must get everything I have got if I don't make it'. Paula dies two days later of her injuries. It transpires that Paula made a formal will a month before she died in which she left all her property to her partner, Quentin.

Advise Rita, Paula's mother.

University of London LLB Examination
(for External Students) Succession June 1998 Q5

General Comment

A two-part question in which part (a) is very different from the usual mutual wills question. It requires the student to discuss the law during the joint lives of the parties, rather than after the death of the first to die. Part (b) is the usual privileged will scenario.

Skeleton Solution

a) Doctrine of mutual wills.

b) Privileged will.

Suggested Solution

a) Mutual wills are wills in similar terms made by two or more persons containing an agreement that the survivor is to be bound by those terms. The doctrine of mutual wills ensures that on the death of the first to die, the survivor becomes bound by a constructive trust to dispose of his/her estate in the manner agreed upon: *Dufour* v *Pereira* (1769) 1 Dick 419.

Norma and Oswald may therefore make wills benefiting each other first, with a gift over to Polly. However, it is not necessary that their wills should confer reciprocal benefits (*Re Dale* [1994] Ch 31); instead they could agree to each make Polly the sole beneficiary of their estates.

They must ensure that there is a clear agreement for the survivor to be bound by the terms of the mutual wills. Such agreement should ideally appear on the face of the will as in *Re Hagger* [1930] 2 Ch 190 but could be proved using extrinsic evidence.

In the absence of such an agreement, Norma and Oswald should note that the mere fact of their having made wills containing similar terms at the same time is inconclusive proof of the existence of mutual wills: *Re Oldham* [1925] Ch 75.

During the testators' joint lifetimes, the mutual wills doctrine does not apply as no constructive trust has arisen. This means that either party may unilaterally revoke or alter his/her will during their joint lifetimes: *Stone* v *Hoskins* [1905] P 194.

Once revocation has taken place, the other party is released from his promise not to revoke. The 'innocent' party may also have a claim for breach of contract;

although there may be difficulty in assessing damages if the mutual wills did not confer reciprocal benefits.

Alternatively, the mutual wills may also be revoked during the joint lifetimes of Norma and Oswald with their joint consent.

In either case, Polly has no remedy as she was not privy to the contract.

However, in *Goodchild* v *Goodchild* [1997] 3 All ER 63, it was held that even where an agreement to make mutual wills could not be proved but one party was shown to have made her will in the belief of mutual intentions, this gave rise to a moral obligation on the part of the survivor to benefit the ultimate beneficiary which could be utilised in a claim for family provision.

b) Rita would wish to know whether she is entitled to Paula's estate. Although Paula had not made a will complying with s9 of the Wills Act 1837 formalities, she may have made a valid privileged will under s11 of the 1837 Act. A privileged will need not comply with the formalities in order to be valid.

According to s11, a soldier in actual military service is entitled to make a privileged will. The courts have generally given a wide meaning to the word 'soldier' and it includes anyone serving with the forces. As a pilot serving with the British Army, Paula is a soldier.

The next issue is whether Paula was in actual military service when the will was made. She was engaged in routine surveillance operations at the time. According to Denning LJ in *Re Wingham* [1949] P 87, the term applies not only to military service directly concerned with the operations in a war which is in progress or is imminent but also include cases during peacetime when a soldier is in or is about to be sent to a disturbed area. This was later applied in *Re Jones* [1981] 1 All ER 1 where privilege was extended to a soldier serving in Northern Ireland. It is thus reasonable to conclude that Paula was in actual military service when she made the will.

For the will to be valid, Paula's statement must have been an expression of her wishes to be carried out on her death; ie animus testandi. In *Re Knibbs* [1962] 1 WLR 852 it was held that the deceased's words could not amount to a privileged will as it was spoken as an exchange of family gossip without animus testandi.

In Paula's case, on the other hand, she clearly had the animus testandi when uttering those words. The conclusion is that she had made a valid privileged will benefiting Rita. The privileged will effectively revokes the formal will Paula made a month before she died.

Chapter 3

Incorporation by Reference

3.1   **Introduction**

3.2   **Key points**

3.3   **Key cases**

3.4   **Questions and suggested solutions**

3.1 Introduction

Incorporation by reference is rarely examined on its own. It is a short chapter worth revising as it could be examined in a combination of a number of other key areas of the syllabus.

3.2 Key points

a) Unexecuted document is incorporated into will provided:

   i) document in existence at date of will or at date of republication of will: *Singleton v Tomlinson* (1878) 3 App Cas 404; *In the Goods of Lady Truro* (1866) LR 1 P & D 201;

   ii) document referred to in will as being in existence: *In the Goods of Smart* [1902] P 238;

   iii) document clearly identified in will. Extrinsic evidence is admissible to identify document.

b) Incorporated document is admitted to probate as part of will.

3.3 Key cases

* *Allen* v *Maddock* (1858) 11 Moo 427
  Parol evidence is admissible to identify a document claimed to be incorporated

* *Edwards, Re* [1948] Ch 440
  Conditions for the incorporation of settlements into wills

* *Singleton* v *Tomlinson* (1878) 3 App Cas 404
  Conditions for a successful incorporation by reference

- *Smart, In b* [1902] P 238
  Reference to a document to come into existence in the future will not result in effective incorporation of the document into the will

3.4 Questions and suggested solutions

QUESTION ONE

In 1980 Roger duly executed a will which reads:

'I leave all my estate

a) to the person or persons who shall be specified in such memorandum signed by me as shall be found in my safe at my death; or

b) in default of any such memorandum to my sister Sally.'

Roger died last month and a document was found in his safe signed by him which reads, 'This is the memorandum referred to in my will. All my property is to go to my fiancee Mildred'.

Roger married Mildred in 1981.

Advise Sally.

University of London LLB Examination
(for External Students) Succession June 1985 Q3(a)

General Comment

A straightforward question on incorporation by reference. This question is interesting as it requires a discussion on what happens when the incorporation does not work. It is important in this type of question to apply the conditions carefully.

Skeleton Solution

Can the document be incorporated? – conditions to be met – decision – if the document is not incorporated, effect of marriage on will?

Suggested Solution

A document can be incorporated into a will, so as to become part of it and admissible to probate, if the paper is in existence at the date of the will, if the will refers to it as an existing document, and if the will makes identification of the paper possible.

The problem here is the way the will refers to the document. It states that the estate is left to the 'person ... who *shall be* specified in such memorandum ... as *shall be found* in my safe'. This description does not seem to confine itself to existing documents only, but could include documents coming into existence in the future. This means the document cannot be incorporated, even if it existed when the will was signed. It certainly cannot be incorporated if it was made after the will was signed.

This leaves the gift to Sally. There is a difficulty of construction here. She is given the property 'in default of any such memorandum'. There is a memorandum, even though it cannot be incorporated. So the condition attached to her gift is not satisfied. On the other hand, the gift might be construed as meaning 'in default of any memorandum that actually disposes of the property'. There is no such memorandum.

In any event, marriage revokes all existing wills. So the 1980 will was revoked by the 1981 marriage.

QUESTION TWO

Eric has recently died and his will is found in the following condition.

The attestation clause and the signatures are on the last page which contains no other writing.

The second page is only two thirds of the size of the others and had been cut in half and taped together.

Under the heading in the will 'pecuniary legacies' is a note 'see the attached memorandum for details'. A paper headed 'memorandum' is found with the will, listing a number of pecuniary legacies.

Discuss.

University of London LLB Examination
(for External Students) Succession June 1988 Q2(b)

General Comment

Most of this question deals with other issues. However, the incorproation by reference point is crucial to concluding the answer correctly. Having said that, all that is required is a simple application of the conditions.

Skeleton Solution

Section 9 WA 1837 and s17 AJA 1982 – intention to give effect – revocation of part – incorporation by reference

Suggested Solution

Section 9 WA 1837 as substituted by s17 AJA 1982 has altered the law on the formal execution of wills. One must consider each of the matters in the question to see whether they affect the validity of the will.

Consider first the fact that the will is written on several unattached sheets of matching paper. Under the old law the matter was considered in the case of *In the Estate of Little* [1960] 1 WLR 495. There the court was dealing with a will comprising several unattached pages. The issue was whether the signature on the last page, which was on top of the other pages at the time of execution, was sufficient to make all the sheets a testamentary document. The judge applied a presumption that the will should, in such circumstances, be admitted to probate if it was in the room and under the control of the testator at the time of execution. This case was interpreted under the 'foot or end' provisions of the Wills Act 1837 and the Wills Act Amendment Act 1852. On a similar line is *In the Estate of Long* [1936] P 166 where the testatrix made a will contained on two sides of a sheet of paper. On one side was a list of bequests while on the other was the heading of the will, the appointment of executors and the testatrix's signature. The will was read as beginning with the bequests and ending with the appointment of executors and the signature.

Although these cases would probably be divided the same way today under s9(b) all that is now necessary is that the testator should intend by his signature to give effect to his will. Thus the fact that the attestation clause and the signatures are on the last page which contains no other writing is of itself inconclusive, if it can be shown that the requisite intention is present – ie to validate the will.

The second page is only two-thirds of the size of the others and had been cut in half and taped together. A number of points arise here; one might ask whether the fact that two-thirds of the second sheet only exist indicates that the remainder has been revoked. There can be revocation by destruction of a part of the will only as opposed to the whole will. If the court is satisfied that the testator intended the remainder to be effective, it will be admitted to probate. In *Re Everest* [1975] Fam 44 the testator directed that his residuary estate should be held on trust but the parts of the will dealing with the trusts were found cut away at his death. However the will was complete in all other respects. Probate was granted to the mutilated will on the basis that the trusts had been cut out but not such as to raise the inference that the whole will was intended to be revoked. Also *In b Nunn* [1936] LJP 57 it was held that there was partial revocation only in a case where part of the will was cut and the remaining parts stitched together. It can be argued on the basis of these cases that the intention in the instant case is not that the will should be revoked, indeed one might read the second page as complete notwithstanding the fact that it has been taped together.

The final point that one must deal with is in regard to the memorandum detailing the manner in which the pecuniary legacies are to be held. The question which arises here is in connection with the doctrine of incorporation by reference. Three conditions must be satisfied before the doctrine can be successfully invoked.

Firstly, the document must be in existence at the time the will was made: *Singleton* v *Tomlinson* (1878) 3 App Cas 404. See also *In b Lady Truro* (1866) LR 1 P & D 201. This condition may be satisfied on the facts here.

Secondly, the document must be referred to as being in existence. On the facts here this condition is satisfied – there is no difficulty as there was in the case of *University College of North Wales* v *Taylor* [1908] P 140 where the will referred to the document to be drawn up at some future date.

Thirdly, the document must be clearly identified; again it would appear that on the facts this condition has been satisfied. Vague references would be insufficient per *In b Garnett* [1894] P 90.

However, parol evidence is admissible to identify a document claimed to be incorporated: per *Allen* v *Maddock* (1858) 11 Moo 427.

Thus it will be the case here that the attached 'memorandum' will be deemed to form part of the will such that the pecuniary legacies cited therein will be treated as though they were expressed in the will itself: eg *In b Balme* [1897] P 261.

Chapter 4

Animus Testandi

4.1   Introduction

4.2   Key points

4.3   Key cases and statutes

4.4   Questions and suggested solutions

4.1 Introduction

This chapter is an essential part of the study of succession. Once it is determined that s9 Wills Act 1837 has been complied with, it is necessary to consider if the will was made with sufficient animus testandi. You should consider capacity as well as those matters that affect the knowledge and approval of the testsator, such as undue influence, fraud and suspicious circumstances. It is important to cover all aspects of the area and to be able to write an answer that is concise. The danger in the examination is often having too much to write and running out of time.

4.2 Key points

Mental capacity

To make a will valid, a testator must have mental capacity and intention.

a) Testator must understand nature of his act and its effect; extent of his property; any moral claims he should consider: *Banks* v *Goodfellow* (1870) LR 5 QB 549.

b) Propounder of will must prove testator had mental capacity when the will is executed.

c) Sufficient if testator had capacity at time of instructions and the will complies with the instructions and signs will believing it gives effect to the instructions: *Parker* v *Felgate* (1883) 8 PD 171.

d) Presumption of capacity if will is rational.

e) Presumption of continuance of testator's mental state.

vi) Insane delusions: a distinction should be drawn between delusions that do and those that do not have any effect on the validity of the will: *Banks* v *Goodfellow* (above).

f) Lucid intervals: a will may still be valid if it was made during a lucid interval by a testator who would normally lack mental capacity.

Animus testandi: knowledge and approval

a) Testator must intend to make a will (see, eg, *Corbett* v *Newey* [1995] 1 All ER 570), and know and approve of the contents of his will. The propounder has the onus of proving this.

b) Knowledge and approval presumed if testator had capacity and will duly executed unless:

   i) Suspicious circumstances, ie where the person or a close friend or relative of the person who prepared the will benefits from it: *Barry* v *Butlin* (1838) 2 Moo PC 480; *Tyrell* v *Painton* [1894] P 151; *Wintle* v *Nye* [1959] 1 WLR 284.

   ii) Mistake:

   - That is, words present without testator's knowledge, not where testator is mistaken in his belief as to their effect: *Collins* v *Elstone* [1843] P 1.

   - *Re Morris* [1971] P 62, *Re Phelan* [1972] Fam 33 and *Re Finnemore (Deceased)* [1991] 1 WLR 793.

   - Section 20 Administration of Justice Act 1982 gives court power to rectify a will if has been a clerical error or failure to understand instructions. See *Wordingham* v *Royal Exchange Trust Co & Another* [1992] 2 WLR 496. Section 20 applies if testator dies after 1982.

   - Testator is blind, dumb or illiterate – need evidence of knowledge and approval, eg will read to testator and attestation clause shows this.

c) Animus testandi: testator must have exercised free choice in making the will, ie no undue influence.

d) Undue influence is present where the testator has been coerced into doing something which he did not wish to do: *Hall* v *Hall* (1868) LR 1 P & D 481.

   Must draw a distinction between undue influence, which invalidates a will, and mere persuasion, which does not affect a will.

e) Statutory Will: under s103 Mental Health Act 1983, Court of Protection may order execution of will for an adult who lacks capacity: see, eg, *Re C (A Patient)* [1991] 3 All ER 866.

f) Drink and drugs: will be a lack of capacity if affect testator's ability to make a sound judgment and makes his will while so affected.

4.2 Key cases and statutes

- *Ayrey* v *Hill* (1824) 162 ER 269
  The effect of drink and drugs on testamentary capacity

- *Banks* v *Goodfellow* (1870) LR 5 QB 549
  Requirements for mental capacity and the effect of insane delusions on capacity

- *Barry* v *Butlin* (1838) 2 Moo PC 480
  If a will is rational on its face there is a presumption of mental capacity

- *Battan Singh* v *Amirchand* [1948] AC 161
  Effect of illness on capacity

- *Cartwright* v *Cartwright* (1793) 1 Phill 90
  The effect of lucid intervals on capacity

- *Christian* v *Instiful* [1954] 1 WLR 253
  Effect of blindness on knowledge and approval

- *D(J), Re* [1982] 2 All ER 37
  The five propositions that apply to the making of a statutory will

- *Davey (Deceased), Re* [1981] 1 WLR 164
  On death of the patient the Court of Protection's powers end and thus the statutory will cannot be set aside

- *Fulton* v *Andrew* (1875) LR 7 HL 488
  Applicability of the doctrine of suspicious circumstances to all cases where the will leaves all or part of the estate to the party preparing the will

- *Guardhouse* v *Blackburn* (1866) LR 1 P & D 109
  The six propositions in relation to knowledge v approval

- *Harwood* v *Baker* (1840) 3 Moo PC 282
  Requirement of sound understanding

- *Killick* v *Poutney and Another* (1999) The Times 30 April
  The burden of proof in allegations of undue influence rest with the party making the allegation

- *Parfitt* v *Lawless* (1872) LR 2 P & D 462
  Explains the difference between the probate doctrine of undue influence and the equitable doctrine of undue influence

- *Parker* v *Felgate* (1883) 8 PD 171
  Capacity is required at the time of execution or when instructions were given so long as at the time of execution the testator understands that he is signing a will for which he previously gave instructions

- *Wilkinson* v *Joughin* (1886) LR 2 Eq 319
  Any form of deception practised on the testator which affects his will will amount to fraud

- *Wingrove* v *Wingrove* (1885) 11 PD 81
  Defines undue influence as requiring coercion

- *Wintle* v *Nye* [1959] 1 WLR 284
  Nature of evidence required to remove suspicioius circumstances

- Administration of Justice Act 1982, s20 – rectification of mistakes

- Wills Act 1837, s7 – precludes infants from making valid wills

4.4 Questions and suggested solutions

QUESTION ONE

In 1990 Ada, aged 70, made a will leaving all her property to her husband, Harold, and her two sons, David and Colin, in three equal shares. In 1992 she was admitted to a hospice as she was suffering from terminal cancer. A week before she died, Ada was visited by David who had prepared a new will following consultations with Harold and Colin. Under the new will David was to receive half of Ada's estate, the residue to be shared equally by Harold and Colin. The will contained a revocation clause revoking all prior wills.

When Ada was shown the will she was in a comatose state as the result of the drugs administered to her. She read through the will and said, 'Are you sure this is all right?'. David replied, 'Well … perhaps we should change one thing'. He then altered the amount of the gift to himself, increasing it from a half to three-quarters of the estate. He showed the altered will to Ada who asked him to read it through to her as she was too tired to do it herself. David read it out twice and then suggested that Ada should sign the will. She did so in the presence of David's wife and two nurses, all of whom then signed the will as witnesses. Ada died leaving an estate valued at £400,000.

You are consulted by Harold and Colin who now think that only the 1990 will should receive probate.

Advise them.

University of London LLB Examination
(for External Students) Succession June 1993 Q3

General Comment

This is a typical animus testandi question. The main difficulty is assuming this question is coping with the volume of material required. It is vital that the answer is well structured, dealing first with issues of capacity, before moving on to knowledge and approval.

Skeleton Solution

Animus testandi – tests of *Banks* v *Goodfellow*. – want of knowledge and approval – suspicious circumstances – witnessed by wife but no s15

Suggested Solution

Ada's 1990 will is only revoked if the 1992 will is valid and Colin and Harold should consider a challenge to the 1992 will by questioning the testamentary capacity of Ada to make a will and, secondly, on whether she lacked knowledge and approval of the will together, with the suspicious circumstances appertaining to its preparation and execution.

As regards mental incapacity the test in *Banks* v *Goodfellow* (1870) LR 5 QB 549 should be applied. It consists of three essentials. The testator must be of sound mind, sound memory, and sound understanding. As regards sound mind, it is meant that the mind must be free from disease or defect which would affect the testator's ability to make a will. Persons who are under the influence of drugs do not have sound mind. Senility, if at an advanced stage, may be such as to affect the capacity to make a will: *Den* v *Vancleve* 2 Southard 660. Physical illness which affects the brain may also affect the soundness of mind: *Battan Singh* v *Amirchand* [1948] AC 161.

Sound memory means a capability of recollecting the property to be bequeathed, the manner of distributing it and who it is intended to benefit, not necessarily in detail, but at least in broad outline.

Sound understanding refers to a comprehension of the transaction, an ability to understand the claims of various relatives and friends, and the effect of the dispositions to be made.

The issue here is whether the testatrix knew that she was only giving a quarter of her estate to her husband, and one son, and giving three-quarters to David, and she deliberately formed an intelligent purpose so to do: *Harwood* v *Baker* (1840) 5 Moo PC 282.

Harold and Colin would need to find evidence to support a challenge and should question the doctors and nurses who attended on Ada in the hospice to find out whether her medical condition of suffering from terminal cancer would have affected her mind or whether the drugs she was prescribed would affect her. She is described as being in a comatose state as a result therefrom and this gives rise to the suggestion that she did not possess animus testandi at the time she read the will brought to her by David.

The time for satisfying the test is the time of execution of the will.

The circumstances of this case raise considerable doubts as to whether Ada had testamentary capacity as laid down in the test of *Banks* v *Goodfellow*.

The will itself must have the knowledge and approval of the testatrix, and this is most important where a will is drawn up on her behalf by a third party, as in the case in the question.

We are not told in this case whether Ada gave any instructions at all, only that there were consultations by David with Harold and Colin. Maybe Ada knew nothing about this. We are not told what conclusion the consultations reached, or even whether David's new will contained terms reached in such consultations. He may have devised the will entirely on his own initiative.

At any rate, it is not for third parties to decide on the terms of a will. This must represent 'the offspring of her own volition and not the record of someone else's as Lord Penzance said in *Hall v Hall* (1868) 1 P & D 481 which was a case on undue influence.

In this case the testatrix was not unduly influenced but seems to have been presented with a fait accompli. This must raise serious doubts as to whether she had knowledge and gave it her approval if the only time she was shown the will was when she was in a comatose state, which makes it extremely dubious as to whether she was in a fit state to comprehend its contents.

Although she may have known and approved the contents of the will, probate would be refused if it could be proved that any fraud had been purposely practised on the testatrix.

As for David reading the will over to Ada, it was held in *Re Morris* [1971] P 62 that reading over was only evidence that there *may* have been knowledge and approval, and much will depend on how the reading over took place. Again with a tired, sick testatrix as in this case, and moreover in a comatose state, this reading over by an interested party who had just made a substantial alteration in his own handwriting, in his own favour, would, it is submitted, most certainly not be enough to prove knowledge and approval.

The circumstances are suspicious on this account and fall within Parke J's description in *Barry v Butlin* (1838) 2 Moo PC 480 where he says: 'If a party writes or prepares a will under which he takes a benefit, that is a circumstance that ought generally to excite the suspicion of the Court … and it ought not to pronounce unless the suspicion is removed and it is judicially satisfied that the paper propounded does express the true will of the deceased.'

The doctrine of suspicious circumstances is obviously intended to avoid fraud by the party who wrote or drew up the will on the testator, and is particularly applicable in cases where the will leaves the testator's estate or part of it to the party who prepared the will: *Fulton v Andrew* (1875) LR 7 HL 448.

Similarly, in *Tyrrell v Painton* [1894] P 151 a will prepared by a beneficiary's son which left the testatrix's estate to the father shortly before the death, and revoking a previous will in favour of the plaintiff, was refused probate on appeal because there were suspicious circumstances surrounding the execution of the will. The evidence of the son and his friend, who had visited the testatrix to secure the execution of the will, was not sufficient to remove this suspicion.

The fact that David's wife was one of the three witnesses to the will might add to the suspicion in the mind of the judge but would not invoke the consequences of invalidity as there are two independent witnesses, namely the nurses, and s15 of the Wills Act 1837 would therefore not apply as the Wills Act 1968 now reverses the decision in *In the Estate of Bravda* [1968] 1 WLR 479 whereby witnesses lost their beneficial interests even though two independent witnesses also attested.

In the event, therefore, Harold and Colin, subject to deducing satisfactory evidence, may well have a good case for contesting this will for the reasons given.

No mention has been made as to whether a solicitor drew up the will or even if it was in David's handwriting.

QUESTION TWO

Walter was a civil servant and was rather formal in his behaviour. In 1985, his wife Betty died. Having no children, Walter asked his solicitor friend, Sam, to prepare a will for him under which he left all his property to his nephew Peter (his nearest relative). Walter duly executed this will early in 1986.

In about 1990, Walter became friendly with a woman called Sybil. He gradually became more and more absent-minded and forgetful.

Peter has just discovered that in 1992 Walter went through a ceremony of marriage with Sybil. Walter did not tell anyone about this and does not appear to remember getting married.

Upon further investigation, Peter has discovered that, in 1993, Walter appears to have made a home-made will. Peter does not know for certain what this will provides, but he suspects that it gives all Walter's property to Sybil. Sybil has the will and has refused to let Peter see it. She says that it is none of his business. Peter has spoken to the two people (Horace and Wendy) who were present on the day when the home-made will appears to have been executed. They say that Sybil brought Walter to their house with a paper which Walter appeared already to have signed. Walter seemed more absent-minded than usual. Wendy was in the kitchen and witnessed Walter's signature after Sybil had pointed to it and Walter had nodded to signify that it was his signature. In the meantime, Horace was in the garden cutting flowers but could vaguely see what was going on, through the window. Sybil then brought Walter out into the garden and Horace witnessed Walter's signature. Wendy watched this from the kitchen window.

Advise Peter.

University of London LLB Examination
(for External Students) Succession June 1997 Q3

General Comment

A complicated question involving many different issues, including capacity and knowledge and approval. This question demonstrates the need to make a quantative judgment about the best course of action based on the burden of proof. This point is often missed by candidates.

Skeleton Solution

Effect of marriage on will – validity of 1993 will – Walter's mental capacity – issue of animus testandi – compliance with formalities.

Suggested Solution

Peter as Walter's nearest relative would wish to clarify two issues; firstly, whether his uncle's 1986 will has been revoked by his marriage to Sybil and secondly, whether the 1993 will is valid.

It is presumed that the 1986 will was valid as it was duly executed. However, Walter's later marriage to Sybil would automatically revoke the earlier will: s18(1) Wills Act 1837.

Although Peter may wish to contend that the marriage was not valid as his uncle did not remember getting married, he may have difficulty doing so as a person does not require a high level of mental competence in order to get married. *In the Estate of Park* [1954] P 112, where the testator got married and executed a complicated will on the same day, the will was held to be invalid due to his lack of competence but his marriage was declared to be valid.

The next issue is to decide on the validity of the 1993 will. The validity of a will depends on the s9 Wills Act 1837 formalities being complied with and on the testator having the requisite mental capacity and animus testandi at the time of its execution.

In discussing s9 of the Wills Act 1837, it is clear that the will was in writing and signed by Walter plus there is nothing in the facts to suggest that he did not intend his signature to give effect to the will.

Although Walter had not signed the will in the presence of two witnesses, he may have acknowledged his signature to Horace and Wendy. Walter had nodded while Sybil pointed out his signature to Wendy. He did not have to say anything as acknowledgment may be effected by gestures: *Re Davies* (1850) 2 Rob Ecc 337. Horace was in the garden at the time but he could see what was happening. Witnesses are not required to actually see the signature so long as they had the opportunity to see it: *Daintree* v *Butcher* (1888) 13 PD 102. There must be a line of sight between the signature and Walter at the moment of acknowledgment: *Re Groffman* [1969] 1 WLR 733.

However, both witnesses must also be aware of what was going on. This means that they must be mentally as well as physically present. Even, if there was a line of sight between Horace and the signature, he may not have been aware of what was happening.

The above requirements would have been met when Walter went out to the garden to enable Horace to witness his signature. However, the testator must acknowledge his signature to the witnesses before they sign or acknowledge their signature in his presence. This means that Wendy who had signed before must acknowledge her signature to Walter before Horace witnessed the will. The essential sequence of events must be followed: *Couser* v *Couser* [1996] 3 All ER 256.

The execution of the will seemed not to have complied with s9 formalities unless it could be shown that while Horace was in the garden he had been aware of what was going on when Walter first acknowledged his signature.

Walter's mental capacity at the time of execution is also questionable as the two witnesses claim he was even more forgetful than usual. The testator must be of sound mind, sound memory and sound understanding when executing the will; this means that he must understand the nature and effect of the will, realise the extent of the property he is disposing and be aware of the claims of his loved ones: *Banks* v *Goodfellow* (1870) LR 5 QB 549.

The onus is on the propounder of the will to prove that Walter had the required level of mental competence at the time. The degree of mental capacity required is a question of fact to be decided according to the circumstances of each case, eg the complexity of the will as in the case of *Park* (above).

In the absence of any medical evidence as Walter's mental capacity, the court will have to rely on the presumption of continuance of his mental state as well on the evidence of the witnesses.

Finally, Walter have must the intention (animus testandi) to make the will. This essentially means that Walter must know and approve the contents of his will and he must have exercised free choice in making the will.

Once the propounder had successfully proven that Walter had the required level of mental competence, he may rely on the presumption that Walter had known and approved the contents of his will: *Barry* v *Butlin* (1838) 2 Moo PC 480.

However, if there are suspicious circumstances, the propounder will have to prove knowledge and approval. To show suspicious circumstances, Peter will have to prove that the will was prepared by Sybil and benefited her. In that case, the court will be more vigilant and not admit the will to probate unless the suspicion has been removed by the propounder: *Wintle* v *Nye* [1959] 1 WLR 284.

The degree of suspicion will by very high if it turned out that Sybil is the main beneficiary and that the will was written in her hand plus the evidence from the two witnesses that it was her who was directing the execution of the will.

Alternatively, Peter may wish to allege that his uncle had been unduly influenced by

Sybil in the making of the will in that he had been coerced into doing something which he did not desire to do: *Hall* v *Hall* (1868) 1 P & D 481. Although, according to *Parfitt* v *Lawless* (1872) LR 2 P & D 462, there is no presumption of undue influence based on the relationship between Walter and Sybil, the court may decide otherwise due to his extreme absent-mindedness and dependence on her following *Simpson* v *Simpson* (1989) 19 Fam Law 20.

However, Peter must be warned that if he is alleging undue influence, the onus will fall on him to prove it: *Craig* v *Lamoureux* [1920] AC 349. It would be better if he challenged the validity of the will either based on lack of formalities, Walter's mental incompetence or lack of knowledge and approval.

QUESTION THREE

Gemma, aged 75, is partially blind and severely incapacitated following a serious stroke. She is a resident at the Happy Valley Nursing Home. Harold, the owner and manager of the home, knows that Gemma has no relations or close friends. He suggests that she should make a will leaving her assets (she has considerable funds in bank and building society accounts) to the home, since it faces closure as the result of its critical financial position. Gemma agrees to do so as she is very happy at the home and does not wish to be moved. She does not know that, contrary to Harold's assertion, the home is financially sound.

Harold prepares a will which leaves all her property to the Happy Valley Nursing Home. He reads it over to her twice and the will is then validly executed. He tells Gemma that he is going to keep the will in his office. Gemma agrees.

A few days later Gemma asks to see the will as she has changed her mind as to whom to benefit (but she does not tell Harold of her change of heart). When Harold brings the will, Gemma looks at it and then suddenly starts to tear it to pieces. Harold snatches it from her, sellotapes it together and leaves it on his office desk. While Harold is away from the office, a cleaner throws the will away with the rubbish, not realising that it is a will.

Gemma has just died of natural causes. Her will cannot be found.

Advise Harold.

University of London LLB Examination
(for External Students) Succession June 1998 Q3

General Comment

Once again, a question on animus testandi, but this time mixed with revocation. The main difficulty with this type of question is the volume of material. It is important to be concise and not to 'waffle' in the answer.

Skeleton Solution

Issue of validity of will – mental capacity – animus testandi – revocation – presumption of missing will

Suggested Solution

Harold would wish to know whether Gemma had died leaving a valid will.

The validity of a will depends on the formalities having been satisfied and on the testator having the capacity and intention to make it. Section 9 of the Wills Act 1837 would not need to be discussed here as the question makes it clear that the will was validly executed.

A testatrix is deemed to have the mental capacity to make a valid will if she is of sound mind, sound memory and sound understanding. Following the case of *Banks* v *Goodfellow* (1870) LR 5 QB 549 this means that she must appreciate the nature and effect of the will, recollect the extent of her property and understand the claims of her family and friends.

The onus is on the propounder (Harold) to prove Gemma's mental competence at the time of the execution of the will. In the absence of any medical evidence, the presumption is of continuance of her mental state. Although Gemma was partially blind and severely incapacitated following a stroke, there is nothing to suggest that she was not mentally competent at the time the will was executed.

Gemma may not have the animus testandi, ie the intention to make the will. In order for her will to be valid, she must have knowledge and approval of its contents and there must be no undue influence or fraud exercised upon her.

Once the propounder is able to prove that Gemma was mentally capable, he may rely on the presumption that she had also knew and approved the contents of her will: *Barry* v *Butlin* (1838) 2 Moo PC 480. Harold would not be able to rely on this presumption due to the suspicious circumstances whereby he prepared the will and is the main beneficiary under it as owner and manager of the nursing home. Another reason is that Gemma is partially blind.

According to *Barry* v *Butlin*, where there are suspicious circumstances, the court will be more vigilant and will refuse to admit the will to probate until the propounder has removed the suspicion. As the degree of suspicion is very high in this case, Harold may have difficulty removing it, as in *Wintle* v *Nye* [1959] 1 WLR 284. Gemma is also partially blind and is therefore more easily taken advantage of.

Harold may show knowledge and approval by adducing evidence of the fact that he read the will over to Gemma twice before it was executed. However, he must be aware that this is not conclusive evidence of knowledge and approval.

Even if Harold succeeded in removing the suspicion, he must be aware that the will may still be invalid due to either fraud or undue influence on his part.

By lying about the financial position of the home, Harold had intentionally deceived Gemma into making the nursing home the sole beneficiary of her will. Harold's actions were clearly fraudulent resulting in Gemma lacking animus testandi when her will was executed.

Undue influence could also be an issue as Harold appeared to have coerced Gemma into making the will so that it was not made of her own free choice: *Hall* v *Hall* (1868) 1 P & D 481.

Apart from the above, Gemma seemed to have revoked her will by destruction when she tore it up. Section 20 of the Wills Act 1837 requires that the will be destroyed by burning, tearing or otherwise destroying by the testator with animus revocandi.

As Harold snatched the will from Gemma it may be that she had not done everything possible in destroying it: *Doe d Perkes* v *Perkes* (1820) 3 B & Ald 489. It seems clear from the facts that Gemma had the intention to revoke her will.

The will is now missing. In the case of *Sugden* v *Lord St Leonards* (1876) 1 PD 154, if a will last known to have been in the testator's possession is missing on the testator's death, the presumption is that it has been destroyed by the testator with animus revocandi. This presumption cannot be applied in this case however, as the will was last with Harold when it disappeared.

Even if Harold manages to rebut the presumption, it is unlikely he will benefit from the will as there is every chance that it is invalid due to the reasons discussed above.

QUESTION FOUR

a) 'In a word, a testator may be led but not driven.' (per Wilde J in *Hall* v *Hall* (1868).

   Explain and comment on this statement.

b) Jim is a young British soldier attached to a United Nations peace-keeping force in the Balkans. He has become friendly with Bill, another soldier with the force. Bill, who is much older than Jim and is of higher rank, suggests that Jim should make a will 'in case anything happens'. Jim says that he does not know how to make a will but Bill informs him that all Jim needs to do is to tell Bill how he would like his property distributed on his death. Jim tells Bill that he can think of no-one in particular to whom he wants to leave his property, whereupon Bill replies, 'Well, what about your Mum, or even me?' Jim looks a little surprised but is reassured when Bill tells him that it is normal for soldiers to leave gifts in wills to colleagues (Bill knows this to be untrue). Jim then says, 'OK – it may as well go to you and my Mum in equal shares.' The following day Jim is killed when his truck is involved in an accident.

   Discuss.

University of London LLB Examination
(for External Students) Succession June 1999 Q3

General Comment

Another question with a large mix of issues, starting in (a) with undue influence – this area is often paid little attention. In part (b) there are several issues to be considered but none are particularly complex.

Skeleton Solution

a) Explanation of the rules on undue influence supported by case law.

b) Privileged will – animus testandi – fraud, undue influence.

Suggested Solution

a) For a will to be valid, in addition to satisfying s9 of the Wills Act 1837, the testator must also have the capacity, the intention and have exercised free choice when making the will. A testator is deemed not to have exercised free choice if he was unduly influence.

A testator who makes a will as a result of undue influence will lack animus testandi. Undue influence in the law of succession has been defined in the case of *Hall* v *Hall* (1868) 1 P & D 481 as pressure or coercion exerted on the testator into making his will.

According to the court in *Wingrove* v *Wingrove* (1885) 11 PD 81, coercion may take many forms, such as threats or violence. However, it is irrelevant that no force or violence was used so long as the testator's free will has been overborne. The will in *Hall* v *Hall* failed because the testator yielded to his wife by making her the sole beneficiary for the sake of peace and quiet.

Undue influence must be distinguished from persuasion, which is allowed. Persuasion appeals to feelings of affection, ties of kindred and a sentiment of gratitude or pity. The test is that the testator may be led but not driven.

The onus is on the person alleging undue influence to prove it: *Boyse* v *Rosborough* (1857) 6 HL Cas 2. Therefore, as was clearly shown in the case of *Wintle* v *Nye* [1959] 1 WLR 284, a person challenging a will is better off relying on any evidence of suspicious circumstances rather than on evidence of undue influence. Once suspicious circumstances have been established, it is for the propounder to prove that the testator did know and approve of the contents of his will.

Unlike in other areas of law, there is no presumption of undue influence based on the relationship between the testator and the beneficiary. In *Parfitt* v *Lawless* (1872) LR 2 P & D 462 the very fact that the main beneficiary of the testatrix's will was her priest did not give rise to a presumption of undue influence.

However, the exceptional circumstances in the case of *Simpson* v *Simpson* [1992] 1 FLR 601 gave rise to such a presumption between the testator and his wife. In that case, the testator had left over two-thirds of his estate to his third wife. Evidence was adduced of the fact that his brain tumour had impaired his mental faculties.

b) The issue here is whether Jim had left a valid will. If Jim was a soldier being in actual military service, he may have made a privileged will under s11 of the Wills Act 1837; ie a will which need not comply with the formalities set out in s9 of the Wills Act 1837. As Jim was a soldier attached to a peacekeeping force, the question is whether or not he was in actual military service when the will was made.

Denning LJ in the case of *Re Wingham* [1949] P 187, defined actual military service to include not only active service during a war or an imminent war but also military operations during peacetime. This was later confirmed in the case of *Re Jones* [1981] 1 All ER 1 where a soldier serving in Northern Ireland was held to have been in actual military service.

Following the reasoning in the two cases discussed above, it is clear that Jim was a privileged testator.

The next issue is whether he made the will with the intention to do so (animus testandi). The testator must have meant for his words to express his wishes on his death: *Re Knibbs* [1962] 1 WLR 852. Jim's will may not be valid if he lacked animus testandi due to either lack of knowledge and approval, fraud or undue influence.

Jim may not have knowledge and approval of the contents of his will due to suspicious circumstances. It is arguable that it was Bill, and not Jim who made the will as the facts show that Bill had directed Jim on what to say. The propounder will have the onus of removing the suspicion before the court will admit the will to probate: *Barry* v *Butlin* (1838) 2 Moo PC 480.

By telling Jim an untruth about the custom of soldiers leaving gifts in their wills to colleagues, it is possible that Bill had acted fraudulently by intentionally deceiving Jim into leaving him half his estate.

Undue influence could also be an issue here as Bill was much older than Jim and is of higher rank. It was Bill who suggested that Jim should make a will. The question is whether Bill had coerced Jim into making the will. The test, according to *Hall* v *Hall* (above) is that Jim may be led but not driven.

If it can be shown that Jim's will was made either as a result of fraud or undue influence on Bill's part, the will is invalid. However, it should be noted that the onus of proving both fraud and undue influence is on the person challenging the will.

QUESTION FIVE

a) Which principles guide the court in making a statutory will on behalf of a mental patient?

b) Andrew and Brian are two brothers, aged 60 and 55 respectively. Andrew has a dominating and extrovert personality, whereas Brian is rather unassertive and shy. These days Brian tends to follow Andrew's advice as regards financial matters in particular.

Recently, Andrew suggested that Brian ought to make a will, and offered to draft one for him. Brian agreed. Andrew drafted a will according to which the bulk of Brian's estate was given to Camfam, a charity which Andrew helps to administer. Brian, who is a bachelor with no close friends or family other than Andrew, was unsure whether he wanted to benefit Camfam as he really preferred to leave his estate to Oxfam. However, when Andrew told him that Camfam was using its funds principally to help orphans in Kosovo, Brian agreed to execute the will since he believed that to be a worthy aim for charitable support.

Brian has just died. It transpires that Camfam has never been involved in helping orphans in Kosovo (or elsewhere).

Advise Camfam.

*University of London LLB Examination
(for External Students) Succession June 2000 Q5*

General Comment

This question reflects the current trend to examine over a wide area of the syllabus by dividing the question into two parts. The issue of statutory wills is probably not studied in any detail by most students as part of their revision of animus testandi and yet the vast majority will most certainly expect to do the animus question in the examination. This question would have been a disaster for someone question-spotting without enough topics for an alternative question. Be warned!

Skeleton Solution

a) Section 103 of the Mental Health Act 1983 – *Re D(J)*; Megarry V-C; five propositions – *Re Davey* – *Re C*.

b) Fraud – undue influence – knowledge and approval.

Suggested Solution

a) Under s103 of the Mental Health Act 1983 the Court of Protection has the power to order the execution of a will on behalf of an adult patient who is unable to make a will himself because of his lack of mental capacity. Section 103A lays down the formal requirements for the execution of such a will. These are not important for the purposes of the current question, which asks about the applicable principles. The best guide to these principles is from the judgment of Megarry V-C in *Re D(J)* [1982] 2 All ER 37 as follows:

   i) It is to be assumed that the patient had a brief lucid interval at the time when the will is made.

ii) During the lucid interval the patient has full knowledge of the past and realisation that once the will is executed he will relapse into the actual mental state he was in.

iii) The court should consider the patient as he was before losing testamentary capacity and do for the patient in the will what he would fairly do for himself as in the case of *Re C* [1991] 3 All ER 866.

iv) During the hypothetical lucid interval the patient must be envisaged as being advised by competent solicitors.

v) In all normal cases the patient is to be envisaged as taking a broad brush to the claims on his bounty.

Such wills are to be regarded as the will of the patient, made by her as if she were of testamentary capacity and thus cannot be later set aside by the Court of Protection whose power over the patient comes to an end at the patient's death: see *Re Davey* [1981] 1 WLR 164.

b) In order to advise Camfam on the potential challenges to their gift under Brian's will, it will be necessary to consider if the will was made with sufficient animus testandi. This will may be challenged on a number of grounds, starting with undue influence. For such a challenge to succeed, the person alleging undue influence would bear the burden of proving that Brian was forced or coerced into executing a document as his will: *Killick* v *Poutney* (1999) The Times 30 April. There must, however, be some coercion as stated in *Wingrove* v *Wingrove* (1885) 11 PD 81. Mere persuasion is not sufficient: *Hall* v *Hall* (1868) 1 P & D 481. The facts given do not disclose any coercion of the type necessary to prove a lack of animus testandi.

A more successful challenge may be mounted on the basis that the will was executed as a result of a fraud. In the context of wills, fraud will be present in cases where the testator has been prompted to make provision in his will, or exclude from his will, a beneficiary because of false statements made to him about that beneficiary as *Wilkinson* v *Joughin* (1866) LR 2 Eq 319. In the present case Andrew has told Brian that Camfam was using its funds principally to help orphans – this was untrue and would appear to have been said for the benefit Camfam, which Andrew helped to administer (so he must have known his statement was untrue). Such a challenge on the basis of fraud would be successful, so long as evidence of Andrew's statements to Brian could be advanced.

The court will normally presume knowledge and approval where the will has been properly executed. This presumption will not apply in cases of suspicious circumstances. The classic example of suspicious circumstances is where the party who prepares or writes the will also takes a benefit under it: *Barry* v *Butlin* (1838) 2 Moo PC 480. In these circumstances, once the suspicion is raised it is up to the party concerned to prove that the testator knew and approved of the contents of his will. The degree of proof will vary depending on the circumstances of each case: *Wintle* v *Nye* [1959] 1 WLR 284. So in this case it will be up to Andrew to bring evidence to remove the suspicion. The difference between the cases mentioned above and the current case is that in those cases the party who benefited was the party who wrote or was involved in the execution of the will. In this case the party who benefits is Camfam and not Andrew personally. There are cases in which the court has been prepared to extend the doctrine to cover cases where the party preparing the will procured a benefit for a close friend or relative or indeed in any other circumstances: *Tyrell* v *Painton* [1894] P 151. This approach has been applied in other cases such as *Thomas* v *Jones* [1928] P 162, *Brown* v *Fisher* (1890) 63 LT 465 and *Re Ticehurst* (1973) 123 NLJ 249. There is little reason why it should not be applied in this case and with some success.

Chapter 5

Revocation of Wills

5.1   Introduction

5.2   Key points

5.3   Key cases and statutes

5.4   Questions and suggested solutions

5.1 Introduction

This chapter should not be studied in isolation. If you intend to prepare this for the examinations, it is advisable to also study Chapters 6 and 7. Revocation questions are very popular in the examinations and the problem questions are normally quite complex and require good fact-management skills.

5.2 Key points

a) A will is ambulatory and revocable until testator's death.

b) Contract not to revoke does not prevent revocation but estate may be liable for breach.

c) Doctrine of mutual wills: see, eg, *Re Dale*, *Proctor* v *Dale* [1994] Ch 31.

d) Methods of revocation:

    i) Marriage of testators: s18(1) Wills Act 1837

- Unless appears from will that when made the testator expected to marry a particular person and he intended the will should not be revoked by marriage: s18(3) Wills Act 1837.

- Where testator's marriage is dissolved will takes effect as though former spouse had died on the day of the divorce: s18A Wills Act 1837.

    ii) Section 20 Wills Act 1837: allows testator to revoke will using another document or by destruction.

- Express revocation by document where duly executed document contains revocation clause: *Re Spracklan's Estate* [1938] 2 All ER 345.

- Implied revocation by document where there are several wills without revocation clause; a later instrument will revoke the earlier to the extent of the inconsistencies.

- Destruction should be burning, tearing or otherwise destroying of will, accompanied by the intention to revoke: *In the Estate of Southerden* [1925] P 177.

- Destruction must be a physical act; need not destroy whole will but must have destroyed vital part: *Cheese* v *Lovejoy* (1877) 2 PD 251; *Hobbs* v *Knight* (1838) 163 ER 267.

- The act of destruction may be by the testator or by another in his presence and by his direction: *In the Goods of Dadds* (1857) 164 ER 579.

iii) Doctrine of conditional revocation: where intention to revoke is conditional, revocation ineffective unless condition is satisfied: *In the Estate of Southerden* (above); *Re Jones* [1976] Ch 200; *Re Finnemore* [1992] 1 All ER 800; *Re Robinson* [1930] 2 Ch 332.

5.3 Key cases and statutes

- *Brunt* v *Brunt* (1837) 3 P & D 37
  Effect of a lack of capacity on revocation

- *Bryan, In the Estate of* [1907] P 125
  Revocation by implication depends on the construction of the will and extrinsic evidence

- *Cheese* v *Lovejoy* (1877) 2 PD 251
  If there is no appropriate act of destruction, couples with an intention to revoke – there can be no revocation

- *Dixon* v *Treasury Solicitor* [1905] P 42
  Conditional revocation will not have effect if the condition is not satisfied

- *Doe d Perkes* v *Perkes* (1820) B & Ald 489
  The testator must do all he intended to do by way of act of destruction for there to be a valid revocation

- *Hobbs* v *Knight* (1838) 1 Curt 768
  The whole will was revoked because the signature, a vital part of the will, had been destroyed

- *Phelan, Re* [1972] Fam 33
  Revocation clauses have no effect if the testator has no knowledge and approval of it

- *Southerden, In the Estate of* [1925] P 177
  Destruction under a mistaken belief that the will is already revoked is not sufficient animus revocandi

- *Spracklan's Estate, Re* [1938] 2 All ER 345
  The document in which the clause is contained need not be in the form of a will

- *Sudgen* v *Lord St Leonards* (1876) 1 PD 154
  The presumption that a will in the possession of the testator that cannot be found on death has been revoked was rebutted as a result of evidence

- Matrimonial Causes Act 1973, s12 – grounds on which a marriage is voidable

- Wills Act 1837, s18 – effect of marriage on a will

- Wills Act 1837, s20 – formalities for the revocation of wills

5.4 Questions and suggested solutions

QUESTION ONE

In 1980 Tom made a will leaving his entire estate to his son Cecil. In 1988, after an argument with Cecil, Tom telephoned his solicitor to say that he wished to make a new will leaving everything to the Newtown Home for the Aged, a registered charity.

The solicitor drew up a new will in accordance with those instructions, which expressly revoked the will of 1980 and left the whole estate to that charity. It was arranged that Tom should attend at the solicitor's office to execute the will, which was to be witnessed by a secretary and an articled clerk. On leaving his home on the way to the solicitor's office, Tom tore up the 1980 will and threw it into the back of his writing desk, saying to his housekeeper. 'As my will of 1980 is to be revoked, I may as well destroy it.'

When Tom arrived at his solicitor's office, the solicitor was engaged with another client and Tom was taken into the secretary's office to execute the will.

The secretary said to Tom, 'I am expecting a telephone call and so I had better attest now'. The secretary then signed the will. While Tom was in the middle of signing his name, the telephone rang and the secretary left that room to answer the telephone in an adjacent office which was separated by a glass partition on which were slatted blinds. Tom completed his signature and the articled clerk then signed as well. The articled clerk then left the secretary's office. When the secretary returned, Tom pointed to his signature and said, 'What a pity that the telephone had interrupted the signing'. The secretary said, 'There is no problem, I had already signed my name'.

Tom died a month ago.

Advise which documents, if any, can be admitted to probate.

University of London LLB Examination
(for External Students) Succession June 1989 Q2

General Comment

This is a typical revocation question with two competing wills. The intention to revoke is a crucial point which relies entirely on the proper execution of the new will.

Skeleton Solution

Is the 1980 will revoked by Tom's destruction? – was the 1988 will executed correctly? – did the 1988 will revoke the 1980 will?

Suggested Solution

Tom's 1980 will can be admitted to probate unless he has revoked it. A will is ambulatory and revocable. Circumstances when a will is revoked are inter alia upon the testator's marriage, by destruction, or by express clause of a subsequent will.

If Tom's 1988 will is admissible then it will revoke his 1980 will since it contains an express clause to this effect: s20 Wills Act 1837.

Tom's tearing his 1980 will may have revoked it. Section 20 Wills Act 1837 requires both destruction and animus revocandi for a will to be revoked by destruction. Both elements must be present at the same time: see *Cheese* v *Lovejoy* (1877) 2 PD 251 and *Gill* v *Gill* [1909] P 157.

As to the act of destruction itself, there is a double test; there must be some tearing or other destruction, and the destruction must be all the testator intended. It should be noted that if only a small part of a will is destroyed, eg a line, that part must be so important that the will could not stand without it, if the will is to be revoked.

The double test seems to be satisfied by this question; there was a tearing of the will, and no evidence that Tom intended to destroy it further.

However, it seems that Tom does not intend to revoke his will at the time he tears it up, since he tears it up on the grounds that it is to be revoked later. Since animus revocandi and destruction were not simultaneous, Tom's destroying his will has not revoked it. It will therefore be admissible unless revoked by his 1988 will.

It cannot be revoked by the 1988 will unless this is admissible, which seems to be a question of whether the formalities of execution have been observed.

Section 9 Wills Act 1837 set out the formalities of execution. It requires that a will be in writing; signed by the testator or a person in his presence and by his direction; it must appear that by the signature the testator intended to give effect to the will; either the will must be signed, or the signature acknowledged, in the presence of two or more witnesses present at the same time; and each witness must either attest and sign the will, or acknowledge his signature in the presence of the testator.

The facts here do not doubt that the will is in writing, signed by the testator etc, or that the testator intended to give effect to the will by his signature. The formalities in question are whether Tom signed or acknowledged in the presence of two or more witnesses present at the same time, and whether each witness attested and signed, or acknowledged in the presence of Tom.

The witnesses are the articled clerk and secretary.

Although Tom's pointing to his signature would amount to acknowledgment, he pointed in the presence of one witness only which is not sufficient. It is therefore important to determine if he signed in the presence of the two witnesses.

Witnesses need not actually see the testator sign; the test is whether they could have seen the signing had they so wished. Thus, if the secretary could see Tom's signing through the slatted blind if she wished, then on the assumption that the articled clerk was present, that would be sufficient and Tom may be said to have signed in the presence of two witnesses.

Each witness must either attest and sign, or acknowledge his or her signature in the presence of the testator. The articled clerk clearly attested and signed in Tom's presence.

It is not necessary for witnesses to sign or acknowledge in the presence of other witnesses, so it does not matter whether the secretary could see the articled clerk signing.

The secretary's signature cannot be said to be attestation because she signed before Tom did. However, by her words 'I had already signed my name' she acknowledged her signature and that is sufficient. As stated before, it does not matter that she did not acknowledge her signature in the presence of the articled clerk.

To conclude, the formalities of execution have been observed so the 1988 will is admissible. Consequently, the 1980 will is revoked by the 1988 will, so that the former is not admissible.

QUESTION TWO

a) A died in 1985 leaving two wills with significant differences as to the beneficiaries. The second will did not contain a revocation clause.

b) B's will was found damaged after his death.

c) C's will could not be found after her death but her draft was discovered.

d) D's sister told him his will was invalid because it had not been prepared by a solicitor. In fact it complied with all formalities and was valid. Believing his sister, D burnt his will saying he might as well dispose of it since it was ineffective. D subsequently died without making another will.

e) E destroyed her will after a party, having rowed with her husband. At the time, E was drunk. She later died, leaving no other will.

Advise the executors of A, B, C, D and E.

Written by the Editor

General Comment

This question examines five aspects of revocation. It is important when revising this area that all the issues are carefully studied as questions of this nature are quite common. Candidates often make errors when dealing with lost or mutilated wills and rarely deal with the issues relating to drink and drugs in the execution of revocation of wills.

Skeleton Solution

Revocation by implication – s20 Wills Act 1837 – mutilated will – lost will – destruction – mistake – destruction – drunk.

Suggested Solution

a) The wording of s20 Wills Act 1837 gives a court authority to hold that a will has been revoked by implication. This doctrine will be relevant where there is more than one will and the later will/wills do not contain express revocation clauses, but contain dispositions which treat the same property differently. In such a case, the court may find that an earlier will has been revoked by a later will by implication: *Dempsey* v *Lawson* (1877) 2 PD 98. Thus the fact that A's second will does not contain an express revocation clause will not prevent a court from holding that the first will has been revoked by the second.

Whether a court will find revocation or not in circumstances such as these, depends upon construction of the will – see *In the Estate of Bryan* [1907] P 125 – and where there is doubt on the face of the will, any relevant extrinsic evidence: see *Methuen* v *Methuen* (1816) 2 Phill 416.

A's executors are therefore advised that A's later will may have revoked his first will, and that that will depend upon the construction of his will and possibly extrinsic evidence.

b) There is conflict between the authorities on the position where a will such as B's is found, after death, mutilated. *Lambell* v *Lambell* (1831) 3 Hagg Ecc 568 states that in such circumstances there is a presumption of revocation. But *Cowling* v *Cowling* [1924] P 113 suggests the contrary. Arguably, whether or not a mutilated will is thereby revoked will depend upon the degree of mutilation. B's executors are advised that it is arguable that, if B's will is severely mutilated there may be revocation; but if it is only slightly mutilated, then it may not have been revoked.

c) *Sugden* v *Lord St Leonards* (1876) 1 PD 154 is authority for two points: firstly, that the loss of a will in the testator's lifetime need not revoke a will and secondly, that the loss of the will need not be fatal. As seen in *Re Webb* [1964] 1 WLR 509 a court is prepared to admit a draft or copy will provided the contents and due execution of the will can be shown. C's executors are therefore advised that it is most likely that C's will can be admitted.

d) A will destroyed by a testator who mistakenly believes the will to be ineffective is not revoked thereby: *In the Estate of Southerden* [1925] P 177. The necessary animus revocandi is lacking. For this reason, D's executors are advised that D's will was not revoked by burning.

e) Destruction of a will at a time when the testator is under the influence of drink or drugs does not constitute revocation: *Brunt* v *Brunt* (1873) 3 P & D 37. E's executors are advised that her will was not revoked when she destroyed it.

QUESTION THREE

Alan owned shares worth about £300,000 and a house worth about £250,000. His other property consisted of furniture and other investments worth a further £50,000. He had had a brother, Ben, who had two sons called Cedric and David. Ben was dead. Alan also had a sister, Elsie, and a wife, Freda. Five years ago, Alan made a will bequeathing his shares to Cedric and the residue of his estate to Freda, 'but if she [Freda] shall die before me' the residue was to go to a (named) charity. Two years ago, Alan divorced Freda. He understood that his divorce had revoked his will and so he tore it in half and threw it into a wastepaper basket. On Christmas Day 1995, Alan had too much to eat and drink. He suffered a heart attack and died about a week later.

Discuss.

University of London LLB Examination
(for External Students) Succession June 1996 Q4

General Comment

A very fair problem question involving two different aspects of revocation of a will. The date of the testator's death has deliberately not been identified clearly; if it was before 1 January 1996 a detailed knowledge of one particular case (*Re Sinclair*) would have been very advantageous to the candidate. It is arguable as to whether the facts of a problem question should turn so closely on the analysis of one case but, in principle, there is nothing unfair about this. If, in fact, the death of the testator occurred on or after 1 January 1996 then the effect of *Re Sinclair* will have been superseded by the Law Reform (Succession) Act 1995. The second aspect of the question concerned conditional revocation by destruction of a will.

Skeleton Solution

Bequest of personalty – disposition of residue – effect of a divorce – contrary intention – consequence of substitutional gift – application of *Re Sinclair* – effect of s3 Law Reform (Succession) Act (LR(S)A) 1995 – effect of s20 Wills Act 1837 – case law application.

Suggested Solution

By his will Alan has bequeathed his shares, worth £300,000, to his nephew, Cedric, and the residue of his estate (comprising a house worth £250,000 and investments worth £50,000) to Freda, subject to a condition that in the event of her death before Alan the residue will pass to a named charity.

The events which then take place raise the question of revocation of Alan's will. There are two specific problems involved:

a) whether Alan's divorce from Freda will allow the residue to pass to the charity; and

b) whether the act of tearing his will in half and throwing it into a wastepaper basket is a sufficient act of destruction by Alan as to constitute a revocation of his will, or a part of it.

The first problem involves consideration of s18A Wills Act (WA) 1837, which provides that where, after testator has made will, there is a decree dissolving or annulling his marriage then any appointment of the former spouse as executor is deemed to be omitted, and any gift to the former spouse is deemed to have lapsed. This is subject to any contrary intention expressed in the will. A consolidating provision is contained in s3 Law Reform (Succession) Act (LR(S)A) 1995 in regard to a testator dying on or after 1 January 1996. Alan's death, according to the facts, may have occurred just before or after that date. Accordingly, it becomes necessary to consider the law both as it stood immediately before the introduction of the 1995 Act, in the context of testators dying on or before 31 December 1995, and as it stood for testators dying after that date.

On the basis that Alan died before 1 January 1996, Freda, now divorced, loses the benefit of Alan's residue; but does the residue pass to the charity? The statement in s18A(1)(b) that the gift to the former spouse shall be deemed to have lapsed is not to be construed as if Freda had predeceased the testator, Alan. This may have an unfortunate effect on the substitutional gift to the charity. The facts correspond to the events in *Re Sinclair* [1985] 1 All ER 1066 where, in 1958, the testator had made a will leaving his entire estate to his wife absolutely provided she survived him for one month. If she should predecease him, or fail to survive him for that period, his estate was to pass to the Imperial Cancer Research Fund. The testator and his wife divorced in 1962. The testator died in 1983 without having changed his will. The question arose as to whether the subsequent gift to the charity should take effect. The Court of Appeal considered the word 'lapse' was not synonymous with 'predecease'. Accordingly, as the former wife was still alive the condition for the contingent gift to charity was not satisfied. The whole estate therefore devolved upon intestacy.

Applying *Re Sinclair* to the facts here, Alan's residue will not pass to the charity but into partial intestacy.

There was a general consensus that *Re Sinclair* left the law in an unsatisfactory state and the Law Commission were invited to look at the problem. In September 1993 they presented a report *Family Law: The Effect of Divorce on Wills* (Law Com No 217). This report recommended that the law should be amended so that where there is a divorce or annulment, the former spouse should be deemed to have predeceased the testator (with the exception that the former spouse should be treated as being alive for the purpose of benefiting as an appointee under a special power of appointment).

The Law Commission's report was implemented in s3 of the 1995 Act, substituting new paras (a) and (b) for the original paras (a) and (b) in s18A(1) WA 1837, as amended (and as applying to testators dying on or after 1 January 1996) so as to read:

'(1) Where, after a testator has made a will, a decree of a court of civil jurisdiction in England and Wales dissolves or annuls his marriage ...
(a) provisions of the will appointing executors or trustees or conferring a power of appointment, if they appoint or confer the power on the former spouse, shall take effect as if the former spouse had died on the date on which the marriage is dissolved or annulled, and
(b) any property which, or an interest in which, is devised or bequeathed to the former spouse shall pass as if the former spouse had died on that date,
except in so far as a contrary intention appears by the will.'

It is the substituted s18A(1)(b) which is the key subsection, and which effectively negatives the effect of *Re Sinclair*. Applied to the facts of the question, Freda, the former wife, would now be deemed to have died on the date of the divorce, with the consequence that Alan's residue would pass to the named charity and not devolve into a partial intestacy. But it must be re-iterated this is only true to the extent that Alan died on or after 1 January 1996 (about which, from the facts, we cannot be certain).

The second problem posed here concerns the tearing in half of the will. For revocation by actual destruction there must be a 'burning, tearing, or otherwise destroying the same by the testator, or by some person in his presence and by his direction, with the intention of revoking the same': s20 Wills Act 1837. There is clearly here a tearing by Alan, but his reason for doing so is that he believes his divorce has revoked his will, whereas the divorce has the effect of revoking the provisions in favour of Freda only while leaving intact the bequest to Cedric. Alan was therefore under a misapprehension as to the legal effect of the act of destruction. Has he the necessary animus revocandi? According to *Re Southerden* [1925] P 177, he has not. In that case the testator believed, mistakenly, that on his death intestate his widow would be entitled to the whole of his property and he therefore destroyed the will by burning. As he had misunderstood the effect of the intestacy rules the revocation was ineffective.

In *Re Davies* [1928] Ch 74, the testatrix thought she had made a valid second will, and in this belief she destroyed her first will. In fact, the second will was invalid and the first will was held to be effective. This is an illustration of the doctrine of conditional revocation.

By comparison a revocation was held to be effective in *Collins v Elstone* [1893] P 1, where a testator mistakenly failed to appreciate the consequence of a revocation clause.

The principle in *Re Southerden* would be applied here. This means that the provision in favour of Cedric would stand. The will, to that extent, would not be revoked by the tearing in half and throwing it into the wastepaper basket. For probate purposes it may be necessary to reconstruct the will under r54 Non-Contentious Probate Rules from a draft, copy, reconstruction or some other evidence of its contents if it proves difficult, or impossible by putting the two halves together. The registrar, in any event, is likely to require an affidavit of due execution under r12.

In summary, Cedric takes the shares. But the residue will fall into partial intestary if Alan died on or before 31 December 1995, in the event for the benefit of the issue of his deceased brother Ben (in equal shares on the statutory trusts of the Administration of Estates Act 1925) and his sister, Elsie. This assumes Alan had no parent living (who would have been entitled in higher degree). On the other hand, if Alan died after 1 January 1996 the residue will pass to the named charity.

QUESTION FOUR

a) In what circumstances may an express revocation clause be held not to revoke earlier wills?

b) John made a will two years ago but recently decided to revoke it. He got it out of his desk, where he kept his papers, and started to tear it up. He was interrupted by a telephone call from his mother which lasted over an hour. When the call was finished, John completed tearing the will but then had second thoughts. He decided that he wanted the will to operate after all, so he stuck the pieces together and wrote, 'This will is now revived'. He took the will to his neighbours, a married couple, and signed it in their presence, having shown it to them.

John has just died. The will cannot be found but his neighbours can recall what its terms were.

Discuss.

University of London LLB Examination
(for External Students) Succession June 1999 Q5

General Comment

This question requires some thinking – especially for part (a). It is important to spend time reading and understanding what you are asked before you begin to write an answer. This is yet another example of a number of topics and issues being mixed in a part question. This pattern is likely to be on the increase for the University of London examinations – especially since the probate aspects of this subject are no longer on the syllabus.

Skeleton Solution

a) Conditional revocation – contrary intention: *Re Wayland* – lack of knowledge and approval – lack of mental capacity.

b) Revocation by destruction: *Perkes* v *Perkes* – revival – missing wills.

Suggested Solution

a) In general, express revocation clauses operate to revoke all previous wills so long as the revocation clause is executed in accordance with s9 formalities: see s20 Wills Act 1837. It is even irrelevant if the testator was misled as to the effect of the clause as in *Collins* v *Elstone* [1893] P 1.

Of course, such a clause would have no effect if the testator did not know and approve of its presence as in *Re Phelan* [1972] Fam 33. Other restrictions on the effectiveness of a revocation clause include situations where the testator has insufficient mental capacity to execute a will. This lack of capacity will equally affect the execution of an express revocation clause, as the same mental capacity is required for both.

Revocation clauses may also be limited in their ambit or even be conditional on the happening of certain events. In the case of *Re Wayland* [1951] 2 All ER 1051 the express revocation clause was limited in its application by a clear contrary intention as expressed by the testator. In this case, the testator left a will with a revocation clause that declared that it was intended only to deal with the testator's property in England. The court held that the revocation clause could not then apply to the testator's estate in Belgium.

Of course, when dealing with conditional revocation – even though there may be an express revocation clause – it will only apply if the particular condition is satisfied – if not the clause is ineffective as in *Dixon* v *Treasury Solicitor* [1905] P 42. In all of the circumstances above an express revocation may not always have the effect of revoking earlier wills.

b) Section 20 of the Wills Act 1837 makes it quite clear that a will may be revoked by 'burning, tearing or otherwise destroying' coupled with 'the intention of revoking the same.' In the given case John has decided to revoke an earlier will and begins to tear the will up before he is interrupted by a telephone call. At the time of tearing it would appear that John has the intention to revoke. The act of destruction must be completed, that is the testator must do all he intends to do by way of destruction. If he does not complete the necessary act of destruction then the will will not be revoked – as in *Doe d Perkes* v *Perkes* (1820) 3 B & Ald 489. In this case, as John has completed the act of destruction and clearly had the necessary intention to revoke at the time his will is revoked by destruction.

In any event he has second thoughts and attempts to revive the will by sticking the pieces together, writing that it is now revived on the face of the will and re-executing the will as per s9. Revival is governed by s22 of the Wills Act 1837. The section limits the ways in which a will may be revived. The method that applies in this instance is the re-execution of the will in accordance with s9. There seems to be no problem with the re execution of John's will.

The difficulty that now arises is that John has died and the will cannot be found. In such circumstances, where the will was known to be in the testator's possession, the court will presume that the will was destroyed by the testator with the intention of revoking it: *Welch* v *Phillips* (1836) 1 Moo PCC 299. Such presumptions may of course be rebutted – as in *Sugden* v *Lord St Leonards* (1876) 1 PD 154. This case raises two important points: first, that a will may be lost or destroyed in the testator's lifetime without being revoked; and, second, that the loss of a will is not necessarily fatal. In these cases the court is prepared to admit a draft of the contents of the will or a copy thereof to probate so long as it can be proved that the will was duly executed and what the contents of the will were by reliable evidence. In this case the evidence of the neighbours may be sufficient proof of the terms of the will.

Chapter 6

Alterations in Wills

6.1   Introduction

6.2   Key points

6.3   Key cases and statute

6.4   Questions and suggested solutions

6.1 Introduction

This chapter must be studied with the preceding chapter and the next chapter. Issues on alterations of wills will normally be examined in the context of a revocation question. It is crucial that the requirements in s21 Wills Act 1837 are fully understood. However, the questions may also examine other issues such as the formalities and s15, as will be seen in Question 1.

6.2 Key points

a)   Section 21 Wills Act 1837 must be complied with if alteration is to be valid.

   i)   Alteration must be executed as required by s9 Wills Act; testator must sign and witnesses attest in margin or opposite or near to the alteration, or there is a memorandum on the will as to the alteration which is signed and attested.

   ii) Alterations not executed per s21 presumed to have been made after execution of will or codicil and not admitted to probate.

b)   An invalid obliteration is effective in revoking obliterated words unless original words decipherable using natural means: *In b Ibbetson* (1839) 163 ER 431; *Ffinch v Combe* [1894] P 191; *Townley v Watson* (1844) 3 Curt 761.

c)   Doctrine of conditional revocation applicable: see *In b Itter* [1950] P 130.

6.3 Key cases and statute

* *Horsford, In the Goods of* (1874) LR 3 P & D 211
  The effect of obliterations

* *Ibbetson, In b* (1839) 2 Curt 337
  The test to determine if words are not apparent

- *Itter, In b* [1950] P 130
  Meaning of 'apparent' and effect of the application of the doctrine of conditional revocation

- *White, In re* [1991] Ch 1
  The effect of the lack of compliance with s21 Wills Act 1837

- Wills Act 1837, s21 – formalities to be met in order to create a valid alteration

6.4 Questions and suggested solutions

QUESTION ONE

In 1980 Alan wrote on a sheet of paper 'The will of Alan Brown. I bequeath £5,000 to my sister Mary and the residue of my estate to my brother John' turned the sheet over and wrote 'A Brown' on the back. He then called his brother John and his friends George and Edward into the room and said 'I must have my signature witnessed.' They signed on the right of 'A Brown' and Edward went out. John next said 'I think you ought to sign your full name'. Brown erased 'A' and wrote 'Alan'. John said that he and George did not have to sign again, and George agreed.

On Brown's death, a week ago, the document was found with £5,000 completely obliterated with ink, and in the margin opposite was written '£10,000, Alan Brown'. Brown is known to have made another will in 1982 which was in his safe a week before his death, but it cannot be found and there is no evidence of its contents.

Advise John.

University of London LLB Examination
(for External Students) Succession June 1985 Q2

General Comment

This is quite a complex question dealing with a variety of issues. It is very important to take each event, analyse it and conclude, before moving on to the next. When dealing with questions of this nature a brief plan is advisable.

Skeleton Solution

Discuss valid execution – discuss effect of altering signature; does this revoke the will?; intention? – is second execution valid? – the problem of the supernumerary witnesses – validity of alteration to bequest – is the second will admissible to probate?; effect on first will.

Suggested Solution

The first issue is whether or not the will is executed in accordance with s9 of the Wills Act 1837. As the testator died a week ago, it is the new s9 that applies, as amended by the Administration of Justice Act 1982. This demands, inter alia, that the testator sign the will, or acknowledge his signature, in the joint presence of two witnesses. It no longer matters whereabouts on the will the signature is, but s9 demands that the testator must have intended by his signature to give effect to the will.

Case law seems to suggest that almost anything will suffice as a signature, if the testator intended it to represent his signature, or to authenticate his will: see *In the Estate of Cook* [1960] 1 All ER 689 – 'your living mother'.

Certainly, 'A Brown' is sufficient, if the testator intends that to be his full signature. An incomplete version of the name would only fail if the testator intended to write his full name, but was interrupted. He has not then put on the will what he intended to be his signature, but only part of it. (See the discussion in *In the Goods of Chalcraft* [1948] P 222.)

At the time he signs the will for the first time, Alan intends 'A Brown' to be his signature. He then acknowledges it in the joint presence of three people. In *Daintreee v Butcher* (1888) 13 PD 102 it was said that if a paper bearing the signature of the testator was put before witnesses who were then asked to sign as witnesses, this amounts to an implied acknowledgement of the signature. It is essential in these circumstances that the witnesses should be able to see the signature that is being acknowledged. This seems to be satisfied here.

The witnesses then attest. At this point, the will seems to be properly executed.

As a result of John's advice, Brown then alters his signature. The only way that this could seem to be of significance would be if it amounted to a revocation of the will, and re-execution. If re-execution is relied upon, the re-execution may be void. Is the new signature 'Alan', or 'Alan Brown'? If the former, the will has been signed in the presence of two witnesses. If the latter, only part of the signature has been written in the presence of the witnesses so the signature must again be acknowledged.

After this, the witnesses must either sign, which they do not, or acknowledge existing signatures to the testator. Can they acknowledge their existing signatures here? Probably not, as they were not put on the will to attest to the second signature, but to the first.

But is re-execution necessary anyway? A will can be revoked by the testator destroying his signature, or by obliterating it: see *Hobbs* v *Knight* (1836) 1 Curt 768 (totally cut out) and *Re Adams* [1990] Ch 601 (signature obliterated. But this must be done with the intention of thereby revoking the will.

In this case, the signature is not obliterated, it is only crossed through in part. (In *In the Goods of Godfrey* (1893) 69 LT 22 the signature of the testator was crossed out, but still legible. It was held that the will was not revoked.) Any alteration was not made with the intention of revoking the will. The alteration was only made because the testator feared that the existing signature was not good enough. He hoped to validate something he thought to be invalid; he had no intention to invalidate something he believed to be valid. The alteration to the signature has not, therefore, had any effect on the validity of the will.

John is one of the witnesses to the will. As his signature is on the will, there is a presumption that he signed as witness (*In the Estate of Bravda* [1968] 1 WLR 479) and he does indeed seem to have signed in that capacity. Section 15 Wills Act 1837 says that if a beneficiary witnesses the will, his beneficial interest fails. This would prevent John taking the residuary estate, and it would have to be distributed on the intestacy rules. However, s1 Wills Act 1968 provides that the attestation of the will by the beneficiary is to be disregarded if without him the will is properly executed. In other words, the gift to John remains valid, if there are two other non-benefitting witnesses. If the will is validated by the first signature, therefore, John will keep the residue.

At Brown's death, the will is found with the legacy altered. The alteration was made after the date of execution, and is therefore void, unless according to s21 of the Wills Act 1837, it has been signed and witnessed, or the original words are no longer apparent on the face of the will. As '£5,000' is obliterated, it is no longer apparent, and would seem to be revoked. However, the testator did attempt to substitute another figure, '£10,000'. This figure is a void alteration, as although it has been signed it has not been attested. It is of significance, however, because it is evidence that the intention of the testator to revoke the gift of £5,000 was not absolute, but only conditional. It is probable that he only intended to revoke the gift of £5,000 to Mary, if the substituted gift of £10,000 was valid. As the condition is not yet met, the gift of £5,000 has not been revoked. As it has not been revoked, it is entitled to probate provided it can be proved that that is what the will said. Proof may come from the evidence of witnesses, (although in this case the witnesses did not apparently see the legacies) or from a copy of the will, or from the will itself. As the obliterated gift is, in fact, valid the court will allow interference with the will (eg by removing the obliterating marks) or will look at an infra-red photograph. (See *In the Goods of Horsford* (1874) LR 3 P & D 211 – pasted slips of paper removed.)

A later will was made in 1982. This was in Brown's control, but could not be found at his death. In these circumstances, there is a presumption that the will has been destroyed by the testator with the intention of revoking it: *Allen* v *Morrison* [1900] AC 604. It is a rebuttable presumption, eg if an accident destruction can be proved, but there seems to be no evidence to rebut the presumption here. But what effect did the later will have on the earlier one? It may have revoked it, either by an express revocation clause, or by implication.

If so, Alan has died intestate. The contents of the second will are unknown. It will only be treated as revoking earlier wills if there is reliable evidence as to its contents. If there is no such evidence, the earlier will must be taken as unrevoked. (See *Re Wyatt* [1952] 1 All ER 1030 – solicitor could not give evidence that every will be drafted contained a revocation clause – so earlier will unrevoked.)

The result seems to be that the 1980 will will be admitted to probate; Mary will be entitled to £5,000, and John to the residue.

QUESTION TWO

a) 'Dependent relative revocation is a wholly fictitious creation of the judges designed simply to prevent an intestacy.'

Discuss.

b) Frank made a will in 1980 and the solicitor who drafted it produces a copy which shows that the will originally was in the following form:

  i)   £100 to Greta;

  ii) £100 to Harry;

  iii) £100 to Ivor;

  iv) The residue to Keith.

The will produced on death is in the following condition:

In legacy (i) '£100' has been crossed out and '£1000' substituted; in (ii) a piece of paper has been stuck across the whole bequest and the words '£500 to Jack' written on top; in (iii) a blank piece of paper has been stuck across the whole bequest. The whole of the residuary bequest has been cut out.

Discuss.

Would your answer differ if the solicitor also produced a validly executed codicil dated 1985 which contained an additional bequest to Keith and stated 'in all other respects I confirm my will of 1980'?

University of London LLB Examination
(for External Students) Succession June 1988 Q3

General Comment

Conditional revocation is often examined as an essay-style question and can normally be successfully pre-prepared as the same issues are repeatedly examined. The rules on obliteration are required for the second part of the question and this area is often avoided in revision. In fact, once you have mastered s21 and the few cases dealt with in the solutions, this is a relatively simple question.

Skeleton Solution

a) Section 20 Wills Act 1837 – policy behind conditional revocation – situations: *Dixon v Treasury Solicitor*; *Re Jones*; *Campbell v French* – revival – animus missing – construction of wills – judicial technique – submission.

b) Section 21 Wills Act 1837 – scribble and intention to revoke – apparent?; if not, obliteration with intent? – codicil: republication; presumption; rebuttal.

Suggested Solution

a) A will is, by its very nature, ambulatory, ie it can be revoked by the testator at any time up to the date of his death. However, s20 of Wills Act 1837 sets out the methods by which a will can be revoked. Apart from these the only other ways of revoking a will are those contained in ss18 and 18A of the Wills Act 1837 and obliterations under s21 of that Act.

This part of the question requires a consideration of the policy motivating factors behind the doctrine of dependent relative revocation (conditional revocation). The fundamental difficulty that is faced in such circumstances relates to the point that a testator must, if his revocation is to be effective, possess the requisite animus revocandi. The law requires that the degree of mental capacity necessary to revoke be equivalent to that which is necessary to make a will in the first place. However, what of testators who do not fully intend to revoke their wills (or part of them) or who only intend to revoke on the occurrence or non-occurrence of a specified event (express or implied). The latter is a true instance of conditional revocation. In the former situation since there is not a sufficient animus revocandi then any purported revocation will be ineffective. In the context of a 'conditional revocation' if the condition is not fulfilled then the will remains unrevoked.

There are a number of situations in which the courts have found the doctrine may be applicable. If the testator has made an earlier will but now decides that he should make a new one however, before the new will has been drawn up or executed the old will is 'revoked' by destruction; then, in such a case the court may find that any intention to 'revoke' was qualified only.

This is exemplified by *Dixon* v *Treasury Solicitor* [1905] P 42 where evidence showed that but for his mistaken belief (that he could not make a new will until his old one had been revoked) the testator would have allowed the old will to remain effective up until his new will was executed.

However, as a contrast to *Dixon*, see *Re Jones* [1976] Ch 200 in which case the revocation was held to be absolute and unconditional since there was nothing on the facts to show that the testator believed she had to destroy her old will in order to make a new one. This case is quite a strict application of the principles for the court refused to infer a conditional revocation from the manner of the will's mutilation or from various statements made by the 'testatrix' before her death as to bequests. Thus it cannot be used to support a general thesis that the courts are motivated by a policy desire to avoid intestacy in this area.

An alternative fact situation in which conditional revocation might exist is where, if a will is destroyed because of a mistaken belief by the testator as to the operation of the law or as to certain facts, this will not amount to revocation – the justification for such result being that the mistake negatives any animus revocandi: eg *In the Estate of Southernden* [1925] P 177 and *Campbell* v *French* (1797) 3 Ves 321.

Further the doctrine has been held to apply in the cases of revival. It is a general rule (s22 Wills Act 1837) that a will can only be revived by re-execution of s9 and not by revocation of a will which itself revoked an earlier will. However, if a will is made in 1980 (Will A) and Will B was made in 1985 then the testator may revoke Will B under a mistaken belief that such revocation will be effective to revive the original will. The doctrine of conditional revocation will apply in such circumstances: eg *Powell v Powell* (1866) LR 1 P & D 209. On a similar line, the doctrine of conditional revocation may apply where an old legacy in a will has been obliterated (revoked) in an erroneous belief that a new legacy which has been substituted is effective: eg *In b Horsford* (1874) LR 3 P & D 211.

It is submitted that the doctrine of conditional revocation can be viewed in one of three ways. Firstly, it might be seen as no more than an application of the principle that for a revocation to be effective the testator must possess the requisite animus revocandi. If he acts under a mistaken belief as to his actions then such animus may be absent.

Secondly, the doctrine may be no more than a vigorous application of the doctrine of construction of wills: eg *Re Robinson* [1930] 2 Ch 332.

Finally, it could be argued that the doctrine is a judicial technique, motivated by policy considerations, to avoid an intestacy.

It is submitted that the cases reveal that the true position lies somewhere between the first and second alternatives.

b) The main 'thrust' of this question is directed to a consideration of the doctrine of alterations and of how they affect the formal validity of wills. The matter is dealt with by the Wills Act 1837 s21 which provides, inter alia, that no obliteration, interlineation or other alteration made in any will after its execution is valid except so far as the words or effect of the will before such alteration shall not be apparent, unless the alteration is executed in a manner in accordance with the execution of the will itself. However, the section goes on to provide that if the alteration is so executed, eg by the testator and the witnesses initialling it (in the margin) then such alteration will be valid.

On the facts here one does not have such an execution as is required by s21 so the question therefore arises as to whether the alterations which have been made are valid or not.

However s21 recognises that if a testator has scribbled over part of his will such that it cannot be deciphered then these acts if combined with an intention to revoke will be sufficient to revoke the parts so obliterated: eg *In b Horsford*.

Thus the question which will arise in relation to the items (i) – (iv) is, initially, whether the gifts (earlier gifts) are 'not apparent' and if they are not so apparent then did the testator obliterate them with the intention of revoking them. It appears settled that 'apparency' is to be construed strictly such that only natural means of identification can be used, eg magnifying glasses, etc per *In b Ibbetson* (1839) 2 Curt 337 and the use of such devices as infra-red photography to discover what is beneath the obliteration is not permissible per *In b Itter* [1950] P 130. However, if it is clear that the obliteration occurred only by accident, eg by the testator spilling ink onto his will, as in *Townley* v *Watson* (1844) 3 Curt 761 then it is permissible to use any means available in order to discover what the words used were.

Thus taking the individual gifts here. As regards the legacy in (i), £100 has been crossed out and £1000 substituted. If the £100 is not apparent in the sense discussed above then this gift will be revoked with the effect that the gift to Greta will be of no effect. Greta will not take the larger gift of £1000 which has been substituted for the original gift for this has not been validly executed.

If, however, the original gift of £100 is still apparent and there was no animus revocandi on Frank's part then this gift may still be effective.

In relation to (ii) the gift to Harry will be revoked by the piece of paper having been stuck on the top so long as it was accompanied by the requisite animus. This is the case of *Itter*.

However, the conclusion there reached may be reached here also, ie because the testatrix had not pasted strips of paper over the names of the legatees (but only over the amounts of certain legacies in her will and wrote on them new amounts) it was possible to infer that she had intended to revoke the original amounts only if the new amounts were effectively substituted.

This conclusion is unlikely to be reached on the facts here for it is not just the amount of the gift which has been substituted but rather the whole bequest. The gift to Harry will be revoked if the obliteration makes that part of the will not apparent. The test is that it must not be optically apparent on the face of the will and cannot be deciphered by natural means: *Ffinch* v *Combe* [1894] P 191. If the pasted strip of paper makes that part of the will not apparent then the alteration is valid and the substituted words will take effect.

As for the gift to Ivor, similarly if the alteration makes the will not apparent then the alteration is valid. However, here there is no substitute gift. It could be argued that this may be a conditional alteration but see the case of *In b Itter* (above). In relation to (iv) the whole of the residuary bequest has been cut out. One method of revoking a will is by burning, tearing or otherwise destroying the will under Wills Act 1837 s20 accompanied by the requisite animus revocandi. The testator must do all that he intends to do by way of destruction but if this is so then the will (or that part of it intended to be revoked) is effectively revoked: *Cheese* v *Lovejoy* (1877) 2 PD 251. Thus the residuary gift to Keith will be revoked.

As regards the 1985 codicil, if the alterations were made after the will was executed but before it was for some reason re-executed or republished, then a rebuttable presumption applies that all alterations were made after execution so as to bring them with s21: *Cooper* v *Bockett* (1846) 4 Moo PC 419, also *In b Shearn* (1880) 50 LJP 15. It is also well established that where a codicil is made to a will it will have the effect of republishing it and confirming it at the time of execution of the codicil. This brings the will forward to the date of execution of the codicil. This may affect the unattested alterations in the will but a presumption exists that an unattested alteration (as here) was made after the execution of the codicil: *In b Sykes* (1873) LR 3 P & D 26.

However, this presumption may be rebutted. Under the 1985 codicil to the 1980 will it would thus appear that the additional bequest to Keith will be valid and the confirmation of the 1980 will may be such as to rebut the presumption re the earlier unattested alterations in (i) and (ii) so validating the substituted amounts. It will however be of no assistance in relation to (iii) for revocation of a revoking document cannot revive the original document so revoked.

QUESTION THREE

a) Mary has recently died and her will has been found in the following condition. Several legacies have been heavily crossed out with a ball-point pen. Above some of the legacies alternative provisions have been written. In one case the amount of the legacy only has been crossed out and a new amount written above. At the end of the will the original signatures in the attestation clause have been crossed out and below written: 'Re-executed with alterations in July 1988'. The signatures of the two witnesses are rewritten below that. One of the witnesses is dead. The other one states that he remembers being asked by Mary if they would re-execute her will by re-signing as witnesses. Mary said that she didn't need to re-sign as she had already signed the will. The witnesses then re-signed.

    Discuss.

b) Nick has recently died and his will made in 1990 has been found on a printed will form. The printed revocation clause has been crossed out. The dispositive parts of the will are hand written in very shaky writing and some of it is illegible. Above some of the writing the text has been rewritten in a different hand in capital letters. The will is signed by Nick and two witnesses, Marvin and Owen.

    Marvin states that after the will had been signed by the three of them Owen left. Marvin then told Nick that some of Nick's writing was illegible and that it should be made clearer. He went through the will with Nick and as Nick told him what the words were, Marvin wrote the words in capital letters above the text. Marvin asked Nick about the revocation clause and Nick told him that he had crossed it out as he had not made any previous wills and so it was not needed. Marvin said that the will was not valid without a revocation clause so Nick told him to put it back in. Marvin rewrote the revocation clause above the original.

    Marvin then told Nick that they had better re-execute the will so he wrote

'Corrected and rewritten by Marvin with Nick's consent' at the end of the will. Nick and Marvin then signed below. Marvin told Nick that Owen must also sign.

Owen's signature is rewritten below that of Marvin and Nick.

A relative has produced a will in his favour, made by Nick in 1980, correctly written and executed.

Discuss.

University of London LLB Examination
(for External Students) Succession June 1991 Q3

General Comment

This is another two-part question which covers a wide variety of issues dealing with s21 and revocation and re-execution generally. The questiion is long and requires good management of the facts and a clear and concise answer. Without this the chances of success are slim.

Skeleton Solution

a) Alterations must be made in accordance with s21 – either s9 formality or original words no longer apparent – contrast additions and deletion to will – conditional recovation and *In b Itter* – effect of re-execution – presumptions as to alterations.

b) Is original execution valid? – effect of Marvin's additions?; extrinsic evidence to aid interpretation? – re-execution: is it effective?; apparently Nick signed in presence of single witness – effect of 1990 will with and without recovation clause.

Suggested Solution

a) A will may only be altered by complying with Wills Act 1837 s21 which requires that the alteration is executed with the formalities of s9 or that the original words shall be no longer apparent. In this case the alterations were originally made without formality so the question is whether the original words are still apparent. The new alternative provisions added to the will cannot be effective unless executed with formality as it is only possible to make deletions informally. If the original provisions are still apparent on the face of the will, they will still be effective. It is only possible to attempt to decipher the words by natural means such as holding up the document to the light: see *Townley* v *Watson* (1844) 3 Curt 761.

If the original words are no longer apparent it may be possible to argue in those cases where the testatrix has attempted to insert new provisions that the deletion of the original words was conditional on the new provisions being effective. In *In b Itter* [1950] P 130 the testatrix pasted strips of paper over the amounts of some legacies and wrote in new amounts. The new amounts were not effective as they had been added informally and the original amounts were no longer apparent. It was held that the testatrix had only intended to delete the original amounts if the new amounts were effective and that since they were not, the original amounts were still valid and could be deciphered by any means. Thus where the amount of a legacy has been crossed out and a new amount added, the decision in *In b Itter* would allow the original amount to be ascertained in any way and provided that this could be done, the original amount would be valid.

It would be more difficult to apply the decision in *In b Itter* if an entire provision had been deleted and a completely different one substituted. In such a case it is more likely that the testatrix's intention would have been to delete one provision and make another one and not for the deletion to be conditional on the new provision being effective. For example, if the testatrix has crossed out a legacy of £100 to Tom and written £500 to Jack instead, it would be unlikely that she only wanted Tom not to have £100 if Jack had £500. Of course if the original words are still apparent they will still be valid.

Mary has then crossed out the original signatures in the attestation clause and attempted to re-execute the will. Re-execution must be done with the formalities of s9. Mary herself did not sign the will at the time of the re-execution but it could be argued that she has acknowledged her original signature to the will. A valid acknowledgement requires the testator to acknowledge his signature by words or conduct and the witnesses must have the opportunity of seeing the signature: *Daintree* v *Butcher* (1888) 13 PD 102. Assuming that Mary's signature was visible to the witnesses at the time of re-execution and that both witnesses were present together, has there been enough for an acknowledgment by Mary when she says that she does not need to re-sign as she has already signed? It is suggested that Mary has sufficiently acknowledged her signature to the will. The final requirement is that the witnesses sign in Mary's presence and although this is not expressly stated in the question there is nothing to indicate that they did not do so.

If the re-execution is valid, does it validate all the alterations? The presumption is that unattested alterations are made after the execution of the will, but in this case the re-execution itself refers to the alterations. The difficulty may be to establish whether all the alterations had been made before the re-execution or only some of them. The evidence of the surviving witness will be very important as will any other persons who may have seen the will. Thus the will may be valid with all the alterations if the re-execution is effective, but if the re-execution is not effective none of the new provisions added to the will are effective, although some of the deletions may be effective subject to the doctrine of conditional revocation.

b) Initially Nick's will appears to be correctly executed. The revocation clause seems to have been crossed out before the execution of the will and thus it does not matter whether the original words are still apparent on the face of the will. Marvin has written out the parts of the will which were illegible after the execution of the will. It is suggested that this does not affect the validity of the will. Wills Act 1837 s9 requires that the will is in writing but extrinsic evidence has been allowed to interpret a will written in code in *Kell* v *Charmer* (1856) 23 Beav 195 and would be allowed to interpret a will written in a foreign language. It is suggested that extrinsic evidence should be allowed to decipher the illegible parts of the will and Marvin's writing is simply evidence of the will of Nick.

Marvin has added back the revocation clause after the original execution of the will and there has been an attempt at a re-execution but it appears that Nick signed in the presence of Marvin alone as the question states that Owen had left after the first execution of the will and does not indicate that he returned before the re-execution. Although Owen did sign the will, the re-execution will only be effective if before he signed, Nick acknowledged his signature in the presence of Marvin and Owen and Owen then signed in Nick's presence and Marvin acknowledged his signature in the presence of Nick. If not, it is suggested that the will is valid without the revocation clause but including the illegible parts.

If the re-execution is valid it does not matter that Nick only included the revocation clause because Marvin wrongly told him that the will would not be valid without it. In such a situation the testator does know and approve the words used although he does not understand their effect: see *Collins v Elstone* [1893] P 1.

If the re-execution is effective the 1990 will has revoked the 1980 will, but if it is not effective, the 1980 will is still valid except to the extent that it is inconsistent with the 1990 will. Both wills would be read together. This would be particularly important if the court decided not to admit Marvin's writing as evidence to decipher the illegible parts of the 1990 will, since in that case the 1990 will may well fail to deal with all of Nick's estate.

Chapter 7

Revival and Republication

7.1   Introduction

7.2   Key points

7.2   Key cases and statute

7.3   Questions and suggested solutions

7.1 Introduction

Once again this chapter must be studied along with the two preceding chapters. There may, however, be questions set entirely on republication. It is important to focus both on s22 Wills Act 1837 as well as the cases.

7.2 Key points

Revival of revoked will possible under s22 Wills Act 1837

a) Method: by re executing the revoked will, or executing a codicil which shows intention to revive: see *In b Steele* (1868) LR 1 P & D 575.

b) For a will to be revived by codicil, the document containing the will must be in existence.

c) Main effect is that revived will is read as at time of revival.

Republication of a will possible under s22 Wills Act 1837

a) Method: re executing the will or confirming it by codicil.

b) Main effect is that will is read as at date of republication: *Goonewardene* v *Goonewardene* [1931] AC 647.

c) Thereby affects construction.

d) Witness deprived of benefit by s15 Wills Act will obtain benefit if will republished and different witnesses attest.

e) Note limitations of republication.

7.3 Key cases and statute

- *Goonewardene* v *Goonewardene* [1931] AC 647
  On republication the will is read as if executed on the date of republication

- *Hardyman, Re* [1925] 1 Ch 287
  The will and the reviving codicil are to be read together and take effect on the date of the reviving instrument re the object of the gift

- *Hodgkinson, In b* [1893] P 339
  An earlier will may not be revived simply by the revocation of a later will

- *Rogers* v *Goodenough* (1862) 2 Sw & Tr 342
  Revival of a will by codicil will only take effect if the will is in existence at the time – it may not be used where the will has been revoked by destruction

- *Steele, In b* (1868) LR 1 P & D 575
  Where a codicil is used to revive a will it should show an intention to revive the same

- Wills Act 1837, s13 – no requirement for will to be published

- Wills Act 1837, s22 – conditions for the valid revival of a will

- Wills Act 1837, s34 – effect of a revival or republication on a will

7.4 Questions and suggested solutions

QUESTION ONE

a) G's will contained blanks where paper had been pasted over the amounts of pecuniary legacies and no substituting amounts inserted. The legatees ask for your advice.

b) i) A executed a will in 1980 which left property to B and C. B and C were the only witnesses to the will. In 1985 A executed a codicil making various legacies and in other respects confirming his original will. D and E witnessed the codicil execution.

   ii) In his will, A left his racing horses to his nephew, E. At that time he had a nephew who died the same year in a car accident. In 1988, before A's death, a brother to the deceased nephew was born, F. Advise F.

   iii) What formalities are necessary for republication?

Written by the Editor

General Comment

A simple question testing knowledge of conditional revocation within a brief problem context as well as ss15 and 22 Wills Act 1837. This is a good example of the potential for mixing issues and a warning to candidates about topic spotting.

Skeleton Solution

a) Conditional revocation – In *b Gilbert*.

b) Section 15 Wills Act.– *Anderson* v *Anderson* – construction – Section 22 Wills Act 1837.

Suggested Solution

a) Parts of a will may be obliterated subject to conditions. If these are not satisfied, then the obliteration is not a valid revocation of those parts of the will and, further, any means may be used to determine the original wording: see *In b McCabe* (1873) 3 P & D 94. G's position is similar to the testator in *In b Itter* [1950] P 130. There, it was held that because names of legatees had not been obliterated, it could be implied that she had intended to revoke the original words only if new figures were inserted. So here, G's legatees would take the original legacies if the figures can be determined. The decision in *In b Gilbert* [1893] P 183, that chemicals could be used to remove strips of paper, is relevant.

b) i)   The effect of s15 Wills Act 1837 is that witnesses cannot take benefits under the will. According to this rule, B and C would be prevented from taking their legacies as they were A's witnesses. However, if the will is republished and the witnesses are different, then the original witnesses may after all take beneficiaries under the will: see *Anderson* v *Anderson* (1872) LR 13 Eq 381. B and C are therefore advised that because A's will was republished by a codicil which was witnessed by others, they may take their legacies.

   ii) It seems that where a gift under a will is expressed by reference to a relationship to the testator as opposed to a specifically named person, republication may save the gift if at the time of the testator's death he has such a relation.

   This is so even though that particular relation was not contemplated when the original will was made: see *Re Hardyman* [1925] 1 Ch 287. This case is authority for advising D that though he was not a nephew and therefore not in A's contemplation when the will was originally executed, nevertheless the republication extends the will to include him. As a result, D will take the racing horses.

   iii) Under s22 Wills Act 1837, republication must be by either re executing the will, or by executing a codicil confirming the will. In each case, the formalities set out in s9 Wills Act must be observed.

QUESTION TWO

a) Richard made his will in 1970 when he was married to Stella and the couple had one child. In this he left his estate to Stella for life with the remainder divided equally between 'my children'. In 1980 Richard and Stella were divorced. In 1985 Richard married Tessa and the couple had two children born in 1987 and 1988. In Richard's 1970 will all references to 'Stella' have been crossed out and the word 'Tessa' written at each point. There is no evidence when this was done. There is another will, undated but apparently correctly executed, which simply leaves all of Richard's property to Tessa. In 1989 Richard made a codicil to 'my will in favour of my wife and children', adding a legacy to a charity and otherwise confirming his will. This codicil is correctly executed.

Discuss.

b) Robin made his will in 1972 when he was a bachelor. In 1974 Robin crossed out the residuary clause in his 1972 will and wrote below 'All residue to Sheila who is to be my wife'. He signed the will and so did two witnesses. In 1975 he married Sheila. In 1980 Robin and Sheila were divorced. Robin then tore his will in half telling his friend Tom who was present that the will was cancelled by the divorce and that he was keeping the parts for future reference. In 1985 Robin and Sheila were reconciled and resumed living together, although they did not remarry. Shortly after Robin stuck the two halves of his will back together with sellotape telling Sheila that the will was 'OK' again. Tom told Robin that he had better re-sign the will. Robin wrote at the end of the will 'Certified by me, Sheila and Tom that this will is now restored to effect'. He signed below and so did Sheila and Tom. Tom then said that it would be better if someone other than Sheila signed. Robin crossed out 'Sheila' and in the 'certified by etc' clause and wrote 'Vera' instead and Sheila crossed out her signature. Two days later at Robin's request Vera (Tom's wife) signed below Tom's signature.

Discuss.

University of London LLB Examination
(for External Students) Succession June 1991 Q4

General Comment

This is a typical question examining revival and republication but in combination with the effect of divorce and marriage. There is little point in studying either of these areas in isolation as so many of the questions are mixed.

Skeleton Solution

a) Divorce doesn't affect validity of will – informal additions to will ineffective, erasure effective if original words no longer apparent – marriage revokes will – does codicil revive old will?; s22 requirements – problems of undated wills: *Re Howard*,

b) Old law applies to wills executed pre 1983 – is will as a whole made in contemplation of marriage? – divorce causes gift to spouse to fail but doesn't revoke will – requirements for revocation by destruction; doubtful if necessary intention present here – does codicil revive will?: probably yes, but problem of Sheila as witness and s15; doubtful if can claim here as will wouldn't work in her favour but for codicil.

Suggested Solution

a) When Richard and Stella are divorced in 1980 this has no effect on the validity of the will. Had Richard died after 31 December 1982 the will would have been valid, but the gift to Stella would have failed and thus the estate would have passed to their child immediately by s18A Wills Act 1837. When Richard marries Tessa in 1985 the 1970 will is revoked by s18 Wills Act 1837. The only exception is for wills made in contemplation of marriage and this clearly does not apply. The alteration of the 1970 will again does not have any effect. Alterations are only valid if executed in accordance with s21 Wills Act 1837 and in any event the will has been revoked by the marriage. The will in favour of Tessa is apparently validly executed, but the effect of the 1989 codicil is not clear.

Although the 1970 will has been revoked it may be revived by re-execution or by codicil showing an intent to revive by s22. Wills Act 1837 Does the codicil show an intent to revive the 1970 will? Strong evidence of intention is required for revival and evidence of the surrounding circumstances is admissible to prove intention as in *Re Davis* [1952] P 279. In *In b Steele* (1868) LR 1 P & D 575 it was held that it is not sufficient to refer to the revoked will by its date as this could be the result of a draftsman's error, but the codicil should refer to the terms of the revoked will. In this case Richard refers in the codicil to 'my will in favour of my wife and children' which seems to be a reference to the 1970 will rather than the will in favour of Tessa alone. Although it was said in *In b Wilson* (1868) LR 1 P & D 575 that 'the court ought to be slow to conclude that a testator has manifested a desire to revoke his last will' it is suggested that there is at least a strong argument that Richard has shown the necessary intention here. It seems unlikely that he would have referred to a will in favour of Tessa as a will in favour of his wife and children, since one of his children is not even Tessa's child.

If the 1970 will is revived, what are its terms? A codicil which revises a revoked will may validate previously unattested alterations as in *Neate* v *Pickard* (1843) 2 N & C 406. There is a presumption that unattested alterations are made after execution of the will and after execution of any codicils to the will but this presumption is rebuttable. The question states that the date of the alterations is not known but the circumstantial evidence suggests that they were made before the codicil, as it seems unlikely that Richard would refer in 1989 to a will bearing Stella's name as a will in favour of his wife. It is not clear whether this circumstantial evidence would be enough to overcome the presumption. If not, then if the will is given effect, Tessa would be unable to claim under it, as the addition of her name was by an unattested alteration and Stella would be unable to claim because of the divorce. Thus the children of Richard would be entitled to the estate.

Assuming that the 1989 codicil has revived the 1979 will, what is the effect of the undated will in favour of Tessa? There is no indication that either will contains an express revocation clause but a later will revokes an earlier will to the extent that they are inconsistent with each other. It may be possible to establish by the evidence of the witnesses when the will in favour of Tessa was executed and if so it will either revoke or be revoked by the 1970 will and codicil. In *Re Howard* [1944] P 39 the testator executed two wills with different dispositions and it was impossible to establish the order of execution. It was held that the testator had died intestate (a will earlier than these two had certainly been revoked). Therefore it may be that if it proves impossible to ascertain the date of the will in favour of Tessa, the court will hold that Richard died intestate. In this case his estate will be divided between Tessa, the surviving spouse, and the children.

b) The alteration of the will in 1974 appears to have been executed in accordance with s21 Wills Act 1837 as it has been signed by Robin and attested by two witnesses. The execution of the alteration should be opposite or near to the alteration itself, or there should be a memorandum referring to the alteration. It is not clear from the question whether this is so and if not, the alteration may be ineffective. Assuming that the will has been validly altered, what is the effect of Robin's marriage to Sheila? The normal rule is that marriage revokes an earlier will by s18 Wills Act 1837 but there is an exception for wills expressed to be made in contemplation of marriage by s177 Law of Property Act 1925. The old law applies here as the will was executed before 31 December 1982.

In the altered will Robin refers to 'Sheila who is to be my wife' which shows that he was contemplating marriage to a specific person, Sheila, at the time. However, the decision in *Re Coleman* [1976] Ch 1 shows that the will as a whole must be expressed to be made in contemplation of marriage. In that case the testator made a will containing gifts to 'my fiancee' but Megarry J held that the will as a whole was not expressed to be made in contemplation of marriage, but only the gifts to the fiancee. In this case only the residue is given to Sheila and there are no general words indicating a contemplation of marriage. In *Re Coleman* the part of the estate not given to the fiancee was substantial, but the question does not indicate the size of the residuary gift here. It is suggested that if the residuary estate comprises virtually the whole or at least a very large part of the estate, it would be possible to distinguish *Re Coleman* and hold that the will as a whole was expressed to be made in contemplation of marriage and thus not revoked by the marriage. This would not be so if the residuary estate was only a small part of the estate.

When Robin and Sheila are divorced in 1980 this has no effect on the validity of the will, although if Robin had died after 31 December 1982 having made no further changes to his will, the gift to Sheila would have lapsed. In order to revoke a will by destruction the testator must comply with s20 Wills Act 1837. There must be a physical act of destruction by the testator and an intention to revoke. Robin has torn the will but he has not done so with the intent to revoke it, but in the mistaken belief that it was already revoked. In *Clarkson v Clarkson* (1862) 2 Sw & Tr 497 a will was held not revoked when it was destroyed in the mistaken belief that it had already been revoked. Thus the will, if not revoked by the marriage, is not revoked by the tearing. Robin's act of sticking the will together again has no effect on its validity, nor does his telling Sheila that the will is 'OK' again.

At this point the will may be wholly revoked by the marriage, or if still valid, the gift of residue to Sheila will be ineffective due to the divorce. Robin then attempts to make the will wholly valid again by writing 'Certified ... that this will is now restored to effect' at the end. This seems to show the necessary intention for revival under s22 Wills Act 1837 and the statement is signed by Robin and witnessed by two witnesses. It was held in *Rogers v Goodenough* (1862) 2 Sw & Tr 342 that it is not possible to revive a will which has been destroyed as there is then no 'writing' to satisfy s9, but in this case the will is still physically in existence although torn and revival should be possible. Sheila's signature is crossed out and Vera signs instead. If Vera signs in the presence of Robin and Robin first acknowledges his signature in the presence of Tom and Vera and Tom acknowledges his signature in the presence of Robin, there will be a proper revival of the will. If Robin then dies Sheila would be able to claim the residuary estate despite s18A as the will would show an intention that she would be able to benefit. However it seems unlikely that the correct formalities were followed by Robin, Tom and Vera.

Is the execution by Robin, Tom and Sheila effective? Sheila's signature has been crossed out (by Sheila but on Robin's direction) but it remains part of the will unless it is no longer apparent on the face of the will by s21. If the signature is still legible the attestation is valid, but if Sheila's signature is no longer apparent on the face of the will, the attestation is only effective if Robin, Tom and Vera complied with the s9 formalities. Assuming that Sheila's signature is valid, will s15 prevent her claiming? This section stops a witness to a will benefiting under it. In this case Sheila has attested not the will itself but a codicil to it. In *Re Marcus* (1887) 57 LT 399 a beneficiary was entitled to claim when he had witnessed the will and one codicil but not another codicil. The beneficiary could claim under the codicil which he had not witnessed. Sheila's position is more difficult as although she did not witness the will itself, she would be unable to claim under it if there had been no codicil because of s18A. In *Re Marcus* the judge said the test was whether the legatee could point to a document not attested by himself giving him his legacy. Arguably Sheila cannot do this since the legacy under the will would be lost by s18A but for the codicil. There seems no direct authority on this point but it would seem consistent with *Re Marcus* to hold that Sheila would not be able to claim.

QUESTION THREE

a) 'Republication is a trap for the unwary – it can lead to unexpected and unwelcome consequences.'

Discuss.

b) John and Mary, brother and sister, executed their wills in 1990 on the same day. John made some small bequests to charities and left the residue of his estate to Mary. In her will she left a large gift to her friend, Alma, and the residue to John.

After a furious row with Mary, John phoned his bank manager and asked him to destroy the will (John kept it at the bank). The bank manager carried out the instructions. Mary decided to alter her will by increasing the amount to Alma. She did this by covering the original amount with Tipp-Ex fluid and writing the new amount over the erasure. She placed her signature close to the alteration. Later that day she had an upsetting phone call from Alma and decided that she would totally exclude Alma from her will. She cut out the gift to Alma with scissors and sellotaped the two parts of the will together. It transpires that Mary had been drinking heavily that day.

Advise John and Mary about the legal effect of their actions.

University of London LLB Examination
(for External Students) Succession June 1995 Q5

General Comment

This was an excellent, well-constructed question. The first part required considerable thought from candidates and the second part involved analysis of a problem which covered primarily revocation of a will, but also an element of constructive trusts.

Skeleton Solution

a) Nature of republication – contrary intention present – republication where revocation clause – republication and position regarding lapse.

b) Facts suggesting mutual wills – effect of constructive trust – requirements for alteration of will – reconstituting destroyed will – dependent relative revocation – factors establishing intention to revoke.

Suggested Solution

a) A testator may 'republish' a will or codicil, but the term 'republication' is an anachronism since s13 Wills Act 1837 made publication of a will unnecessary. The term 'confirmation' would be more apt. By republication is meant re-execution of the will with the proper formalities, or the execution of a codicil containing some reference to the will. In order to republish a will a codicil need only contain some reference to the will and in practice normally ends with the phrase: 'In all other respects I confirm my will'.

A republished will operates as if it had been executed at the date of its republication.

There are indeed certain traps for the unwary. Republication must not defeat the intention of the testator by, for instance, invalidating a gift which was valid at the date of the will: see, for instance, *Re Moore* (1907) 1 IR 315. Republication of a will containing a revocation clause can produce anomalies. In *In the Goods of Rawlins* (1879) 48 LJP 64 a will was executed which contained a revocation clause in general terms; a codicil was then executed and later the testator deleted one clause in the will and re-executed the will. This should have had the effect, strictly, of revoking the codicil but the court held that the codicil was not revoked by the republication of the will containing the revocation clause because the will was re-executed so as to give effect to the deletion and it was not the testator's intention to revoke the codicil. Another court might have held otherwise, justifiably in principle.

Where the republication rule applies it can certainly lead to unanticipated consequences, whether or not unwelcome. In *Re Hardyman* [1925] 1 Ch 287, the testatrix made a will leaving property to her cousin's wife. After the will was made the cousin's wife died, and the testatrix thereafter made a codicil republishing the will in general, but without particular reference to the gift. The cousin subsequently remarried, and it was held that his second wife could benefit.

A gift which fails through lapse cannot be saved by republication of the will so as to allow it to take effect as a gift to the donee's personal representatives. Although the will is read as if executed at the time of its republication the donee's death before the earlier will determines the destination of the gift. This may well be a trap for the unwary, imagining that the rule would be otherwise.

b) The act of John and Mary, brother and sister, executing their wills on the same day in 1990, with common gifts of residue to each other, may suggest they have created mutual wills, if it can be established the wills were executed pursuant to a common agreement, or arrangement. If this is the position a constructive trust would arise on the death of the first of either John or Mary, thereby preventing any unconscionable revocation by the survivor and imposing upon each an obligation not to revoke his/her will without notice to the other during that other's lifetime: *Birmingham* v *Renfrew* (1937) 57 CLR 666.

John's action in telephoning his bank manager and asking him to destroy the will raises the question of whether the will has been validly revoked. Under s20 Wills Act 1837 a will may be revoked by a burning, tearing or otherwise destroying of the will with the intention of revoking (animus revocandi) by the testator or someone else in his presence and at his direction. Accordingly, the bank manager's destruction of the will is not a revocation of it since it has not taken place in the presence of John. The result is that John's will remains unrevoked and would have to be reconstituted through a draft, copy, or some other evidence of its contents, such as the evidence of any person who could depose to the provisions of the will: r54 Non-Contentious Probate Rules 1987.

Mary's decision to increase the gift to Alma by erasing the original amount and replacing it with the new amount involves consideration of the rules relating to alteration of wills. By s21 Wills Act 1837 any alteration made subsequent to the execution of a will (as is the case here) is invalid unless executed in the same manner as the will itself, that is in compliance with the requirements of formal validity: s9 Wills Act 1837, as substituted. Although Mary has signed the alteration it appears that the witnesses have not; accordingly, the altered figure is invalid. The consequence is that since there has effectively been an obliteration with an attempted (but invalid) substitution the doctrine of dependent relative revocation can be invoked to establish the original figure from extrinsic evidence; such as infra red, chemical ink or the testimony of witnesses. If the original figure cannot be deciphered by such means then probate issues with a blank space and Alma receives nothing; if the original figure can be deciphered Alma takes it.

As regards the purported exclusion of Alma by the means described Alma would seek to establish that Mary could not have had the required animus revocandi necessary to bring about a revocation, unless Mary's executors are able to claim successfully that Mary's true intentions had been established by the upsetting telephone call, and that her heavy drinking did not affect Mary's capacity to form the intention to revoke. If this were so the cutting with scissors and sellotaping is still an invalid alteration since it was not properly executed: see *In b Itter* [1950] P 130. The doctrine of dependent relative revocation would be unavailable because there is no attempted substitution of another gift. Accordingly, it would have the effect of enlarging the residue passing to John.

There remains the issue of whether, in any event, Mary's will would have to be construed on the basis that Alma's entitlement is set by the constructive trust under the mutual will (if that is the interpretation) at the time of execution so that the proportions of the estate as between Alma and John are unalterable. This would depend on the availability of more detailed factual evidence.

Chapter 8

Legacies and Devises

8.1   **Introduction**

8.2   **Key points**

8.3   **Key cases and statutes**

8.4   **Questions and suggested solutions**

8.1 Introduction

It is important when studying this area that you learn to identify the particular gifts involved. A mistaken identification of a gift can lead to the entire question being answered wrongly. By and large the questions in this area often examine the same issues each year. This area is very popular in the examinations and is worth revising well. You may wish to consider combining the study of this chapter with construction as it is not uncommon to have a mixture of issues from the two areas in one question.

8.2 Key points

a) Distinction between different types of gift in a will is relevant because of the doctrine of ademption.

b) Types of gift

    i)   Specific legacy: gift of particular property.

    ii) General legacy: gift out of general estate.

    iii) Demonstrative legacy: a general legacy which testator requires to be paid out of a specific fund.

    iv) Pecuniary legacy: gift of money.

    v) Devise: gift of real estate.

c) Ademption. A specific devise or specific legacy will fail by ademption if the property no longer exists at testator's death eg has been sold: *Ashburner* v *MacGuire* (1786) 29 ER 62 and *Re Dorman* [1994] 1 All ER 804.

    i)   Specific legacy of shares adeems wholly or pro tanto if testator sold all or part of shares. Ademption also takes place where there has been a substantial change in the nature of the shares, as opposed to change in name and form: *Re Slater* [1907] 1 Ch 665; *Re Clifford* [1912] 1 Ch 29; *Re Gibson* (1866) LR 2 Eq 669.

   ii) Specific gift which is subject-matter of a contract of sale entered into, or has an option to purchase granted by, the testator after the will would fail by ademption: *Re Edwards* [1958] Ch 168; *Lawes v Bennet* (1785) 1 Cox Eq Cas 167.

d) Lapse. If a beneficiary predeceases testator, a devise or legacy fails.

   i) Section 184 Law Property Act 1925. If two or more people die in circumstances where it is uncertain who died first, then the younger is deemed to survive the older.

   ii) Section 33 Wills Act 1837 as amended by s19 Administration of Justice Act 1982: a gift to a beneficiary who is the testator's issue or descendant and predeceases but leaves issue who survive the testator will not fail by lapse but will go to the surviving issue. Subject to contrary intention.

e) Uncertainty. If the subject or object of a gift are uncertain, the gift fails.

f) Section 15 Wills Act 1837. A beneficiary cannot take under a will if he is also a witness, nor can his spouse.

g) Forfeiture. As a matter of public policy, a person cannot take under the will of someone he has killed. Note: 1982 Forfeiture Act gives the court discretion to grant relief: see, eg, *Re H* [1990] 1 FLR 441; *Jones v Roberts* [1995] 2 FLR 472; *Re K (Deceased)* [1985] 2 All ER 833; *Re Jones (Deceased)* (1997) The Times 29 April; *Dunbar v Plant* (1997) The Times 13 August.

h) Lapse by divorce. The effect of 18A Wills Act 1837 is that, where the testator is divorced after making a will, any property left to the former spouse shall pass as if the former spouse had died on the date of divorce.

i) Disclaimer. A beneficiary may refuse to take a benefit under the will.

j) Effect of failure. Legacies and devises fall into residue or go on intestacy.

8.3 Key cases and statutes

- *Ashburner v MacGuire* (1786) 2 Bro CC 108
  Defines a demonstrative legacy

- *Bothamley v Sherson* (1875) LR 20 Eq 304
  Defines a specific legacy

- *Bravda, In the Estate of* [1968] 1 WLR 479
  Application of s15 Wills Act 1837

- *Crippen, Re* [1911] P 108
  Application for the forfeiture rule

- *Dorman, Re* [1994] 1 All ER 804
  Money moved to a more profitable bank account will not adeem where the change of account was not substantial

- *Durrant v Friend* (1851) 5 De G & S 343
  Where a specific gift is adeemed the beneficiary is not entitled to any insurance monies

- *Harker's Will Trust, Re* [1969] 1 Ch 339
  The doctrine of acceleration

- *Hickman v Peacey* [1945] AC 304
  Application of the commorientes rule

- *K (Deceased), Re* [1985] 1 All ER 403
  The forfeiture rule may not apply to some cases of manslaughter, such as unintentional killing

- *Land v Devaynes* (1793) 4 Bro CC 537
  A gift of a chattel in a particular place will not adeem if the chattel is moved

- *Lawes v Bennett* (1785) 1 Cox Eq Cas 167
  Where an option to purchase is impressed on the gift after the will, the beneficiary is not entitled to the gift

- *Leeming, Re* [1912] 1 Ch 828
  Stocks and shares will not adeem if there has only been a change in name and form

- *O'Connor, Re* [1948] 1 Ch 628
  Defines a general legacy

- *Sweeting (Deceased), Re* [1988] 1 All ER 1016
  A contract of sale entered into by the testator after the date of the will, but not completed until after death, will cause the gift to adeem

- *TWGS v JMG and Others* [2000] 2 All ER 83
  The forfeiture rule does not require the court to treat the murderer as having predeceased the victim for the purposes of s47(1)(i) of the Administration of Estates Act 1982

- Administration of Estates Act 1925, s46(2A) – consider the effect of this on s46(3) of the Administration of Estates Act 1925

- Forfeiture Act 1982, s2(1) – passed to provide relief from the Forfeiture Act

- Law of Property Act 1925, s184 – commorientes rule

- Wills Act, s15 – loss of benefit under a will if the attesting witness or his/her spouse witnesses the will

- Wills Act 1837, s18A(1) – effect of divorce on a will

- Wills Act 1837, s24 – specific gifts speak from the date of death

- Wills Act 1837, s32 – exception to the doctrine of lapse

- Wills Act 1837, s33 – operation of exception of doctrine of lapse vis-à-vis the testator's issue

- Wills Act 1968, s1 – exception to s15 if there is an additional independent witness

8.4 Questions and suggested solutions

QUESTION ONE

Alfred, an aged bachelor, made a will in 1990 in which he devised and bequeathed his property as follows.

'(i)   I give and bequeath unto my sister, Barbara, 52,300 ICI shares and to my brother Charlie, 41,000 BP shares now standing in my name.
(ii)   I give my Rolls-Royce car to my sister Dora's eldest son,
(iii) I give all my shares in Easyprofit Limited to my brother Fred.'

The following events then occurred.

a) At the time when he made his will, Alfred had owned exactly 52,300 ICI shares and 41,000 BP shares. He sold both lots of shares in 1993.

b) Dora's eldest son, at the time when Alfred made his will, was Gregory. But in 1994, Gregory was driving Alfred's Rolls-Royce car and crashed it, destroying the car and killing himself. Alfred then bought another Rolls-Royce car which he owned at the time of his death. Dora's eldest son at the time of Alfred's death was Harry, Gregory's brother.

c) Alfred and his sister Barbara were killed in a car crash when they were being driven in Alfred's (new) Rolls-Royce by Harry. Barbara was younger than Alfred. The car was a write-off. Harry was later charged with, and convicted of, causing death by reckless driving.

d) In 1995 Alfred had granted Fred's son John an option to buy any or all of his shares in Easyprofit Limited (the family company) at 90 per cent of their market price – option to be exercised within one year of Alfred's death, at the latest.

Advise as to the effect of the dispositions.

University of London LLB Examination
(for External Students) Succession June 1996 Q8

General Comment

This was a longish question raising a number of issues centred round the doctrine of ademption. In the course of it, two different Rolls Royces are crashed and written off, and several people get killed. The question fails to state the date of the testator's death (which would have been helpful for candidates) and omits any reference to the destination of the deceased's residuary estate; in the event, this may be considered unfortunate because Harry can only inherit, if at all, as a residuary beneficiary. But is he one?

Skeleton Solution

Consequence of ademption on specific legacy – contrast general legacy – construction summons – effect of commorientes (joint deaths) – date from which will speaks – status of Harry as a beneficiary – effect of forfeiture rule – option to purchase: effect on specific gift.

Suggested Solution

The advice as to the effect of the dispositions made by Alfred will depend upon the nature of each of the gifts he has made. With regard to the shares bequeathed, the use of the phrase 'now standing in my name', referable to the 41,000 BP shares given to Charlie, clearly suggests a specific legacy of those shares. The principal feature of such a legacy is that the gift is adeemed, so that the specific legatee receives nothing if the subject-matter is not in existence at the testator's death. Alfred sold the shares in 1993 and appears not to have replaced them. Accordingly, Charlie receives nothing and cannot compel the personal representatives of Alfred to acquire a similar number of BP shares from the residuary estate.

The gift of ICI shares to Barbara, on the other hand, is not qualified by the phrase 'now standing in my name'. This would suggest that the legacy is a general legacy, rather than a specific legacy: yet it is curious that Alfred owned the precise number of shares (52,300) which he has bequeathed to Barbara. This may raise a claim from Alfred's executors that Barbara's legacy was also specific and therefore likewise adeemed by the sale in 1993.

A construction summons may be taken out by Alfred's executors to determine whether they should construe the words 'now standing in my name' as reflecting back to Barbara's gift as well as to Charlie's. Without that intervention, the gift to Barbara is to be construed as a general legacy.

Accordingly, the death of Alfred and Barbara in a car crash will be significant because the circumstances may raise the issue of 'commorientes', or joint deaths. Under s184 Law of Property Act (LPA) 1925, if two or more persons die in circumstances where it is uncertain as to the order of deaths, the younger shall be deemed to have survived the elder. If the evidence of the car crash is that it is not possible, on medical or other relevant evidence, to determine which of Alfred and Barbara died first, Barbara, being younger than Alfred, will, under s184 LPA 1925, have survived. This means that Alfred's executors will be required to purchase 52,300 ICI shares and transfer them into Barbara's estate, to be administered by her personal representatives, according to the terms of her will or intestacy.

The bequest of Alfred's Rolls Royce car, to his sister Dora's eldest son, raises further issues of ademption. The eldest son at the date of the will is Gregory, but he crashes the car and kills himself. A will is construed to speak from death when identifying or describing property, but from the time of its making when identifying or describing persons. Section 24 Wills Act 1837 is the key provision here, but is subject to any contrary intention, of which no evidence is presented on the facts. The consequence is that the gift of 'my Rolls Royce to my sister Dora's eldest son' can only be construed as a gift to Gregory who, if he had lived, would have been able to inherit the new Rolls Royce (if it had not also been crashed). In the event, if the new (written-off) car has a salvage value or an insurance equivalent, as will be likely, that value will pass into the residuary estate.

Is Harry a residuary beneficiary, in whole or in part, of Alfred's estate? The question gives no indication. Harry's being convicted of death by reckless driving may disqualify him from inheriting if he is such a residuary beneficiary; it has already been seen that Harry does not, in principle, inherit as 'my sister Dora's eldest son'. A judge-made forfeiture rule, based on public policy, establishes that someone who commits murder (see *Re Crippen* [1911] P 108) or some forms of manslaughter (*Gray* v *Barr* [1970] 2 QB 554) is debarred from taking any benefit from his victim's estate. It is probable, although not certain, that the forfeiture rule does not apply to a case where there is a conviction for causing death by reckless driving: see, for example, AJ Oakley, *Constructive Trusts* (2nd edn, 1988) pp25–26. Even if it were to, the Forfeiture Act 1982 gives the court power to modify the effect of the forfeiture rule if the court is satisfied that the justice of the case so requires, having regard to the conduct of the offender and of the deceased and of any other material circumstances.

Alfred's gift of all his shares in Easyprofit Ltd to his brother Fred has to be considered in the context of the option Alfred gave in 1995 to Fred's son, John, to be exercised within one year of Alfred's death, to buy all or any of the Easyprofit shares.

Under the rule in *Lawes* v *Bennett* (1785) 1 Cox Eq Cas 167, the exercise of the option by John within the permitted period after Alfred's death would operate to adeem the specific gift of the shares in Easyprofit to Fred, pro tanto. An option to purchase which is exercised after a testator's death (Alfred) adeems a specific gift in the same way as a binding contract for sale made by the testator before his death, and see *Re Carrington* [1932] 1 Ch 1. If John does exercise the option, therefore, to that extent the money arising therefrom will pass into Alfred's residuary estate and not pass to the specific legatee.

QUESTION TWO

a) When does the forfeiture rule apply?

    Discuss.

b) Malcolm made a will in 1992 in which he bequeathed all his money in Midshire Bank to his son, Tom, and the residue of his estate to his daughter, Rachel. In 1994,

Malcolm transferred his bank account to the Royal Bank of Wales, a subsidiary of the Midshire Bank. Rachel died a few weeks before Malcolm, survived by her illegitimate daughter, Alison.

Advise Alison and Tom.

University of London LLB Examination
(for External Students) Succession June 1997 Q7

General Comment

A good question to answer requiring a simple explanation of the forfeiture rule and a simple problem on ademption. Candidates who revised this area of legacies and devises would have had little difficulty in producing excellent answers.

Skeleton Solution

a) Explanation and discussion of the forfeiture rule.

b) Doctrine of ademption – lapse and s33 of the Wills Act 1837.

Suggested Solution

a) The forfeiture rule is based on the public policy rule that a person should not be allowed to benefit from his crime. This translates in the law of succession as the following: a beneficiary who unlawfully kills the testator/intestate should lose his interest under the will or on intestacy: *Jones v Roberts* [1995] 2 FLR 472.

The rule applies to all unlawful killings but case law seems to have confined it to murder and manslaughter. However, the cases are inconsistent as to whether forfeiture applies to all forms of manslaughter.

The Court of Appeal in *Re Hall* [1914] P 1 held that application of the rule did not depend on the moral guilt of the killer. In *Re Royse* [1984] Fam 22 the Court of Appeal applied the rule to a wife convicted of the manslaughter of her husband on the grounds of diminished responsibility.

In *Gray v Barr* [1971] 2 QB 554 however, the court held that the rule does not apply to manslaughter unless the killer was guilty of deliberate, intentional and unlawful violence or threat of violence.

The court in *Jones v Roberts* (above) refused to follow the test laid down in *Gray v Barr* but instead based its decision on *Re Royse* (above) which states that moral culpability is irrelevant. The son was therefore held not to be entitled on his father's intestacy as he had been found guilty of manslaughter on the grounds of diminished responsibility.

On balance, the *Re Royse* reasoning appears to be more sound in that the rule should apply to all manslaughter cases with the *Gray v Barr* distinction to be utilised only when considering relief.

Relief may be allowed under s2 of the Forfeiture Act 1982 which gives the court a discretion to modify the application of the rule. An application must be made within three months from the date of conviction. The Act does not apply to applicants who have been convicted of murder.

An illustration of the way the court could use its discretion could be seen in the case of *Re K (Deceased)* [1985] 2 All ER 833, where a wife was allowed to benefit from her husband's will despite having been convicted of his manslaughter. The court was satisfied that she had spent many years caring for him and had suffered abuse at his hands. Also, there were no other persons for whom the deceased was under any moral duty to provide.

b) Alison and Tom would wish to find out their entitlement, if any, under Malcolm's will.

Malcolm had left all his money in Midshire Bank to Tom. This appears to be a specific bequest (a gift by will of personalty forming part of the testator's estate at the date of death) rather than a demonstrative one (a general gift directed to be paid from a particular account). The test is deciphering Malcolm's intention; which in this case is that Tom is entitled only to the money in Midshire Bank.

As Malcolm transferred his account to the Royal Bank of Wales, the question is whether Tom's gift has adeemed.

A specific gift would fail by ademption if the subject matter of the gift has been destroyed or converted into something else at the testator's death: *Ashburner* v *MacGuire* (1786) 29 ER 62.

Whether ademption has taken place or not would depend on whether the change in this case is in name and form only or in substance: *Re Slater* [1907] 1 Ch 665. In *Re Dorman* [1994] 1 All ER 804, where the account which was the subject matter of a gift was closed and the money transferred to another account in the same bank, the court held that there was no ademption as the change was only in name and form. The court recognised that this decision was borderline based on the unusual facts.

Re Dorman can be distinguished from the facts here as the new account was opened in a different bank altogether albeit a subsidiary. The better conclusion would be that the change is a substantial one and Tom's gift has adeemed. The money in the account falls into the residue.

Rachel, who is entitled to the residue, predeceased her father. The general rule where a beneficiary predeceased the testator is that the gift to that beneficiary lapses.

Section 33(1) of the Wills Act 1837 as amended by s19 of the Administration of Justice Act 1982 provides an exception to the doctrine of lapse. As the testator was Rachel's father and Rachel was survived by her daughter Alison, s33 provides that Alison becomes entitled to the residue unless a contrary intention appears by the will. Her illegitimacy is irrelevant: s33(4)(a) of the 1837 Act.

QUESTION THREE

Alan, who has recently committed suicide, made a will in 1994 in which he gave:

i)   £10,000 to Michael 'to be paid out of my Government Stock';

ii) a complete original set of the collected works of Charles Dickens to Oliver;

iii) 'my leasehold interest in the property at 10 High Street, Oldtown' to Trevor; and

iv) 'the residue of my estate to my three children in equal shares'.

The will was witnessed by Trevor's wife and Trevor's two brothers.

It transpires that before his death Alan sold his Government Stock and used the proceeds to buy a valuable stamp collection for investment purposes; made an inter vivos gift of the works of Dickens to a friend; and acquired the freehold of No 10 High Street, Oldtown.

When he made the will Alan had three children: Colin who is still alive; Marion who died before Alan without children; and Peter who also predeceased Alan but who was survived by Rachel, and whom Peter and his wife had adopted. Colin wishes to disclaim any interest that he may have under the will as he does not believe in inherited wealth.

Trevor has been convicted of aiding and abetting Alan's suicide and sentenced to six months community service.

Advise on the effect of the gifts in Alan's will.

University of London LLB Examination
(for External Students) Succession June 1999 Q6

General Comment

A long question covering most aspects of legacies and devises. Candidates should consider brief plans dealing with each gift before answering the question. There is usually an issue of the residuary gift, the answer to which will depend on accuracy on all the preceeding points.

Skeleton Solution

Identify types of gifts – doctrine of ademption – s24 Wills Act 1837 – lapse and s33 Wills Act 1837 – disclaimer – forfeiture rule – s15 Wills Act 1837.

Suggested Solution

Whether Michael is entitled to the £10,000 would depend on the type of gift it is. A specific legacy is a gift of a particular part of the testator's personalty, distinguished from the rest of the assets whereas a demonstrative legacy is a general legacy to be paid out of a particular fund.

A specific gift would fail by ademption if the subject matter of the gift has been destroyed or converted into something else at the testator's death: *Ashburner v MacGuire* (1786) 29 ER 62. If the gift to Michael was specific it would fail by ademption as the stock was sold by Alan.

Whether the gift is specific or demonstrative is a matter of construction but the court generally leans against specific legacies. If the gift was construed to be demonstrative, the doctrine of ademption does not apply and Michael would receive the £10,000 out of the residue.

The gift of a set of the collected works of Dickens to Oliver is a general bequest due to the use of the word 'a' as opposed to the word 'my'. Therefore, it is irrelevant that Alan had given his set of the works of Dickens to a friend. The personal representatives would have to purchase another set for Oliver out of the general estate.

The gift of the leasehold of '10 High Street, Oldtown' is a specific devise but the problem is that Alan acquired the freehold before he died. The specific devise to Trevor would fail by ademption unless s24 of the Wills Act applies.

According to s24, every will is to be construed, with reference to property comprised in it, to speak and take effect as if it had been executed immediately before death unless a contrary intention shall appear by the will.

In the absence of contrary intention, according to s24, Trevor would be entitled to the freehold property. The test is whether the use of the word 'leasehold' was an essential part of the description or whether it was a mere addition to the description. The facts suggest that it was a mere addition to the description of the property which means that Trevor should be entitled to the freehold.

Section 15 of the Wills Act may apply to void Trevor's gift as his wife witnessed the will. However, as Trevor's wife was a supernumerary witness, s1 of the Wills Act 1968 provides an exception to s15.

Trevor may still be disallowed from benefiting by virtue of the forfeiture rule as he had helped in Alan's suicide. However, the case law on this area have so far confined the forfeiture rule to cases of murder and manslaughter. Trevor had not been convicted of either.

Even if the forfeiture rule is applied to Trevor, he may still apply for relief under s2 of the Forfeiture Act 1982 which gives the court a discretion to modify the rule.

The final issue is the residuary gift. Out of his three children, only one (Colin) had survived Alan. Marion's share in the residue would lapse as she had predeceased her father. Peter's share would also lapse but for the exception provided by s33(1) of the Wills Act 1837 as amended by s19 of the Administration of Justice Act 1982.

Following s33(1), Peter's adopted daughter Rachel would receive her father's share. The fact that she was adopted is irrelevant as s39 of the Adoption Act 1976 states that a child adopted by a married couple is treated as a child of that marriage.

The residue would therefore be divided equally between Colin and Rachel. Colin, however, wishes to disclaim his interest. The general rule is that so long as Colin has not unequivocally accepted the gift, he may disclaim his interest and, once he has done so, the disclaimer can only be retracted if no one has altered his position in reliance: *Re Cranstoun's Will Trusts* [1949] Ch 523.

A disclaimer may be made orally, in writing or by deed. On Colin's disclaimer, Rachel would become entitled to the whole residue.

QUESTION FOUR

Three months ago Ron went on a coach holiday abroad with four close friends, Jack, Alan, Bill and Derek. The coach overturned on a steep bend in the Alps. Ron survived but all his friends were killed. It transpires that all made a gift to Ron in their respective wills:

a) Jack left his London home to Molly for life, and thereafter to Ron. Molly was Jack's wife when he made the will but they were divorced a few months before the fatal coach accident. Molly has since remarried.

b) Alan left his vintage sports car, 'Red Streaker', to Ron. When Alan's executors informed him of this, Ron told them that he really did not want the car as he could not drive. The executors then allowed Alan's son, Nigel, to use the car and enter it for a vintage car rally. Ron has now changed his mind: he has started driving lessons and would like to have 'Red Streaker' after all.

c) Bill left a legacy of £5,000 to Ron. Bill's will was witnessed by Ron's wife, Ethel, and by Bill's neighbours, Arthur and Mavis. In his will Bill left £500 to Arthur 'for the purposes of the Clifton Chess Club'. Bill was a keen member of the club and Arthur is its President. Neither Ron nor Ethel had any idea, when the will was executed, that Ron was a beneficiary under it.

d) Derek left Ron 'my deposit account in Barclay's Bank, Notting Hill, London'. Several months after Derek executed his will he moved to Manchester. He closed the deposit account in Barclay's Bank, Notting Hill and used the proceeds to open a current account in a branch of the NatWest bank in Manchester.

Advise Ron.

University of London LLB Examination
(for External Students) Succession June 2000 Q7

General Comment

This is a very popular area for the examiner – the only danger is leaving out small parts of the syllabus. This question is not untypical and covers four aspects of this part of your syllabus. Many students do not favour this area. However, once you revise all the crucial points the questions are never very difficult and as such this is a worthwhile topic.

Skeleton Solution

Application of s18A Wills Act 1837: the effect of divorce – disclaimer of gifts – retraction of disclaimer – s15 and exceptions – ademption: *Re Dorman* and *Re Slater*.

Suggested Solution

a) This question requires discussion of the impact of divorce on the gift to Molly. Section 18A of the Wills Act 1837 provides that any devise or bequest to the former spouse will lapse on divorce, unless there is some contrary intention that appears in the will. The remaining dispositions in the will are not effected by this lapse. In essence the lapse requires that the ex spouse be treated as having died at the date of the divorce.

   The next issue to be addressed is the impact of the above rule on Ron's entitlement. As Molly is treated as dead, s18A(3) provides that the remainder will take effect immediately on the testator's death. Thus Ron will take Jack's London home absolutely.

b) A person is entitled to disclaim his interest under a will and, if no one has altered their position in pursuance of the disclaimer, he may retract it at any time. In this case Ron has clearly disclaimed the gift of the car as he does not know how to drive. In reliance of this, the executors have allowed Alan's son to use the car and enter it into a rally. In *Re Cranstoun's Will Trusts* [1949] Ch 523 Romer J considers the possibility of the person who disclaims a gift and then changes his mind. Romer J suggests that he should be allowed to change his mind if no one has acted on the disclaimer.

   In the present case, Nigel has been 'allowed to use the car'. This suggests that this is a temporary measure and that the car has not yet been transferred to Nigel. In this situation, it may be possible to argue that Ron's entitlement to the car still survives and that he may by way of compromise wait until the end of the vintage car rally before claiming his gift. There is no authority for this suggestion.

c) In this scenario Ron may be at risk of losing his legacy of £5,000 from Bill's will as Ron's wife was a witness to the will. Section 15 Wills Act 1837 provides that no benefit may be taken by a beneficiary who either witnesses the will himself or whose spouse witnesses the will under which the benefit is derived. There are, however, several exceptions to this rule. One exception that applies in this case is s1 Wills Act 1968, which allows a beneficiary in these circumstances to take the benefit so long as there are a further two independent witnesses. In this case, the will was witnessed by Arthur and Mavis as well as by Ron's wife.

   The next issue that arises here is the gift to Arthur for the Clifton Chess Club. Clearly s15 applies equally to Arthur who witnessed the will and therefore Arthur may not rely upon s1 Wills Act 1968 as there is only one supernumerary independent witness – Ethel. However, it would appear that Arthur takes the gift as a trustee for the use of the Chess Club – it is not a gift to him personally and as such will not fail: see *Cresswell v Cresswell* (1868) LR 6 Eq 69.

d) The gift of the deposit account is a specific legacy. As such the doctrine of ademption will apply. The effect of the doctrine is to cause the failure of a gift by ademption if the subject matter of the gift no longer exists at the date of death. Where there is a change in name and form alone, which leaves the subject matter of the gift substantially the same, no ademption occurs. However, the assessment of whether a substantial change has occurred is up to the particular court and may lead to contradictory findings. In *Re Slater*[1907] 1 Ch 665 the change was to the name of the company (the original company was acquired by a new company) and the area over which they supplied water. This was regarded as a change in form and the gift adeemed. However, in *Re Dorman* [1994] 1 WLR 282 the change was to a bank account but the money remained at the same bank and had simply been moved to a different account, which earned more interest. The court held that the gift did not adeem. *Re Slater* is regarded as an unduly harsh decision and was commented upon as such in *Re Dorman*. The distinction between *Re Dorman* and the present case is that here the funds have been moved to a different bank. The question to be asked is whether this is a sufficient change in form. It is submitted that, following *Re Dorman*, the change is not sufficient to adeem the gift.

Chapter 9

Construction of Wills

9.1   **Introduction**

9.2   **Key points**

9.3   **Key cases and statutes**

9.4   **Questions and suggested solutions**

9.1 Introduction

Words in a will may not always be clear. On these occasions the court's assistance may be sought to construe the words used in a will to see what they mean. It is vital that you study the canons of construction and the general rules. In addition, the evidential rules that apply to this area should be considered.

9.2 Key points

a) General principles

   i)   Purpose is to determine the testator's wishes as expressed in the will: *Perrin* v *Morgan* [1943] AC 399.

   ii) Words are given their ordinary meaning, unless that would result in inconsistency, in which case the secondary meaning is used: *Re Smalley* [1929] 2 Ch 112.

   iii) Technical words are given their technical meaning: *Re Cook* [1948] Ch 212.

   iv) Testator's intention as indicated by the will as a whole is paramount: cf *Re Dorman* [1994] 1 WLR 282.

   v)   Court can supply words if there is a blank and the nature of the omission is obvious.

   vi) Alterations to the will by codicil must be clear and unambiguous.

   vii) Court can take into account the style of writing of a will.

b) Evidence

   i)   Evidence as to surrounding circumstances was admissible to explain otherwise meaningless words pre Administration Justice Act 1982: *Re Fish* [1893] 2 Ch 83; *Charter* v *Charter* (1874) LR 7 HL 364.

ii) Evidence as to intention of testator was inadmissable save in the case of equivocation, prior to the Act: *Bennett* v *Marshall* (1856) 2 K & J 740.

iii) Section 21 Administration Justice Act 1982 allows evidence in three circumstances:

- if part of the will is 'meaningless';

- if language in any part of the will is ambiguous on the face of the will;

- if language in any part of the will is ambiguous in light of surrounding circumstances.

c) Presumptions

   i) Satisfaction of portions.

   ii) Satisfaction of debts.

   iii) Ademption of legacies.

d) Section 24 Wills Act 1837: prima facie, gifts must be construed with regard to the testator's estate immediately before death: *Re Champion* [1893] 1 Ch 101; *Re Willis* [1911] 2 Ch 563.

e) Section 27 Wills Act 1837: any general gift extends to property over which testator had a general power of appointment.

f) Class closing rules enable beneficiaries to be ascertained as soon as possible.

g) Statutory rules of construction

   i) Adoption Act 1976.

   ii) Legitimacy Act 1976.

   iii) Family Law Reform Acts 1969 and 1987.

h) Administration of Justice Act 1982

   i) Introduces new rules as to admissibility of evidence; see above.

   ii) Gives the court a limited power to rectify wills namely in case of clerical error or failure to carry out testator's instructions. (Section 20 AJA 1982.)

   iii) Section 22 AJA 1982: where testator makes a gift to his spouse which purports to be absolute, but makes a gift over to his children, then the gift to his spouse is construed as being absolute, subject to contrary intention.

9.3 Key cases and statutes

- *Abbott* v *Middleton* (1858) 7 HLC 68
  Words are to be given their ordinary meaning where this does not lead to any difficulty with construction

- *Allgood* v *Blake* (1873) LR 8 Ex 160
  The armchair principle

- *Andrews* v *Partington* (1791) 3 Bro CC 401
  Rules for the ascertainment of classes

- *Charter* v *Charter* (1874) LR 7 HL 364
  Where the object of the gift is in question, extrinsic evidence is admissible to show what the testator intended

- *Doe d Winter* v *Perratt* (1843) 6 M & G 314
  Technical words must be given their technical meaning

- *Drummond's Settlement, Re* [1988] 1 All ER 449
  Class closing rules dealing with a class gift where a contingency is imposed on each member

- *Emmet's Estate, Re* (1880) 13 Ch D 484
  Class closing rules dealing with a contingent class gift following a life interest

- *Evans, Re* [1909] 1 Ch 784
  Circumstances in which s24 may be excluded

- *Henley* v *Wardell* (1988) The Times 29 January
  The courts' duty is to ascertain the expressed intention of the testator

- *Kell* v *Charmer* (1856) 23 Beav 195
  Application of s21(1)(a) Administration of Justice Act 1982 – power to admit evidence where any part of the will is meaningless

- *Knapp's Settlement, Re* [1895] 1 Ch 91
  Class closing rules dealing with a class gift following a life interest

- *Manners, Re* [1955] 1 WLR 1096
  Class closing rules dealing with immediate class gifts without age requirements

- *Perrin* v *Morgan* [1943] AC 399
  The principle in *Abbot* v *Middleton* does not apply if the word in question has more than one ordinary meaning

- *Ringrose* v *Bramham* (1794) 2 Cox Eq 384
  Class closing rules dealing with individual gifts to each member of a class

- *Segelman (Deceased), Re* [1995] 3 All ER 676
  Application of the rules regarding rectification under s20 of the Administration of Justice Act 1925

- *Watson* v *National Children's Home* (1995) The Times 31 October
  Where the will is ambiguous s21 of the Administration of Justice Act 1982 allows evidence of the testators intention to be admitted

- *Whitrick, Re* [1957] 1 WLR 884
  The court may supply words where there is an omission but only if the nature of the omission is clear

- *Williams, Re* [1985] 1 All ER 964
  Application of s21(1)(b) Administration of Justice Act 1982

- *Willis, Re* [1911] 2 Ch 563
  Application of s24 of the Wills Act 1837

- Administration of Justice Act 1982, s20 – rules of rectification of wills

- Administration of Justice Act 1982, s21 – admissibility of extrinsic evidence

- Adoption Act 1976 – status of adopted children

- Family Law Reform Acts 1969 and 1987 – status of illegitimate children

- Legitimacy Act 1976 – status of legitimated children

- Wills Act 1837, s24 – date from which the will speaks

- Wills Act 1837, s27 – powers of appointment

9.4 Questions and suggested solutions

QUESTION ONE

'It is virtually impossible to produce rules of law which will result in every case in the real, as distinct from the expressed, wishes of the Testator being carried out'. (Law Reform Committee.)

Explain and discuss.

> University of London LLB Examination
> (for External Students) Succession June 1989 Q4

General Comment

Quite a difficult essay question on the rules of construction. This type of question should not be attempted unless the issues have been thought about. The danger is writing an answer on all you know about construction.

Skeleton Solution

Introduction: quote from *Re Whitrick* – rules restricting court to will: strict meaning; secondary meaning; more probable; technical; special group; s27 Wills Act 1837; s24

Wills Act 1837; s28 Wills Act 1837; class closing; children; comment – rules allowing extrinsic evidence AJA 1982: s21; construction; s22; rectification; conclusion.

Suggested Solution

It is not the court's aim to give effect to the 'testator's real as distinct from his expressed wishes'. Such an aim would detract from the fundamental requirement that a will be in writing. 'The court cannot rewrite the testamentary provisions which come before it for construction': per Jenkins LJ in *Re Whitrick* [1957] 1 WLR 884.

It is the court's purpose to interpret the meaning of the will. To this end there are general rules and principles of construction. These are set out below. It will be seen that where possible, the rules do not direct the court beyond the will, or the 'expressed wishes' of the testator.

The rules which do not direct the court beyond the will are as follows.

A word or phrase is given its strict grammatical meaning: see *Villar v Gumey* [1907] AC 310; *Hamilton v Ritchie* [1894] AC 310; *Higgins v Dawson* [1902] AC 1. This may cause a result which the testator did not intend: see *Gilmour v MacPhillamy* [1930] AC 712.

In two circumstances the court will apply the words 'secondary meaning'.

Firstly, if there is a definition in the will. Thus, in *Re Helliwell, Pickles v Helliwell* [1916] 2 Ch 580 the testator showed he intended the word 'nephew' to have a wider meaning than usual. Secondly, if the testator's circumstances show the testator meant a word to have an unusual meaning in which case the court will apply that meaning eg *Re Smalley, Smalley v Scotton* [1929] 2 Ch 112.

If a word is capable of more than one meaning, the court will apply the more probable meaning: see *Perrin v Morgan* [1943] AC 399.

If a word has a technical legal meaning that technical meaning should be given.

If a testator belonged to a special club in which a word has a special meaning, then that special meaning should be given.

The effect of s24 Wills Act (WA) 1837 is that any reference to real estate and personalty comprised in it speaks as if the testator executed the will immediately before death, subject to contrary intention in the will, in the context of construction of gifts. This can result in the real wishes of the testator being overridden. For example, if the gift is specific and construed as contrary intention to s24, and the subject matter is replaced between the date of the will and the death, the gift will adeem and the beneficiary receive nothing.

Section 27 WA 1837 provides that any gift of estate shall be construed to cover property over which the testator has a general power of appointment and shall operate as an execution of that power subject to contrary intention.

As to whether a gift is absolute or for life, s28 WA 1837 provides a devise is construed as passing the fee simple or other whole interest over which the testator had power to devolve by will, unless the will limits the devise or contains contrary intention.

The class closing rules application often runs contrary to the testator's intention since clearly the testator intends all members to benefit.

Similarly the rules as to adopted, illegitimate and legitimated children may achieve a result different to that intended by the testator.

To summarise, the above rules are rules of convenience enabling courts to consistently construct the meaning of wills, but not designed to implement the testator's 'real wishes'.

However, there are certain circumstances in which the construction rules require a court to look beyond the will. These are as follows.

Extrinsic evidence including evidence of the testator's intention may be called upon in three cases. Firstly, it may be used where part of the will is meaningless either because the words do not make grammatical sense or because they do not make sense applied to the particular circumstances.

Secondly, it may be used where the language is ambiguous on the face of the will, eg a word with more than one natural meaning is used: *Re Williams* [1985] 1 All ER 964.

Finally, it may be considered where part of the will is 'ambiguous in the light of the present surroundings'. This paragraph would apply to cases like *National Society for Prevention of Cruelty to Children* v *Scottish National Society for the Prevention of Cruelty to Children* [1915] AC 207.

The above rule is contained in s21 Administration of Justice Act (AJA) 1982.

Further, under s22 AJA 1982, the court has a limited power to rectify a will where it is satisfied that the will does not comply with the testator's intentions, either because of a clerical error or failure to understand the testator's instructions. The court may order rectification to give effect to the testator's instructions and extrinsic evidence is admissible.

To conclude, there are rules of construction which admit evidence as to the testator's 'real wishes' and those which restrict the court's scope to the will, or the testator's 'expressed wishes'. However, as explained at the outset, the court's overriding aim is to interpret the will. It is inevitable that in most cases it will be the expressed wishes and not the real wishes of the testator which will prevail, not least because it is only the minority of wills which reach court.

QUESTION TWO

'You ought if possible to read the will so as to lead to a testacy, not an intestacy.'

To what extent is this 'golden rule' reflected in the principles developed by the courts for the construction of wills and illustrated in decided cases?

University of London LLB Examination
(for External Students) Succession June 1993 Q5

General Comment

Another difficult essay-style question on construction. Candidates who choose this type of question must have a very clear idea of the relevant issues. The last question and this question should not be used as an oppoprtunity to 'write all you know'.

Skeleton Solution

Statement of the rule – examination of the rules of construction, giving instances where it can apply – caveat that the general principles apply and rule only subsidiary.

Suggested Solution

The quotation in the question is an extract from the words of Lord Esther MR in *Re J Harrison, Turner* v *Hellard* (1885) 30 Ch D 390 where he explained the golden rule in his judgment by saying: 'Where a testator has executed a will in solemn form, you must assume that he did not intend to make it a solemn farce – that he did not intend to die intestate when he had gone through the form of making a will. You ought if possible to read the will so as to lead to a testacy not an intestacy.'

The rule is that the court will endeavour to find a construction which gives a sensible meaning to the provisions of the will, and which will not lead to an intestacy. The rule operates where there are two or more possible constructions. An example is *Re Arnould, Arnould* v *Lloyd* [1955] 2 All ER 316 where the court could only make sense of the testator's will by construing his full stops as commas, which in fact was done.

The golden rule is in fact a subsidiary rule of construction and can only operate within the constraints of the general principles of construction, and it may not be possible to apply the golden rule because a court is duty-bound to follow the rules, and the application of these may lead, in certain circumstances, to an intestacy, which the court is powerless to avoid.

Illustrations of the rules, where the subsidiary golden rule is relevant, can be given by reference to case law.

One must start by stating that the court's duty, when construing a will, is to ascertain the expressed intention of the testator. This excludes conjecture as to what the testator might have meant.

The second general principle states that when words and expressions that are used are unambiguous, and their application to the circumstances of the will does not lead to any difficulty of construction, then they are to be given their ordinary meaning. In *Perrin* v *Morgan* [1943] AC 399 a gift of 'all moneys of which I die possessed' was held by the House of Lords to include not only £840 cash, but also stocks and shares worth some £33,000. Thus, the word 'money' was given its popular, rather than a strict legal, meaning and an intestacy was avoided.

Technical words or expressions, however, must be taken as having been used in their technical sense. This is a presumption, and can be rebutted. In *Re Bailey* [1945] Ch 191 the words 'I leave Y as my residuary legatee', when the estate consisted largely of realty, was interpreted as 'residuary beneficiary', thus avoiding an intestacy.

The testator's intention collected from the entire will must be given effect, even if this leads to the literal sense of the words being overturned or extended beyond their usual meaning.

The court may supply words where there is an omission by implication, if the omission is clear. In *Re Whitrick* [1957] 1 WLR 884 a gift of the estate to a husband, but with the words added 'in the event of my husband and myself both dying at the same time' – then such estate to be held in trust for three persons – was held to be a gift over, intended to take effect in the event of the husband predeceasing the testatrix, as well as dying simultaneously, thus again avoiding intestacy.

Codicils should be construed to interfere as little as possible with the dispositions of the will.

A court may also take into account the manner in which the words of the will were written, looking at the original will, for example, to ascertain the punctuation, the effect of a blank, or the introduction of capital letters.

As regards the admissibility of evidence, surrounding circumstances at the date when the will was made is admissible to explain particular words used in the will, when such words may only become apparent in the light of those circumstances. Usually this will concern either the objects or the subject matter of gifts in a will. In *McKeown v Ardagh* (1847) Ir R 10 Eq 445 a gift to a non-existent 'Patagonian Chilean and Peruvian Missionary Society' was held to refer to a 'South American Society' of which the testator knew and had subscribed to, and the legacy was given to them instead of lapsing.

Declared intentions of the testator are inadmissible except in cases of equivocation and the ambit of this has been extended to include not only latent ambiguity, as under the old law, but patent ambiguity by the provisions of s21 of the Administration of Justice Act 1982.

This Act has assisted the courts in widening their approach to the construction of wills by freeing some of the constraints of the prior law.

The general effect of this must be to achieve testacy rather than intestacy in a number of cases and thus enhance the operation of the golden rule.

Statute law itself operates from time to time to implement the golden rule; for example s28 of the Wills Act 1837 provides that a devise to a person without words of limitation passes the fee simple. However if there is an absolute gift to a legatee in the first instance and trusts are engrafted or imposed on that absolute interest which fail, either from lapse, or invalidity, or any other reason, then the absolute gift, it was held in *Hancock* v *Watson* [1902] AC 14, takes effect, so far as the trusts have failed to the exclusion of the residuary legatee or the next-of-kin on an intestacy.

In many instances therefore one can see the golden rule working. However, it must always be emphasised that it can only operate where the principles of construction, as laid down in case law or statute, permit, and it is only within an area of discretion, so circumscribed, that a court is free to implement it, and which it should do to avoid intestacy where it can.

QUESTION THREE

a) 'In formulating rules for disputes about the meaning of a will the law must hold the balance between giving effect to the testator's "true" intentions on the one hand and enabling those concerned to rely on the words actually used in it on the other.' Law Reform Committee's 19th Report *Interpretation of Wills* (1973) para 3.

   Discuss.

b) Terence had three children, Kitty, Milly and John. Kitty married and had a son called Fred. Shortly afterwards John, her brother, was killed in an accident. Terence had been very fond of John (who had, clearly, always been his favourite child) but he began to treat Fred as a substitute for the son he had lost and started to call Fred 'John'. It became his habit always to call Fred 'John'. Then Milly married and she had a son whom she named John. For some unexplained reason, Terence did not like Milly's son and seldom spoke to him or of him. Whenever Terence referred to 'John' he was referring to Kitty's son, Fred.

   Recently, Terence died. In his home-made will he left 'all my money to my beloved grandson John'. Terence's estate consists principally of the house in which he lived and of investments quoted on the stock exchange.

   Discuss.

University of London LLB Examination
(for External Students) Succession June 1996 Q6

General Comment

This was a two-part question. The first part required a candidate to examine rules of construction of wills to resolve disputes which may arise from strict interpretation of a will's wording when it is contended that the testator's true intentions were not given expression in the words used. This was a perfectly fair 'book-work' type question. The second part of the question asked the candidate to consider what might happen if a testator had confusingly referred to children and grandchildren otherwise than by their actual names. It also required knowledge of whether a specific word – 'money' – might have an extended meaning. This was a somewhat convoluted problem but by no means unfair.

Skeleton Solution

a) Primary principle – availability of extrinsic evidence – construe intention from words used – no rewriting of will – words given ordinary meaning – will read as a whole – the dictionary principle.

b) Should gift be construed other than as in will? – availability of extrinsic evidence – three sets of circumstances – application of relevant case law – words to be given ordinary meaning – interpretation of technical words.

Suggested Solution

a) The primary principle of construction of a will is to ascertain the testator's intention, as expressed in the will when it is read as a whole. Sometimes extrinsic evidence, ie evidence not contained in the will, is admissible to assist in the interpretation of the will, but the language of the will is central to its construction because the object is to discover the meaning of the words as intended by the testator.

In *Perrin* v *Morgan* [1943] AC 399 Lord Simon LC declared that:

> '... the fundamental rule in construing the language of a will is to put on the words used the meaning which, having regard to the terms of the will, the testator intended. The question is not ... what the testator meant to do when he made his will, but what the written words he uses mean in the particular case – what are the "expressed intentions" of the testator.'

The difficulty with the quoted section of Law Reform Committee's 19th report on the *Interpretation of Wills* is that the balance referred to is extremely difficult to strike, given that the courts do consciously seek to ascertain the testator's expressed intention from the words actually used.

Certain clear principles have emerged governing issues of construction. These will be set down in outline. The first is that the court cannot rewrite a will. Apart from its power to rectify a will under s20 Administration of Justice Act 1982, the court has no power to rewrite a testator's will because the court's function is to construe the testator's will, not to make a new will for him. As stated by Jenkins LJ in *Re Bailey* [1945] Ch 191:

> '... the function of the court is to give effect to the dispositions actually made as appearing expressly or by necessary implication from the language of the will applied to the surrounding circumstances of the case.'

The second principle of value is that words are given their ordinary meaning. So, for example, in *Re James's Will Trusts* [1962] Ch 226, a testator's children took life interests in his residuary estate, each child taking a life interest in an equal share. As each child died, the share in which he had had a life interest passed to his issue, but if a child died without issue his share passed to 'my surviving children'. The strict and plain meaning of these words was that the share passed to the deceased child's surviving brothers and sisters, but not to the issue of other brothers and sisters who had died before him, however harsh and improbable this interpretation may be. It reflected the ordinary meaning of the words used.

The third principle is that the will must be read as a whole. If the court is faced with a choice between two or more possible meanings of an ambiguous word or phrase, it determines the meaning intended by the testator by considering all the provisions of the will, combined with the aid of admissible extrinsic evidence. Rebutting the presumption in favour of the ordinary meaning – known as the dictionary principle – can often be helpful and is the theme which is at issue on the facts of part (b) of this question.

b) The question raised here is whether a gift of 'all my money to my beloved grandson John' should be construed in a manner other than that which is evident from the ordinary meaning of those words. Terence had a son called John, who was killed in an accident. There is evidence that John's son (and Terence's grandson) Fred was known to Terence as 'John', by which name he had the habit of calling him. The matter is further complicated by the fact that one of Terence's daughters, Milly, does have a son by the name of John, but that for some unexplained reason Terence did not like this son of Milly and seldom spoke to him or of him. Yet it remains the case that 'all my money to my beloved grandson, John' can only be construed as a gift to Milly's son of that name unless evidence can be established on behalf of Kitty's son, Fred, that Terence used the name 'John' deliberately to refer to Fred.

Under s21 Administration of Justice Act (AJA) 1982 (applicable, as here, where a testator has died after 31 December 1982) extrinsic evidence is admissible of the testator's intention only where evidence of surrounding circumstances would have been admissible before the passing into law of the 1982 Act and in three specific sets of circumstances:

1. insofar as any part of a will is meaningless;

2. insofar as the language used in any part of a will is ambiguous on the face of it;

3. insofar as evidence, other than evidence of the testator's intention, shows that the language used in any part of a will is ambiguous in the light of surrounding circumstances.

Clearly, from our facts (1) and (2) appear not to be appropriate; but (3) may be, although the weight of case law is against Fred. In *Re Smalley* [1929] 2 Ch 112, a testator left all his property 'to my wife Eliza Ann Smalley'. Two women claimed to fit the description – one Mary Ann Smalley, who was the testator's lawful wife (with whom he had not lived for many years); the other Eliza Ann Mercer, with whom he had gone through a ceremony of marriage and who lived with him, believing herself to be his wife. The Court of Appeal decided that Eliza Ann Mercer was entitled: the surrounding circumstances showed that the testator had used the words 'my wife' in his will in their secondary meaning of his reputed wife. The description fitted neither of the two women insofar as the testator's wife was not called Eliza and Eliza was not his wife. But s21 AJA 1982 is not of any value if the language of the will is not ambiguous, even where it is read in the light of the surrounding circumstances. Herein lies the difficulty for Fred. Terence's will refers to a grandson, John. There is only one such person. That is not Fred, but Milly's son, John. That conclusion is not diminished by the importance of the adjective 'beloved'. Such a description, particularly in the context of a will, is not uncommon and it will not avail Fred to seek to establish that Milly's son, John, was not beloved of Terence.

It is now important to consider whether the phrase of Terence's home-made will – 'all my money' – could encompass the assets referred to. There can be little question but that the house cannot pass from this wording; arguably, the investments quoted on the stock exchange might since they will have a monetary value when realised. In the usual sense, stocks and shares, and investments, do not come within the word 'money' (see *Re Tetsall* [1961] 1 WLR 938); but there is a well-settled rule that a technical word or expression which does not make sense if read in the light of surrounding circumstances when the testator made his will may be read in a non-technical way if that does make sense. This happened in *Re Bailey* where the words 'residuary legatee' were held to have been used in the wider sense of 'residuary beneficiary'.

QUESTION FOUR

' "When I use the word", Humpty Dumpty said in a rather scornful tone, "it means just what I choose it to mean, neither more nor less." '

To what extent do you consider that the judges behaved like Humpty Dumpty in the following cases?

Perrin v *Morgan* [1943] AC 399

NSPCC v *SNSPCC* [1915] AC 207

Charter v *Charter* (1874) LR 7 HL 364

University of London LLB Examination
(for External Students) Succession June 1999 Q7

General Comment

An interesting question requiring a good knowledge of three major cases in the area. Where the question specifies the cases required, candidates should only attempt the question if they are confident of their knowledge of all the cases.

Skeleton Solution

Principles of construction – analysis of judges' behaviour in cases mentioned.

Suggested Solution

In construing a will, the court can only interpret the testator's intention as expressed in the will itself and should not conjecture. It is not for the court rewrite the will: *Perrin* v *Morgan* [1943] AC 399.

Therefore, in construing a will, the rule is to read it in the ordinary and grammatical sense of the words (*Abbott* v *Middleton* (1858) 7 HLC 68) unless a word has more than one ordinary meaning, in which case the court will try to determine the meaning intended by the testator by construing the will as a whole in the light of any extrinsic evidence.

In *Perrin* v *Morgan* the meaning of the word 'moneys' was in issue. The question was whether the word 'moneys' includes all net personalty including stocks and shares and household goods or should be limited to just cash.

The court in this case decided that as the word has no fixed meaning: the court must decide on the meaning intended by the testator by reading the will as a whole and in the light of all circumstances such as the contemporary use of the English language when the will was made. The House of Lords in this instance decided that the word should include the net personalty.

The general rule is that extrinsic evidence is inadmissible as the court should only look at the words of the will itself in ascertaining the testator's intention. Exceptionally, evidence is admissible at common law under the armchair rule and in cases of equivocation. Note that s21(1) of the Administration of Justice Act 1982 now governs the admissibility of extrinsic evidence.

In the case of *NSPCC* v *SNSPCC* [1915] AC 207 the will contained a legacy to the NSPCC that was claimed by both the English charity and its Scottish counterpart. Although there is evidence to suggest that the testator had intended to benefit the Scottish charity, it was inadmissible as extrinsic evidence should only be admitted where there is ambiguity. To admit the evidence in this instance would create ambiguity rather than resolve it.

The case of *Charter* v *Charter* (1874) LR 7 HL 364 provides an illustration of the armchair principle. This principle allows circumstantial extrinsic evidence to be admitted; ie the court has the right to ascertain all the facts as known to the testator at the time the will was made by placing itself in the testator's position: *Boyes* v *Cook* (1880) 14 Ch D 53.

In *Charter* v *Charter* the testator had appointed his son 'Forster Charter' executor and left him the residue and directed him to pay an annuity to the widow so long as 'they reside together in the same house'. The testator had three sons; Forster Charter who died before the will was made, William Forster Charter who lived away from home and

Charles Charter who was still living with his mother. Based on this evidence, it was held that Charles was the one meant by the testator.

In the three cases discussed above, the court was shown to have behaved rather like Humpty Dumpty in both *Perrin* v *Morgan* and in *Charter* v *Charter*. It is felt that only the decision in *NSPCC* v *SNSPCC* is reasonable, following accepted rules of admissibility of evidence.

Chapter 10

Intestate Succession

10.1   Introduction

10.2   Key points

10.3   Key cases and statutes

10.4   Questions and suggested solutions

10.1 Introduction

When the testator does not leave a will, or fails to dispose of all his property, the rules of intestacy will determine in inheritance. The rules are provided by a number of statutory provisions that must be carefully considered.

10.2 Key points

a) There is total intestacy where there is no will and a partial intestacy where the will leaves part of the estate undisposed.

b) Section 33 Administration of Estates Act 1925 – the intestate's personal representatives hold estate on trust with a power of sale.

c) Succession of interests is governed by s46 AEA 1925.

d) If intestate leaves surviving spouse

   i) If intestate leaves issue, spouse takes personal chattels, a statutory legacy of £125,000 plus interest and a life interest in half the residue. Remainder goes to the issue with half the residue on statutory trust (if the deceased died after 1 December 1993).

   ii) If intestate leaves no issue but leaves a parent or brother or sister of whole blood, spouse takes personal chattels, £200,000 plus interest and half residue absolutely. Half residue to parents then brother and sister on statutory trust.

   iii) If intestate leaves no issue, parent, brother or sister of whole blood or their issue, spouse takes estate absolutely.

e) Spouse may elect within 12 months of grant:

   i) to capitalise life interest;

   ii) to take matrimonial home against the statutory legacy.

f) Section 46(2A) AEA 1925: a surviving spouse is only entitled on intestacy if he/she survives intestate by at least 28 days.

g) NB definition of 'personal chattels'.

h) Subject to spouses' rights, estate goes to:

    i) issue on statutory trust, but if none

    ii) parents, but if none

    iii) brothers and sisters of whole blood on statutory trust.

    If there is no spouse or relative above, then to

    i) half brothers and sisters on statutory trust, if none

    ii) grandparents, but if none

    iii) uncles and aunts of whole blood, if none

    iv) half uncles and aunts, if none

    v) bona vacantia.

i) Partial intestacy: the provisions in the will are applied first, followed by intestacy rules.

j) Section 1(2) Law Reform (Succession) Act 1995 abolished all hotchpot provisions.

10.3 Key cases and statutes

* *Collins, Re* [1975] 1 WLR 309
  The relevant date for the valuation of real property is the date the surviving spouse gives notice of appropriation

* *Crispin's Will Trusts, Re* [1975] Ch 245
  The value of an item is immaterial when determining if it is a personal chattel

* *Hutchinson, Re* [1955] Ch 255 ·
  Twelve race horses kept for recreational purposes held to fall within the meaning of s55 Administration of Estates Act 1925

* *MacCulloch, Re* (1981) 44 NSR (2d) 666
  Dominant purpose rule

* *Ogilby, Re* [1942] Ch 288
  Certain assets can only be regarded as business assets

* Administration of Estates Act 1925, s33 – trust with the power to sell

* Administration of Estates Act 1925, s46(1) – entitlement of the surviving spouse

* Administration of Estates Act 1925, s47(1)(i) – entitlement of the issue on intestacy

- Administration of Estates Act 1925, s47A(1) – redemption of life interest

- Administration of Estates Act 1925, s49(1) – rules on partial intestacy

- Administration of Estates Act 1925, s55(1)(x) – definition of personal chattels

- Intestates' Estates Act 1952, s5 and Sch 2 – rights in respect of the matrimonial home

- Law Reform (Succession) Act 1995, s1(1) – requirement for the spouse to survive for at least 28 days to take on intestacy

10.4 Questions and suggested solutions

Students should note that any discussion of the hotchpot principles in the following suggested solutions is only appropriate taking into account the year of the examination. The position after 1995 is that hotchpot has been abolished.

QUESTION ONE

'The Law Reform (Succession) Act 1995 enacted the Law Commission's recommendation that hotchpot should be abolished but did not enact the recommendation that a surviving spouse should inherit the entire estate. This was the wrong way round. Either recommendation would have simplified the law. But to abolish hotchpot is to prefer simplicity to fairness. Giving the entire estate to the surviving spouse would have been *both* simple *and* fair.'

Discuss.

University of London LLB Examination
(for External Students) Succession June 1996 Q2

General Comment

This was a perfectly fair question requiring a candidate to give a considered view of certain recent changes introduced into the law of succession by the Law Reform (Succession) Act 1995. The merit of such a question is that it assumes a pre-conceived view of the legislation and invites the candidate to affirm or disavow that view by reasoned argument. This type of question tends only to be popular with candidates of more analytical mind and will not have found favour with the weaker candidate; but therein lies its worth.

Skeleton Solution

Law Commission background report – abolition of hotchpot idea – equitable basis – lifetime advancement on intestacy – benefits under will on partial intestacy – contrast with s32 Trustee Act advancement – view on spouse succession – present scheme merits.

Suggested Solution

In 1989 the Law Commission published a report Law Com No 187, *Distribution on Intestacy*, which made three proposals for reform of the intestacy rules. These were:

a) that the statutory hotchpot rules should be repealed;

b) that a spouse should only inherit under the intestacy rules if he or she survived the intestate for 14 days;

c) that a surviving spouse, subject to (b), should in all cases take the intestate's whole estate.

The first proposal has been implemented by s2 Law Reform (Succession) Act (LR(S)A) 1995. The second proposal was accepted in principle, but the period of 14 days was extended to 28 days at the committee stage of the Bill's reading in the House of Lords: the provision is in s1(1) LR(S)A 1995, inserting a new subs(2A) into s47 Administration of Estates Act (AEA) 1925. The third proposal has not been implemented.

The question invites consideration that to abolish hotchpot is to prefer simplicity to fairness, while to give the entire estate to the surviving spouse would have been both simple and fair. It will be argued here that neither of these observations is a true reflection of the prevailing position or of any recommended future position.

The abolition of the statutory hotchpot rules in relation to the deaths intestate of persons dying on or after 31 December 1995 was effected for administrative convenience and simplicity without proper regard to the longstanding maxim upon which it was based, that equity should lean against double portions and attribute to a parent a sentiment that s/he would not wish to prefer one child over another.

The great virtue of the hotchpot principle was that it preserved the idea of flexibility. It also gave proper recognition to the per stirpes method of inheritance through a family line. These ideals have been abandoned in favour of what is thought to be simplicity, irrespective of considerations of fairness. An example will make the illustration.

If a testator died intestate in, say, November 1995 the hotchpot rule of s47(1)(iii) AEA 1925 required certain benefits conferred inter vivos on his child by the intestate to be brought into account on the division of the residuary estate into shares under the statutory trusts. For example, if during his lifetime the intestate had given £20,000 to the eldest of three children on her marriage and then died a widower leaving a residuary estate worth £180,000, under s47(1)(iii) the elder child would receive a one-third share reduced by the amount of the advancement. The other two children would therefore receive £66,666 each and the elder child £46,666, reflecting the amount advanced. The reasoning would be that the deceased felt it appropriate to make a gift of capital to the elder child at a crucial period of that child's life but that such capital provision should be compensated for, if possible, at the end of the deceased's lifetime. It would be the same for any form of permanent capital provision. Section 47(1)(iii) AEA 1925 ensured fair regulation.

Another hotchpot provision, s49(1)(a) AEA 1925, required the issue of an intestate (child or remoter issue) to bring into account on a partial intestacy what had been received under the operative provisions of the deceased's will, to be set against whatever that child may receive under the intestacy provisions of the deceased's estate. A case such as *Re Grover's Will Trusts* [1971] Ch 169 construed this provision to ensure that amounts so received under the will belonging to a certain branch of the family would only be set against that branch's eventual intestate entitlement – an eminently fair and rational approach.

Again, the justification for s49(1)(a) was that not to have such an accounting mechanism by way of hotchpot would be to condone unfairness of distribution at the end of the day and to ride roughshod over the presumed intentions of the deceased.

It is to be noted that no recommendation appears to have been tabled by the Law Commission to modify s32 Trustee Act 1925, permitting trustees to advance up to one-half of the vested or presumptive share of capital to a remainderman, subject to conditions, one of which is that sums advanced should be brought back into account on a final distribution.

The Law Commission's recommendation giving the entire intestate estate to the surviving spouse has not been implemented. Nor should it have been. Such a provision would: be an unwarranted interference in the balance of family succession; deny the evidential reality that some spouses, over the course of a marriage, can come to positively dislike each other; and unnecessarily interfere with the checks and balances written into the family provision legislation, enabling a spouse to challenge a deceased's will or intestacy distribution by seeking provision out of the deceased's net estate.

The present scheme of distribution, set out in s46 AEA 1925, makes a particularly sensible allocation of the deceased intestate's assets, distinguishing between personal chattels, the need for a statutory legacy to the surviving spouse and the prospect of an income from half the residue, which in given circumstances can be converted into capital. The other half of the residue passes on the statutory trusts of the AEA 1925 to the deceased's issue.

Where there are no issue the claims of parents and brothers and sisters of the whole blood come into play. Other classes of collateral relatives also have claims, as appropriate. To abolish this realistic scheme would be grossly unfair and would constitute an attack on the foundation of family relationships. Supposing a surviving spouse, having inherited all, then remarries. Should the new spouse have superior moral claims to the issue of the common spouse? And what might happen if a surviving spouse was judicially separated at the date of death? Would the extant s18(2) Matrimonial Causes Act 1973 remain in place?

Giving the entire estate to the surviving spouse would have made for bad law and been grossly unfair, as has been demonstrated.

QUESTION TWO

Arnold died suddenly from a heart attack on 1 May 1998. He made a will two years ago but it transpires that the will was invalidly executed.

Arnold is survived by his wife, Beryl, a daughter, Christine, aged 25, a son, David, aged 20, and a grandson, Edwin, aged 12 (the child of Arnold's predeceased daughter, Fiona).

At the time of Arnold's death he and Beryl were living at 'The Ridings', a large house which was held in their joint names. In the basement Arnold kept a collection of antique guns. Collecting guns was his main hobby. In the year before he died, Arnold had started to trade in the antique gun business and had made some profit.

Arnold also owned a river cruiser which was used mainly for family holidays but occasionally was hired out to friends at a low rent. The rest of Arnold's estate consisted of shares and money in various equities.

Christine wishes to disclaim any entitlement that she may have in Arnold's estate. She feels that she has already been generously treated because two months ago Arnold settled a large sum on trust for her on the occasion of her marriage.

Discuss. Would distribution be different if Beryl had died on 20 May?

University of London LLB Examination
(for External Students) Succession June 1998 Q2

General Comment

With the abolition of the hotchpot rules, the number of examinable issues for intestacy have been reduced. This question covers most of the crucial issues and interestingly includes a disclaimer point. This type of intestacy question should be a favourite as the issues are quite clear.

Skeleton Solution

Distribution on total intestacy; s46 AEA 1925 – entitlement of surviving spouse – issue of house, personal chattels – entitlement of issue – advancement and disclaimer.

Suggested Solution

It would appear that Arnold has died totally intestate as his will was invalidly executed. According to s33(1) of the Administration of Estates Act 1925 as amended by the Trusts of Land and Appointment of Trustees Act 1996, Arnold's estate will be held by his personal representatives in trust with the power to sell it.

The personal representatives must first pay all funeral, testamentary and administration expenses, debts and other liabilities of the intestate out of any ready money or any net money arising from the sale of any part of the estate.

However, there are certain limitations to the personal representatives' power of sale: any reversionary interest is not to be sold until it falls into possession, personal chattels are not to be sold and if the assets include a house in which the surviving spouse was residing at the intestate's death, it is not to be sold within twelve months of the first grant of administration without the spouse's written consent.

The order of distribution is governed by s46 of the AEA 1925. Arnold is survived by a wife and issue. Beryl, as the surviving spouse is entitled to the personal chattels absolutely, a statutory legacy of £125,000 plus interest payable from the date of death to the date of payment and half the residuary estate for life, remainder to the issue. The other half of the residuary estate is held on trust for the issue absolutely.

Personal chattels are defined in s55(1)(x) of the 1925 Act as including most household and personal items but excluding money, securities for money and chattels used by the intestate for business purposes.

The collection of antique guns may not qualify as personal chattels as Arnold was in the antique gun business before he died. However, if it can be shown that the collection was kept as a hobby as in *Re Reynolds* [1966] 1 WLR 19 and formed no part of the business, Beryl will be entitled to it as personal chattels. It is irrelevant how large the collection is and how much it is worth: *Re Crispin's Will Trusts* [1975] Ch 245.

The river cruiser was used both for business and domestic purposes. In such a situation, it is likely that the court will use the test in *Re MacCulloch* (1981) 44 NSR (2d) 666, the determining factor being the dominant use of the river cruiser. The facts suggest that the dominant use is domestic as the cruiser is only occasionally hired out and at a low rent at that. Beryl would thus be entitled to it.

The shares and money in equities are not personal chattels and form part of the estate.

In determining the value of Beryl's entitlement, it should be noted that The Ridings does not form part of Arnold's estate as it was in the joint names of Beryl and himself. Following the right of survivorship, on Arnold's death, Beryl becomes entitled to the house absolutely. She would not need to appropriate the house under s5 and Schedule 2 of the Intestates' Estates Act 1952.

Beryl may wish to redeem her life interest in her half of the residue under s47A(1) of the 1925 Act. She may do this by giving written notice to the personal representatives within twelve months of the first grant of administration. This would give a capital sum in lieu of the life interest.

Under s47(1) of the 1925 Act, the other half of the residuary estate is held on statutory trusts to be divided equally between the children of the intestate who are alive at the date of death and who have attained the age of 18 or are married. Where a child has predeceased the intestate but leaves issue living at the date of the intestate's death, those issue will take the share which their parent would have taken (per stirpes). This means that the residue would be divided into three equal shares, with Christine and

David getting their shares immediately whereas Edwin's share will be held on trust for him until he turns 18 or marries before that.

Christine received an inter-vivos settlement from her father on the occasion of her marriage. This is an advancement which under the previous law she would have to bring into account in calculating her entitlement under the hotchpot rules. However, the hotchpot provisions have since been abolished by s1(2) of the Law Reform (Succession) Act 1995.

As for her wish to disclaim her entitlement, she may do so according to the case of *Townson v Tickell* (1819) 3 B & Ald 31 but once she has done so, she cannot retract her disclaimer unless no one has altered their position in reliance: *Re Cranstoun's Will Trusts* [1949] Ch 523. A disclaimer may be made orally, in writing or by deed. The effect according to the case of *Re Scott* [1975] 1 WLR 1260 is that her share will pass to the other beneficiaries in the same class, ie David and Edwin.

If Beryl had died on the 20th of May.

According to s46(2A) of the 1925 Act as inserted by the Law Reform (Succession) Act 1995, in order to be entitled on intestacy, the spouse must survive the intestate by 28 days. If Beryl died within 20 days of Arnold, his estate would be distributed on the basis that he left no surviving spouse.

This means that the residuary estate will be held on statutory trust for Christine, David and Edwin equally as above.

QUESTION THREE

Read the following extract from *Distribution on Intestacy* (Law Com No 187, 1989) and answer the questions below:

> 'There are a number of principles upon which the rules of intestacy might be based and in our working paper we canvassed the respective merits of the presumed wishes of the deceased, the needs or deserts of the survivors, and the status of the surviving spouse. The present law is based upon a combination of these, although the underlying object has been to do what the deceased himself, or herself, might have wished.'

a) Illustrate in which ways the present law of intestacy is based upon 'a combination' of the principles outlined above.

b) Do you consider that the present law gives sufficient recognition to 'the status of the surviving spouse'?

c) In which ways, if any, can the present law be said *not* to reflect 'the presumed wishes of the deceased'?

University of London LLB Examination
(for External Students) Succession June 1999 Q2

General Comment

An essay question requiring some thought. This is not a standard question, but the issues here are those commonly discussed in the context of intestacy. Another angle to consider would be the adequate protection of the children. Unless these issues have been considered, it is a difficult question to do.

Skeleton Solution

a) Position of surviving spouse – position of issue – deceased's intention.

b) Entitlement of surviving spouse under s46 – right to appropriate matrimonial home – redemption of life interest.

c) Bona vacantia – cohabitants – per stirpes rule – entitlement of remoter next of kin under s46.

Suggested Solution

a) The Law Commission recognised the fact that the intestacy rules cannot cover every eventuality but it is hoped that the rules will provide a just solution generally. For that to happen, the interests of several parties must be taken into consideration: the needs of the surviving spouse and of the issue; and the presumed intention of the intestate.

According to the Law Commission, the most important of the above factors is the presumed wishes of the deceased and this is reflected in the intestacy rules. The order of distribution is governed by s46 of the Administration of Estates Act 1925. Where there is a surviving spouse plus issue, the surviving spouse will receive a statutory legacy of £125,000 plus interest, all the personal chattels absolutely and a life interest in half the residue with the other half of the residue being held on statutory trusts for the issue. Where the residue is held on statutory trusts for the issue, the per stirpes principle applies whereby the children of a child who predeceased the intestate is entitled to that child's share.

Where there is no issue but the intestate is survived by a parent or brother or sister of the whole blood or their issue, the surviving spouse is entitled to a statutory legacy of £200,000 plus interest, all the personal chattels absolutely and half the residue absolutely. Where there is issue but no surviving spouse, the residuary estate is held on statutory trusts for the issue. The legitimacy or otherwise of the issue is irrelevant in determining entitlement: Family Law Reform Act 1987.

The rules mentioned above clearly favour the deceased's spouse and issue over remoter next of kin. In fact, in smaller estates, the likelihood is that the surviving spouse's entitlement will subsume the entire residuary estate.

Further evidence of the fact that the intestacy rules reflect the presumed intention of the deceased is shown from s33(7) AEA 1925 which states that in cases of partial intestacy, the distribution of undisposed of property is subject to the provisions in the will.

Section 46(2A) AEA 1925 (inserted by s1 of the Law Reform (Succession) Act 1995) applies to intestates dying after 31 December 1995. This subsection states that the spouse must survive the intestate by 28 days in order to be entitled on an intestacy. This prevents the intestate's assets going to the spouse's branch of the family and is presumably in accord with the wishes of most intestates. The change was put forward by the Law Commission although the original survivorship period recommended was 14 days.

b) The surviving spouse must prove that he/she was lawfully married to the intestate at the date of death. A voidable marriage is regarded as a valid marriage so long as it has not been declared null and void. Also, a person is still considered to be a surviving spouse where the deceased died after a decree nisi of divorce has been granted but before the decree absolute was granted: *Re Seaford* [1968] P 53.

As stated in part (a), if there is issue, the surviving spouse is entitled to a statutory legacy, personal chattels and life interest in half the residue. Where there is no issue but the intestate leaves a parent or brother or sister of the whole blood, the spouse receives a larger statutory legacy, personal chattels and half the residue absolutely. This clearly shows the importance of the surviving spouse as in many of the smaller estates, the surviving spouse will probably receive the whole estate minus costs and debts.

Also, the surviving spouse is entitled to all the deceased's personal chattels absolutely. This again is an acknowledgment that apart from the deceased, the surviving spouse is the person to whom the chattels meant something. Personal chattels are defined in s55(1)(x) AEA 1925 and include most personal and household items but exclude chattels used for business purposes and also exclude money or securities for money.

This entitlement to personal chattels could prove lucrative as case law in this area has made clear that the value of an item is irrelevant in deciding its status: *Re Crispin's Will Trusts* [1975] Ch 245. Apart from the everyday household items like furniture and electronic goods, the definition also includes personal items like jewellery. Furthermore, in *Re Hutchinson* [1955] Ch 255, the intestate's 12 racehorses which were used for recreational purposes passed to the surviving spouse as personal chattels.

Section 5 and Schedule 2 of the Intestates' Estates Act 1952 gives the surviving spouse the right to require the personal representatives to appropriate the house in which the he/she was residing at the date of death. The surviving spouse may appropriate the house in or towards satisfaction of any absolute interest in the estate. This would normally mean the statutory legacy and/or the residue. According to *Re Phelps* [1979] 3 All ER 373, where the value of the house exceeds the value of the spouse's absolute interest, the spouse may make up the difference personally. This right enables the surviving spouse to continue residing in the matrimonial home without tying up the estate. The spouse has 12 months from the first grant of representation in which to make a decision regarding the matrimonial home by giving notice to the personal representatives.

Where the surviving spouse is entitled to a life interest in half the residue, he/she may opt to capitalise that life interest again by giving notice to the personal representatives of such intention within 12 months of the first grant of representation: s47A(1) of the 1925 Act. This right would prove useful where the surviving spouse is in urgent need of money and may be useful in the appropriation of the matrimonial home if his/her absolute interest is less than the value of the house.

The final proof of the recognised status of the surviving spouse under intestacy rules is the fact that a cohabitant is not entitled to anything on the partner's intestacy regardless of the length of time they have lived together a husband and wife.

c) The most glaring aspect in the present law which would not reflect 'the presumed wishes of the deceased' is the fact that the estate will pass to the Crown as bona vacantia where there is no next of kin.

With more and more couples preferring to cohabit rather than get married, it is obvious that an intestate would be extremely unhappy at the fact that their partner is not entitled to anything on intestacy and that remoter relatives or even the Crown would benefit instead. The cohabitant may yet benefit by applying for provision under the Inheritance (Provision for Family and Dependants) Act 1975.

In cases where the intestate leaves a surviving spouse but no issue, he/she would presumably want the spouse to have everything rather than for them to share the estate with remoter next of kin.

The intestate may also not agree with the per stirpes principle being applied to the entitlement of issue and of brothers and sisters.

Finally, with many marriages today ending in divorce, an intestate may have children from a former marriage. With a small estate, this may mean the surviving spouse inherits the entire estate, thus leaving out these children.

Chapter 11
Family Provision

11.1   Introduction

11.2   Key points

11.3   Key cases and statute

11.4   Questions and suggested solutions

11.1   Introduction

This is an important area which merits a compulsory question for the London University examination. In other examinations on succession this is a very popular topic. It is important to properly study all the statutory provisions and to have a sound knowledge of the cases.

11.2   Key points

a)   Inheritance (Provision for Family and Dependants) Act 1975.

b)   Applicants. Under s1(1) of the 1975 Act where a person dies domiciled in England and Wales and is survived by any of the following persons:

    i)   the wife or husband of the deceased;

    ii)   a former wife or husband of the deceased who has not remarried;

    iii) the cohabitant of the deceased who has lived in the same household as the deceased as husband and wife of the deceased for at least two years prior to the death: inserted by s2 Law Reform (Succession) Act 1995;

    iv) a child of the deceased;

    v)   any person (not being a child of the deceased) who was treated by the deceased as a child of the family;

    vi) any person who immediately before the death of the deceased was being maintained by the deceased (*Graham* v *Murphy* [1997] 1 FLR 860);

that person may apply to court for an order that the disposition of the deceased's estate is not such as to make reasonable financial provision for the applicant.

See *Moody* v *Stevenson* [1992] Ch 486 and *Re Collins (Deceased)* [1990] 2 All ER 47.

c) 'Maintained'

Section 1(3) provides that a person is 'maintained' if the deceased made a substantial contribution in money/money's worth towards his reasonable needs, other than for full valuable consideration, see, eg, *Bishop* v *Plumley* [1991] 1 All ER 236.

d) Time limit for application is six months from Grant: see *Re McBroom* [1992] 2 FLR 49, *Re C (Deceased) (Leave to Apply for Provision)* [1995] 2 FLR 24 and *Re N (A Minor) (Claim from Deceased's Estate)* [1995] 2 FLR 689.

e) 'Reasonable financial provision'

   i) Objective test.

   ii) Two standards of provision:

- surviving spouse – such provision as is reasonable whether or not for maintenance: see *Moody* v *Stevenson* [1992] Ch 486 and *Re Clarke* [1991] Fam Law 364;

- others – reasonable provision for maintenance: *Re Dennis* [1981] 2 All ER 140.

   iii) the court must take into account the facts as known to it at date of hearing.

f) Guidelines for court

   i) General guidelines:

- financial needs and resources of applicants and beneficiaries: see, eg, *Re Jennings* [1994] 3 All ER 27;

- deceased's moral obligations; see eg *Re Coventry* [1979] 2 All ER 408; *Re Jennings* and *Goodchild* v *Goodchild* (1995) The Times 22 December; *Re Hancock* (1998) The Times 8 May; *Espinosa* v *Bourke* [1999] 1 FLR 747;

- size and nature of estate;

- physical or mental disability of any applicant or beneficiary;

- any other matter, including conduct of applicant or other person.

   ii) Surviving spouse guidelines:

- applicant's age, duration of marriage;

- applicant's contribution to family;

- provision applicant might expect on divorce: *Re Besterman* [1984] 2 All ER 656.

   iii) Cohabitant guidelines:

- applicant's age, duration of time applicant and deceased lived together;

- applicant's contribution to family welfare.

iv) Children and child of the family guidelines:

- education or training;

- for child of the family, consider also whether deceased assumed any responsibility for applicant's maintenance knowing that applicant was not his child and the liability of any other person to maintain the applicant.

g) Orders are made against net estate. For example:

i) periodical payments;

ii) lump sum;

iii) transfer of property.

h) Anti-avoidance provisions in ss10–13 to prevent evasion from the 1975 Act – court gives the power to set aside a disposition or to modify a contract to leave property by will.

Note: The far-reaching nature of the provisions against donee's disposition of property: *Hanbury* v *Hanbury* [1999] 2 FLR 255.

11.3 Key cases and statute

- *Beaumont, Re* [1980] 1 All ER 266
  There is no maintenance when the parties make contributions of equal value

- *Besterman, Re* [1984] 2 All ER 656
  Consideration of the common guidelines

- *Callaghan, Re* [1984] 3 All ER 790
  'Child' in the Act is not to be construed as only covering minors

- *Coventry, Re* [1979] 2 All ER 408
  Discussion of the meaning of maintenance

- *Debenham (Deceased), Re* [1986] 1 FLR 404
  Claim of a disabled child

- *Espinosa* v *Bourke* [1999] 1 FLR 747
  A moral obligation is not a threshold requirement

- *Freeman, Re* [1984] 3 All ER 906
  Determines when time begins to run in terms of s4 of the 1975 Act

- *Fullard, Re* [1981] 2 All ER 796
  Position of former spouses applying under the Act

- *Jelley* v *Iliffe* [1981] 2 All ER 29
  The position of 'other dependants'

- *Salmon, Re* [1980] 3 All ER 532
  Guidelines re the extension of time

- *Sehota (Deceased), Re* [1978] 3 All ER 385
  Wife included a wife under a polygamous marriage

- *Snapes* v *Aram and Others* (1998) The Times 8 May
  It is not necessary for a child to prove a moral claim

- *Whytte* v *Ticehurst* [1986] 2 All ER 158
  The right to apply is a personal right and does not survive for the benefit of the applicant's estate

- *Wilkinson, Re* [1978] 1 All ER 221
  The burden of proof is on the applicant to show that they were being maintained

- Inheritance (Provision for Family and Dependants) Act 1975 – all provisions

11.4 Questions and suggested solutions

QUESTION ONE

'The interests of the children of a deceased testator do not receive adequate protection under the Inheritance (Provision for Family and Dependants) Act 1975'.

Discuss, with particular reference to reported cases of applications by children under the Act.

University of London LLB Examination
(for External Students) Succession June 1993 Q4

General Comment

This is a very focused question requiring a discussion of the position of children under the 1975 Act. This is a welcome change from questions overloaded with issues and allows for a detailed discussion.

Skeleton Solution

The workings of the Inheritance (Provision for Family and Dependants) Act 1975 relating to children – the attitude exemplified in *Re Coventry* – factors to be taken into account – examples: *Re Coventry* (the facts); *Williams* v *Johns*; *Re Collins (Deceased)* – inadequate protection? – the need to legislate.

Suggested Solution

A child of a deceased testator may make application for an order for reasonable financial provision under s1(1)(c) of the Inheritance (Provision for Family and Dependants) Act 1975 (the Act) and under s25(1) 'child' includes an illegitimate child and a child en ventre sa mere at the death of the deceased, though not a stepchild, who would have to apply under s1(1)(d).

There is no age limit for applicants in this category; the term child refers to the relationship between the deceased and the applicant and is not limited to a minor or dependant child. This permits applications, in exceptional cases, such as where a child, although an adult, may be provided for because of a handicap.

The attitude of the courts however, is exemplified by Oliver J in *Re Coventry* [1980] Ch 461 who stated that an application for maintenance of a male child of full age who is able to earn his own living should be entertained only in the most exceptional circumstances.

The courts are thus reluctant to interfere with testamentary freedom in this country even in favour of children who have been disinherited, albeit on a whim. This contrasts with the law in certain continental jurisdictions where spouses and children may not be totally disinherited. It may therefore be questioned whether the time has not come to give children better protection.

The court is given certain guidelines for the exercise of the judge's discretion in s3 of the Act, and these include the applicant's financial needs and resources and those of any other applicant, together with those of any beneficiary of the deceased's estate. Another factor is consideration of the obligations on the deceased towards the applicant. The size of the estate is taken into account, as well as any disability of the applicant, and also the conduct of the applicant. In the case of children the court must also consider the manner in which the applicant was to be educated or trained, and this last guideline is, in the case of these applications, of crucial importance.

The question is, what is reasonable financial provision in all the circumstances of the case?

In *Re Coventry* the deceased was married in 1927 and acquired a house jointly at that time with his wife. In 1931 the deceased's only child was born and up to 1957 he served in the navy but then came home to live with the deceased when the deceased's wife left home. This son lived rent-free in the house but did some domestic work and paid for food. In 1961 he got married and until 1971, when the marriage ended, the wife also lived rent free in the deceased's house, but also did some domestic work. The deceased died in 1976 leaving an estate of £7,000, all of which passed to his widow on intestacy. At that time the son was aged 46 and earning £52 per week, out of which he paid his wife £12 per week maintenance. He had no savings and if required to move would have had to find alternative accommodation. However, the court would not interfere merely because it considered the deceased had acted unreasonably but would if the deceased had not made adequate provision for the applicant.

In order to succeed the applicant would have had to show a moral claim over and above the claim of a blood relationship to be maintained by the deceased. This was not discharged merely because the applicant found himself in necessitous circumstances, and the claim failed.

The son in this case certainly did not receive adequate protection under the Act, particularly if one considers that the father may have died intestate by pure chance and the widow already had a house and a pension.

Another case is *Williams* v *Johns* [1988] 2 FLR 475 concerning a claim by an adopted child – a son. The deceased left the whole of her estate to her natural son, and before her death stated that she thought she had made sufficient provision for the applicant in her lifetime. He made a claim on the basis that he was impecunious, as well as because the deceased had shown him considerable affection during her life. At the time of the application he was aged 43 and unemployed. County Court Judge Micklem dismissed the application, holding that two stages must be given adequate consideration. First, the reasonableness of any provision in the will. It was for the applicant to show that an obligation existed for him to be maintained out of the estate, beyond the mere fact of an adoptive relationship. Second, such test was objective – poor financial circumstances and the deceased's affection for him were not sufficient. Since he was physically fit and capable of taking employment the test was not satisfied.

One is constrained to wonder, in the light of this case, what would satisfy the test. If impecuniosity is not a ground for a disinherited child to claim on a parent's estate then it may be argued that the law is failing to give adequate protection when taking into account all other circumstances.

In *Re Collins (Deceased)* [1990] 2 WLR 161 the facts were that A was the mother of two children, a girl born in 1970 and a boy in 1979. She died intestate in 1980, survived by her husband and leaving an estate of some £35,000. The boy was adopted in March 1987 and in June 1987 both children applied for provision out of the estate, but it was held that the application of the boy would fail, as the right to apply is not preserved on adoption, but the girl was awarded £5,000.

It is thus seen that the workings of the law in this area can be somewhat capricious and further legislation could better protect the interests of children of a deceased testator. It could well be argued that they should have more of a vested interest and not one where an obligation to maintain has to be proved to the satisfaction of a judge, the views of whom may be very narrow.

QUESTION TWO

Arthur died in January 1996 leaving an estate valued at £100,000, consisting mainly of his house worth £90,000. In his will, made in 1992, he left all his property to his illegitimate son, Jack, a wealthy businessman. Arthur had been married to Wendy but the marriage ended in divorce in 1985 when Arthur began an affair with his secretary, Janet.

After the divorce, Janet gave up her rented flat and came to live with Arthur at his suggestion. She insisted on paying him rent and also paid for their holidays but Arthur paid the bills and the day-to-day household expenses.

In 1990 Janet suggested that they should marry but Arthur was unwilling as he had come to regard marriage as pointless. After that their relationship deteriorated and they started to sleep in separate bedrooms. In 1993 Arthur became seriously ill. Janet gave up her job in order to nurse him on a full-time basis. Unfortunately she suffered a nervous breakdown and was placed in a nursing home two weeks before Arthur died. She recovered after his death and went back to live in Arthur's home.

Jack wants her to leave but Janet, who is now aged sixty and has only modest private means, has nowhere to go. In his will Arthur stated that he did not wish Janet to remain in his house after his death because she was a 'woman who lacks human warmth'.

Advise Janet of her chances of success in an application under the Inheritance (Provision for Family and Dependants) Act 1975.

NB: The above question is compulsory.

University of London LLB Examination
(for External Students) Succession June 1996 Q1

General Comment

For the second year running the examiner set a compulsory question on family provision. On this occasion, however, the factual content was specific – arguably too much so. Candidates were invited to consider the basis upon which one particular category of applicant, a dependant, might contest the deceased's estate. No well-prepared student should have been discomforted by the question and high marks would have been expected for the better candidate. As always in this area, the parameters of the question were not sufficiently defined. Was a candidate, for instance, required to consider the property out of which any successful award could have been ordered? Further, should the candidate have refrained from considering any potential claim by the former spouse, Wendy, insofar as this could have been a relevant factor in assessing the claim of the applicant, Janet?

Skeleton Solution

1975 Act the basis – requirement of English domicile – position of cohabitants: the amending law – unavailability of 1995 Act to Janet – basis of claim under s1(1)(e); s1(3) – objective test – time limits for claim – application of key case law – assumption of responsibility requirement – general guidelines available to court – deceased's statements and effect thereof.

Suggested Solution

In order for Janet to proceed under the provisions of the Inheritance (Provision for Family and Dependants) Act (I(PFD)A) 1975 it would have to be shown that the deceased, Arthur, died domiciled in England and Wales (s1(1)), the burden of proof resting on the applicant, Janet: see *Mastaka v Midland Bank Executor and Trustee Co Ltd* [1941] Ch 192. It is presumed that the facts will establish this.

Janet is not married to Arthur, but it would appear that for over five years she cohabited with him. As Arthur died in January 1996, the Law Reform (Succession) Act (LR(S)A) 1995, effective as to deaths of testators taking place after 31 December 1995, would apply to Arthur's estate. Section 2(2) and (3) LR(S)A 1995 have extended s1(1)(a)–(e) of I(PFD)A 1975 so as to permit a claim by:

> '(ba) any person who was living in the same household as the deceased, and as the husband or wife of the deceased, during the whole of the period of two years ending immediately before the date when the deceased died.'

The provision uses the wording 'as husband or wife' to mean 'as if husband or wife'. The difficulty here for Janet is that the cohabitation between herself and Arthur may not have continued for the requisite two-year period terminating with his death. When Arthur's and Janet's relationship deteriorated and they began to sleep in separate rooms it may reasonably be implied (analogous to the family law term 'living apart' but in the same household) that the cohabitation did not continue for the requisite two-year period: indeed, on this basis they ceased to cohabit several years before. Accordingly, Janet has no right to contest Arthur's estate as a cohabitant, but she may have a claim if she can establish she falls within s1(1)(e) I(PFD)A 1975.

That provision allows application to be made by any person who immediately before the death of the deceased was being maintained, either wholly or partly, by the deceased. And by s1(3) a person shall be treated as being so maintained by the deceased only if the deceased, 'otherwise than for full valuable consideration, was making a substantial contribution in money or money's worth towards the reasonable needs of that person.'

The court cannot order provision for Janet as an applicant unless it is satisfied that the disposition of Arthur's estate is not such as to make reasonable financial provision for her maintenance.

The test is an objective one: whether the disposition of the deceased's estate is not such as to make reasonable provision, rather than whether the deceased may be said to have been reasonable towards the applicant, which would import a subjective test.

Arthur died in January 1996. The question is set at early June 1996. Probate to Arthur's estate may have been obtained relatively early after his death. Janet should be made aware that she must make her application not later than six months from the date of grant of representation to Arthur's estate: s4 I(PFD)A 1975. Once that time has elapsed Arthur's personal representatives can distribute the estate. The court, however, has an unfettered discretion to extend the time, a discretion which must be exercised judicially. In *Re Salmon* (1981), for instance, a widow's application for an extension was refused by Sir Robert Megarry VC, where her claim was more than four and a half months out of time and the fault was wholly on the widow's side.

Janet came to live with Arthur, at his suggestion, insisting on paying him rent and paying for their holidays, but with Arthur paying the bills and day-to-day household expenses. The question for determination is whether she has brought herself, as already described, within s1(1)(e) and s1(3) I(PFD)A 1975, so as to have a claim out of the net estate by way of reasonable provision for her maintenance?

In *Re Wilkinson* [1978] Fam 22, the deceased provided board and lodging for her sister, the applicant, who did a share of light housework and cooking, helping the deceased, a crippled arthritic, to dress. She also acted as companion. The deceased's condition gradually deteriorated but so did the applicant's, with the result that a home help was brought in. The applicant never received any payment for her services, but throughout their six years together the deceased paid all household expenses and food bills. In May 1976, she died intestate leaving the applicant £5,000 and the furniture of her choice. The applicant claimed this was 'not reasonable provision' for her continued maintenance in the light of the assistance she had been receiving before the sister died; she claimed reasonable provision under s1(1)(e) on the basis that the free board and lodging she had received at the deceased's home was a 'substantial contribution in money or money's worth towards her reasonable needs'. The residuary beneficiary opposed the application, arguing that the deceased had provided food and accommodation in return for valuable consideration, namely the applicant's services towards the deceased, thereby taking the case outside the ambit of s1(1)(e). Arnold J rejected the residuary beneficiary's contention, stating that whilst the burden is cast upon the applicant to show that he or she falls within the section, the applicant here had done this by showing that the services she had rendered to her sister did not constitute full valuable consideration for her board and lodging.

Re Wilkinson is a salutary and helpful decision. Arnold J did not seek to establish that full valuable consideration would have to be shown under a contract to take an applicant's argument outside the ambit of s1(1)(e), but he did indicate that an applicant's services had to be valued in order to decide whether they constituted full valuable consideration.

For a successful application under s1(1)(e) it is established that an applicant must also prove that before his death the deceased had assumed responsibility for the applicant's maintenance: see, for example, *Re Beaumont* [1980] Ch 44. The reason for this is the presence in the legislation of the particular guideline applicable to a dependant – 'the extent to which and the basis upon which the deceased assumed responsibility for the maintenance of the applicant'. In *Jelley* v *Iliffe* [1981] Fam 128 it was held by the Court of Appeal that the basic fact that the applicant was being maintained by the deceased under an arrangement subsisting at the deceased's death was sufficient to raise a presumption that the deceased had assumed responsibility for his maintenance. Unless the applicant's contribution to the deceased equalled or outweighed the benefit of the rent-free accommodation provided by the deceased the applicant would qualify as a dependant under s1(1)(e).

If Janet, having given up her job in order to nurse Arthur on a full-time basis, continues to pay him rent while Arthur continues to pay the bills and household expenses, it becomes a question of fact and degree whether she can bring herself within the subsection. Further detail would be needed. The fact that Janet has suffered a nervous breakdown and was placed in a nursing home two weeks before Arthur's death would not prevent her from being regarded as a person 'who immediately before the death of the deceased' was being maintained. In *Re Beaumont* the deceased had habitually maintained the applicant but was unable to do so immediately before death as she was in hospital with an illness. The provision is not to be construed absolutely literally, or restrictively. There is no reason why the same principle should not pertain where it is the applicant who is in a home or hospital immediately before the deceased's death.

Section 3 I(PFD)A 1975 requires the court to have regard to a number of general guidelines to assist it in arriving at a view of the merits of the applicant's case. These include:

a) the financial resources and needs which the applicant has or is likely to have in the foreseeable future – Janet is aged sixty and has only modest means;

b) the obligations and responsibilities of the deceased towards the applicant – the sole beneficiary of Arthur's estate is his wealthy illegitimate son, Jack. The court will consider all the circumstances, including the question of Jack's needs and whether to make an award to Janet would unfairly prejudice Jack;

c) the size and nature of the estate – it is significant that the house comprises nine-tenths of the value of Arthur's estate. It may be thought appropriate here for maintenance, if at all, to be ordered by way of a small lump sum payment;

d) disability of any applicant – although Janet has suffered a nervous breakdown this may not be treated as a disability, unless it becomes a permanent condition; and

e) conduct and any other matter – a relevant consideration would be any possible claim by another potential applicant, ie Wendy, as a person who is a former spouse who has not remarried (if that is the case). But Wendy may have accepted a clean break consent order on divorce and debarred herself from applying: see *Re Fullard* [1982] Ch 42 and s15 I(PFD)A 1975.

Arthur stated that he did not wish Janet to remain in the house after his death because she was a 'woman who lacks human warmth'. The Act does not require the court to have regard to the deceased's stated reasons but it is usually prudent to record them. Arthur's statement here is unhelpful and perhaps meaningless. In *Williams* v *Johns* [1988] 2 FLR 475, the applicant, by her behaviour, had caused the deceased distress; the court held that in any event the applicant had failed to establish any obligation in the deceased to maintain her. The I(PFD)A 1975 makes a statement made by the deceased, whether orally or in a document, admissible under the Civil Evidence Act 1968 as evidence of any fact stated in it. Arthur's statement would, therefore, be available to the court, but it is likely to be lightly considered and possibly disregarded.

In conclusion, Janet probably has the basis of a claim under s1(1)(e) I(PFD)A 1975 but much depends upon an analysis of the full facts in the light of decisions such as *Re Wilkinson* and *Jelley* v *Iliffe*, as explained.

QUESTION THREE

John has recently died intestate, leaving an estate worth £40,000. His only relation is his brother, Alan, a wealthy company director, to whom John had not spoke since 1994 following a bitter row between them. Advise the following potential applicants under the Inheritance (Provision for Family and Dependants) Act 1975.

a) Mary, aged 50. She and John married in 1970 and were divorced four years later. Neither ever remarried. John paid her £100 a month by way of the financial settlement following the divorce. He never missed a payment. Mary has a part-time job with a modest salary. She has little capital and lives with her widowed sister. Mary recently won £20,000 on the National Lottery.

b) David, aged 30. He was fostered by John and Mary for two years prior to their divorce, after which he lived with Mary until he joined the Army in 1987. David kept in touch with John. They often went to football matches and usually spent part of Christmas together. John frequently referred to David as 'the son I never had'. David gained rapid promotion in the Army but a few weeks ago was accidentally shot while on exercises. The likelihood is that he will be confined to a wheelchair for the rest of his life.

c) Amanda, aged 30. She and John started living together in 1990 and continued to do so until John's death. They lived in rented accommodation, mostly on Amanda's earnings. Amanda, a promising journalist, was often sent on foreign assignments. Indeed, when John died, Amanda had been abroad for two months. Amanda has just learned that her book on political life, 'An A–Z of Sleaze', has been accepted for publication and that the publishers expect it to be a best-seller.

University of London LLB Examination
(for External Students) Succession June 1997 Q1

General Comment

This is a more typical 1975 Act question requiring discussion of a variety of parties with differing relationships with the deceased, not forgetting the competing interest of the peron entitled under the will. The party entitled either under the will or intestacy is often forgotten in the discussion – he ought to be mentioned at least in the conclusion.

Skeleton Solution

Claims under the 1975 Act – identify categories of applicants – Mary – David – Amanda – consider relevant general and particular guidelines.

Suggested Solution

To make a successful application under the 1975 Act, each applicant must prove the following.

a) John died domiciled in England or Wales.

b) The applicant has locus standi to make the application.

c) John's intestacy has failed to make reasonable financial provision for the applicant.

d) The application was made within six months of the first grant of administration: s4.

As the question does not suggest otherwise, it can be presumed that John had died domiciled in England or Wales and that the applications were made within the time limit.

Locus standi

Each applicant must prove that they fall under one of the categories in s1(1) of the 1975 Act.

Mary

She may have a claim under s1(1)(b) as a former spouse who has not remarried. She would not have received anything under John's intestacy.

The applicable standard of financial provision is the maintenance standard; ie such financial provision as it would be reasonable in all the circumstances of the case for her to receive for her maintenance.

As Mary had been receiving £100 a month by way of a divorce settlement, her application should not succeed unless there has been a substantial change in financial circumstances: *Re Fullard* [1982] Ch 42. An example of such a change could be shown if the periodical payments had stopped on John's death: *Whiting* v *Whiting* [1988] 1 WLR 565.

In considering the relevant general guidelines, it appears that Mary has little capital. Financial resources include earning capacity and Mary does have a part time job.

Mary's age and her contribution to the welfare of the family will be taken into account under the particular guidelines but as she and John had only been married for 4 years, it is unlikely to be of much use to her claim.

According to s3(5), the court must take into account the facts as known at the date of the hearing. Therefore, Mary's recent good fortune on the lottery must be considered. As the win is £20,000, an amount equivalent to half of John's modest estate, it is unlikely that Mary will succeed in her application.

David

David may have a claim under s1(1)(d) if he could prove that John treated him as a child of the family in relation to John's marriage to Mary.

Although David had lived with Mary after the divorce, it seems clear that John had treated him as his own son, by their attending football matches and spending Christmas together. This is further evidenced by the fact that he had frequently referred to David as the son he never had: *Re Callaghan* [1984] 3 All ER 790.

It is clear, therefore, that John had assumed responsibility for David and did so knowing that David was not his own child.

David would not have been entitled to anything under John's intestacy.

The more important general guidelines would be David's financial resources and needs, and his physical disability. As David may now be wheelchair bound, his earning capacity may be severely restricted and it would follow that his financial needs would increase to include medical bills, home help, specialist equipment and renovating his home to suit his wheelchair among other things.

The court would also consider the financial resources and financial needs of Alan, the person solely entitled to John's estate. The fact that he is a wealthy director would strengthen David's claim.

Taking into account the above plus the fact that the other two applicants are unlikely to succeed in their applications, it is likely that David may be awarded a reasonable sum out of the estate. The standard applicable is the maintenance standard: *Re Dennis* [1981] 2 All ER 140 defined maintenance as payments which directly or indirectly enable the applicant to discharge the cost of his daily living at whatever standard is appropriate to him.

Under s2 of the 1975 Act, the court has the power to make either a lump sum order or periodical payments to David. If a lump sum payment is ordered, it may be paid in instalments: s7.

If David is in immediate need of financial assistance, he can apply for an interim order: s5.

Amanda

As Amanda had lived with John since 1990 until his death, she could easily show that she is a cohabitant, a category introduced by the Law Reform (Succession) Act 1995; ie, any person, other than a spouse or former spouse, who was living in the same household as the deceased, for a period of at least two years ending immediately before the date of deceased's death: s1(1)(ba). The fact that she was abroad when John died will not affect her application under this category.

Amanda is still relatively young and is gainfully employed. When John was alive, they lived mainly on her earnings. Although Amanda no longer has to show dependency on John when he was alive, all these factors will be taken into account by the court under the general and particular guidelines. The publication of her book will also be relevant as potential earnings: *Re Ducksbury* [1966] 2 All ER 374.

The court may well award Amanda something taking into account the fact that she had lived with John all those years and will have contributed to the welfare of the home.

However, it is safe to assume that any sum awarded would not be substantial taking into account the factors discussed above, the fact that David is more needy and the size of the estate.

Finally, it should be noted that the intestacy of the deceased will take effect subject to any court order under s2; and that the personal representatives will not be liable if they make payment in accordance with the court's order.

QUESTION FOUR

'The decisions in *Re Besterman* (1984) and *Re Krubert* (1996) show that, in deciding what is "reasonable provision" for a spouse, the courts will regard the imaginary divorce guideline in s3(2) of the Inheritance (Provision for Family and Dependents) Act 1975 as of limited relevance.'

Discuss.

University of London LLB Examination
(for External Students) Succession June 1998 Q1

General Comment

This is another example of a very focused question. Candidates must be clear on *Re Besterman* and *Re Krubert* before attempting this question. Consider the variety of specific issues questions may examine in the future.

Skeleton Solution

Discussion on claims by surviving spouses – court's approach to relying on the imaginary divorce guideline – discuss *Re Besterman* and *Re Krubert*.

Suggested Solution

Certain categories of persons can apply for financial provision under the 1975 Act on the grounds that the deceased's will or intestacy has failed to make reasonable financial provision for the applicant.

One of the categories of people is the surviving spouse of the deceased. The applicant must prove that he/she was married to the deceased and that the marriage was subsisting at the date of death: *Re Peete* [1952] WN 306.

Once it is proven that the applicant has failed to receive reasonable financial provision, the court must then decide how much is reasonable for the surviving spouse to receive.

There are two standards of financial provision in the 1975 Act, the s1(2)(b) maintenance standard applicable to all other applicants and the s1(2)(a) surviving spouse standard; which is such financial provision as it would be reasonable in all the circumstances of the case for a husband or wife to receive, whether or not that provision is required for his or her maintenance. Needless to say, this is a higher standard, enabling the surviving spouse to claim for a share in the deceased's estate instead of for a mere sum sufficient for maintenance.

In the particular guidelines listed, s3(2) provides that the court may use the imaginary divorce guideline, that is the provision which the applicant might reasonably have expected to receive if on the day on which the deceased died the marriage, instead of being terminated by death, had been terminated by a decree of divorce. This means that the court should take into account the spouse's entitlement on divorce under matrimonial law.

Although the guideline appears to be clear enough, the court's approach to it has been far from unambiguous.

The court in *Moody v Stevenson* [1992] Ch 486 held that the amount awarded to the surviving spouse should mirror his prospective entitlement under matrimonial law.

However, in *Re Besterman* [1984] Ch 458, the Court of Appeal felt that the guideline was only one of several factors to be considered, the overriding consideration being what was reasonable in all the circumstances. In *Re Bunning* [1984] 3 All ER 1, the surviving spouse was awarded more than she would have been entitled to on divorce because the husband's future needs no longer have to be taken into account. This is an important point to note and does clearly illustrate the danger in drawing too close an analogy between divorce and death.

The Court of Appeal in *Re Krubert* [1996] 3 WLR 959 made the same point and clearly stated that the approach in *Re Besterman* is to be preferred to that in *Moody v Stevenson*. This means that the imaginary divorce guideline should not be the court's first or most important consideration in deciding what is reasonable financial provision for the surviving spouse.

QUESTION FIVE

Max died recently leaving an estate worth £500,000. In his will he left all his property to various charities.

Advise the following as to their chances of success in applying under the Inheritance (Provision for Family and Dependents) Act 1975.

a) Richard. He is Max's only child and is aged 50. After leaving school, Richard worked in his father's business for some 12 years and contributed to its success. During this time Richard lived at home with his parents rent-free but was never paid a salary. The expectation was that Richard would one day take over as manager of Max's business, but relations between them deteriorated sharply some 20 years ago when Richard married a woman whom Max strongly disliked. As a result Richard stopped working for his father and the two of them had hardly any contact from that time.

Richard, who now runs his own very profitable business, feels bitter that in the circumstances his father left him nothing in his will.

b) Patricia. She is Max's former wife, and the mother of Richard. Patricia is aged 75 and is cared for in a nursing home following a stroke. She divorced Max soon after Richard's marriage and neither married again. Max was very bitter and blamed her for the breakdown of the marriage (she approved of Richard's choice of wife). In 1994 he sold a painting he had long owned, and which Patricia had loved, fearing that she might attempt to claim it on his death. He invested and lost the proceeds in risky share dealings.

Patricia's assets have largely been used up for her nursing home care, so she is hoping for a substantial share in Max's estate.

c) Camilla. She lived with Max for the last 10 years of his life as his partner. They lived in his home but she always insisted on paying him a full rent and funded their expensive holidays together. Camilla is aged 58 and hhas not been employed for many years. Shortly before Max's death Camilla went into hospital for a complex hip replacement and was still recuperating there when Max died.

Camilla would like to remain in Max's home (valued at £300,000). She has insufficient assets to buy her own home.

University of London LLB Examination
(for External Students) Succession June 1999 Q1

General Comment

This is a long question with a number of issues to be covered. The danger in these questions is having enough time to answer the solution suggests how the points general to all the applicants can be dealt with in the beginning before discussing the applications of the individuals.

Skeleton Solution

Claims under the 1975 Act – identify categories of applicants – Richard – Patricia – Camilla – consider relevant general and particular guidelines – relevant anti-avoidance provision.

Suggested Solution

To make a successful application under the 1975 Act, each applicant must prove the following.

a) Max died domiciled in England or Wales.

b) The applicant has locus standi to make the application.

c) Max's intestacy has failed to make reasonable financial provision for the applicant.

d) The application was made within 6 months of the first grant of administration: s4.

As the question does not suggest otherwise, it can be presumed that Max had died domiciled in England or Wales and that the applications were made within the time limit.

Locus standi

Each applicant must prove that they fall under one of the categories in s1(1) of the 1975 Act.

Richard

Richard would be applying as the child of the deceased who had not been given reasonable financial provision under his father's will.

The standard of financial provision relevant to Richard would be the s1(2)(b) maintenance standard, that is, such financial provision as it would be reasonable in all the circumstances of the case for the applicant to receive for his maintenance. Although the Act does not define 'maintenance', the case of *Re Dennis* [1981] 2 All ER 140 defined it as payments which directly or indirectly enable the applicant to discharge the cost of his daily living at whatever standard is appropriate to him.

In considering the general guidelines, Richard's financial resources appear to be sound as he has a very profitable business, plus it seems unlikely that he has any financial needs. In fact, the court in *Re Coventry* [1980] Ch 461 made it very clear that an application for maintenance by a child of full age able to earn his own living should be entertained only in the most exceptional circumstances.

Despite that, Richard may be able to show that the deceased had a moral obligation to provide for him as he had helped out in his father's business and contributed to its success for twelve years.

However the recent case of *Re Hancock* (1980) The Times 8 May made it clear that it is not necessary for an adult child to establish a moral obligation or exceptional circumstances in order to succeed in a claim. If that is the case, Richard may have a strong claim for provision taking into account the fact that Max's estate is a large one.

Finally, it is unlikely that Richard's conduct in marrying against his father's wishes would be taken into account as it is hardly abnormal conduct as required by the courts: *Re Snoek* (1983) 13 Fam Law 18.

From the above, it is likely that Richard would be entitled to financial provision from his father's estate although it is not likely to be a large amount due to his comfortable financial resources.

Under s2, the court has the power to make certain orders. In Richard's case, a lump sum payment seems the most appropriate.

Patricia

Patricia would be applying as the former wife of the deceased who has not remarried.

As with Richard, the applicable standard of financial provision is the s1(2)(b) maintenance standard.

The facts do not state whether Patricia received a divorce settlement. If she did, her application would not succeed unless there has been a change in her financial circumstances: *Re Fullard* [1981] 2 All ER 796.

In considering the general and particular guidelines, it is clear that her financial resources are limited as she is obviously no longer able to work due to her age and her health following the stroke. Her main financial needs are her daily living expenses and nursing home fees.

Apart from her age, the court will also consider the duration of her marriage to Max and the contribution she made to the welfare of their family.

As for the painting, the court has the power under s10 of the 1975 Act to set aside a disposition intended to defeat an application provided certain conditions are satisfied. There was a disposition in that Max did sell the painting in 1994, within the six year period before his death. His intention was to defeat a claim by Patricia. However, it must have been sold for otherwise than for full valuable consideration. If it can be shown that Max was not given full valuable consideration for the painting, the court may set aside the disposition if it would facilitate the making of financial provision for Patricia.

By virtue of s2, the court has the power make an order out of the deceased's net estate of specified periodical payments to cover Patricia's nursing home care and daily living expenses. The court may also acquire the painting out of the assets from the net estate for her.

Camilla

Camilla may apply two possible categories, as a dependant of Max or as cohabitant.

Although Camilla was living in Max's home, she will not be able to show that she was being maintained, either wholly or partly, by him as she paid him a full rent and shared their holiday expenses.

The better option, therefore, is to apply as his cohabitant, which is a new category introduced by the Law Reform (Succession) Act 1995. She will fall under this category so long as she can show that they have been living together in the same household as husband and wife for at least two years before his death. As they have been living together for the past ten years, it is irrelevant that she was in hospital when he died.

Camilla is 58, has not worked for many years and does not have enough money to buy her own home. She is almost of retirement age and is unlikely to have any earning capacity, especially after undergoing a hip replacement. Apart from that, there is no other information on her financial resources. The court will also consider the contribution she made to the household in the ten years she lived with the deceased.

Camilla's application is likely to succeed although the court is unlikely to continue to allow her to remain in Max's home as it forms a large part of his net estate.

It is more likely that she will be awarded a lump sum payment to enable her to either purchase or rent a smaller house.

Finally, it should be noted that the deceased's will will take effect subject to any order made by the court under s2 and the personal representatives will not be liable for distributing the deceased's estate in accordance with the order: ss19 and 20.

Chapter 12

Executors and Administrators

12.1   Introduction

12.2   Key points

12.3   Key cases and statutes

12.4   Questions and suggested solutions

12.1 Introduction

It is important to have a working knowledge of the basic elements of the appointment of executors and administrators. The information studied here can be of help when answering a wide variety of questions. You must have some knowledge of the Non-Contentious Probate Rules (NCPR) 1987.

12.2 Key points

Executor is appointed by testator to administer his estate

a) Appointment may be express or implied.

b) On death of executor, office passes to his executor by transmission.

c) Court has power to pass over an executor: s116 Supreme Court Act 1981.

d) Restrictions on appointment of inter alia partnerships, infants, criminals.

e) Executor may renounce office.

Administrator is appointed by court to administer the estate

a) Circumstances: inter alia, intestacy, executors renounce, executors predecease.

b) Priority for obtaining a grant of letters of administration is contained in rr20 and 22 NCPR 1987.

c) Rule 20 applies where deceased left a will:

   i)   executor

   ii) residuary legatee/devisee on trust

   iii) any other residuary legatee/devisee

iv) PR of residuary legatee/devisee

v) any other legatee/devisee

vi) PR of any other legatee/devisee

d) Rule 22 applies where intestacy:

i) surviving spouse

ii) children of the deceased or issue if predecease

iii) father or mother

iv) brothers and sisters of whole blood or issue if predecease

and if none:

i) brothers and sisters of half blood or issue if predecease

ii) grandparents

iii) uncles and aunts of whole blood

iv) uncles and aunts of half blood

and in each case, person must have a beneficial interest to qualify.

e) Clearing off is process whereby person with priority does not want grant and person with lower priority does.

f) Capacity similar to capacity for executor.

g) Administrator may renounce.

h) Number: no minimum, not more than four.

i) Court may pass over.

j) Executor de son tort – a person who has no grant but acts as though he did: see s28 Administration of Estates Act 1925. See also *Pollard* v *Jackson* (1994) 67 P & CR 327.

12.3 Key cases and statutes

- *Adamson, In b* (1875) LR 3 P & D 253
  The principal duties of an executor

- *Attenborough* v *Solomon* [1913] AC 76
  The office of executor is generally for life

- *Bigger, Re* [1977] 2 WLR 773
  Capacity to be an executor

- *Holland, In the Estate of* [1930] 3 All ER 13
  The number of executors in respect of the 'same' property shall not exceed four

- *Mathew, Re* [1984] 2 All ER 396
  The court has the power to pass over executors

- *Morant, In b* (1874) LR 3 P & D 151
  Probate may be renounced in writing and filed

- *New York Breweries Company Ltd* v *Attorney-General* [1899] AC 62
  Considers the acts that can lead to a person being regarded as an executor de son tort

- Administration of Estates Act 1925, s5 – provides that an executor is not bound to take up office

- Administration of Estates Act 1925, s7 – provides for the transmission of office when the executor dies

- Administration of Estates Act 1925, s22 – appointment of special executors for settled land

- Non-Contentious Probate Rules 1987

- Supreme Court Act 1981, s114 – maximum number of executors

- Supreme Court Act 1981, s116 – court's power to pass over executors

12.4 Questions and suggested solutions

QUESTION ONE

See Chapter 14, Question 1(b).

QUESTION TWO

See Chapter 14, Question 2(a).

QUESTION THREE

See Chapter 19, Question 2(a).

QUESTION FOUR

See Chapter 19, Question 3(a).

QUESTION FIVE

See Chapter 14, Question 3(a).

Chapter 13

Grants of Probate and Administration

13.1   **Introduction**

13.2   **Key points**

13.3   **Key cases and statutes**

13.4   **Questions and suggested solutions**

13.1 Introduction

It is vital that the personal representatives obtain the necessary authority to act – both for their own protection as well as for the protection of the estate and any third parties dealing with the estate.

13.2 Key points

Necessity for grant

a) Production necessary to establish right to recover/receive deceased's estate in United Kingdom.

b) Under Administration of Estates (Small Payments) Act 1965 order, grant not necessary where asset less than £5,000.

Common form business

a) Defined s128 Supreme Court Act 1981.

b) Business is conducted in Principal Registry of Family Division of High Court and District Probate Registries of Family Division.

c) Conduct governed by Non-Contentious Probate Rules 1987.

Procedure

a) Solicitor lodges at selected Registry:

  i)   oath duly sworn by PRs;

  ii) will duly marked;

   iii) Inland Revenue Account if necessary, signed by PRs and bearing self-assessment to Inheritance Tax;

   iv) cheque for tax and court fee.

b) Registrar may refuse Grant, or require further evidence, or refer to judge.

c) When Registrar satisfied papers are in order, the Grant will be issued.

Inheritance Tax

a) PRs have duty to collect and value deceased's estate for Inheritance Tax.

b) Must deliver an account to the Revenue within twelve months after end of month of death of all property comprised in deceased's estate before death.

c) Tax payable on delivery of account subject to special provisions for instalment payments in case of large sums.

The oath

a) An affidavit sworn by the PRs.

b) Contents inter alia:

   i)   date of deceased's death;

   ii) whether testacy or intestacy;

   iii) title of applicant for grant;

   iv) gross value of estate.

Solemn form business

a) Includes cases where will is challenged, right of an applicant for grant is contested, application for revocation.

b) Assigned to Chancery Division.

c) Writ action, procedure similar to common form business save for rules of evidence.

Caveats

a) A notice to the Registrar not to let anything be done in connection with the will or estate without notice to the person lodging.

b) Main purpose is to prevent issue of grant.

Citations

a) Used to speed up issue of grant.

b) Citation to take probate, to accept or refuse probate, to propound a will.

13.3 Key cases and statutes

- *Bowman* v *Hodgson* (1867) LR 1 P & D 362
  To prove the due execution of a will it is essential to call at least one of the attesting witnesses

- *Moran* v *Place* [1896] P 214
  Explanation of caveats

- *Webb, Re* [1964] 1 WLR 509
  All acts are presumed to have been done rightly and regularly

- Non-Contentious Probate Rules 1987

- Supreme Court Act 1981, s108 – the entering of caveats

- Supreme Court Act 1981, s112 – citation to accept or reject probate

- Supreme Court Act 1981, s117 – grant of letters of administration pending suit

- Supreme Court Act 1981, s120 – surety's guarantee

- Supreme Court Act 1981, s122 – the court has the power to examine the person in open court

- Supreme Court Act 1981, s123 – power of the court to issue subpoenas to any person believed to have knowledge of the testamentary

- Supreme Court Act 1981, s128 – meaning of common form/non-contentious probate business

13.4 Questions and suggested solutions

QUESTION ONE

John has been appointed Harold's executor by the will. He wishes to know the procedure for obtaining a grant of representation, and the consequences of a caveat which he is informed has been entered by the Registrar. Advise John.

Written by the Editor

General Comment

This is a simple question requiring a discussion of all the steps required of an executor. A good revision aid.

Skeleton Solution

Documents to be lodged – issue/refusal – affidavits – inheritance tax – oath – caveat.

Suggested Solution

If there is nothing contentious in the matter of Harold's will and estate then the business of obtaining probate and administration will be 'common form business' under s128 Supreme Court Act 1981, and as such will be conducted in the Principal Registry of Family Division of the High Court and District Probate Registries of the Family Division. Its conduct will be governed by the Non-Contentious Probate Rules 1987, which confer discretions on Registrars.

John or his solicitor must lodge the following at the selected Registry: the oath for executor duly sworn by John and exhibiting the will; the will and any codicils, duly marked; the Inland Revenue Account signed by John and bearing self-assessment to Inheritance Tax; and a cheque for Inheritance Tax and the court fee.

The Registrar may refuse the Grant, or ask for further evidence as to knowledge and approval, as to due execution, and as to plight and condition. Alternatively he may refer the matter to the judge, otherwise, he will issue the Grant to John with office copies as requested.

The oath will contain the following information: details of extracting solicitors; true name of deceased; date of death and domicile at death; executors' capacity and duties; statement as to whether Inland Revenue account is needed and if so, value of the estate; and the jurat.

John's duty is to ascertain and value Harold's estate for Inheritance Tax purposes and deliver the account to the Revenue within twelve months after the end of the month of death. Interest on unpaid tax runs after six months. Tax is due six months after the end of the year unless a right to pay instalments is exercised.

As to the caveat, John is advised that this may be entered by any person who opposes the issue of a Grant to prevent sealing of a Grant in favour of an applicant without notice to caveator.

A caveat is valid for six months. If a person applies for a grant, such as John, but is refused because there is a caveat, the applicant sends a 'warning' which gives the caveator eight days to do the following. He must withdraw the caveat, or enter an appearance if for example he has a contrary interest or better title to the grant, or enter a summons for directions, or do nothing. If the caveator does nothing then after eight days the caveat is said to be 'warned off' and the issue of grant may take place.

QUESTION TWO

See Chapter 14, Question 3(b).

Chapter 14

Types of Grant

14.1   Introduction

14.2   Key points

14.3   Key cases and statutes

14.4   Questions and suggested solutions

14.1   Introduction

There are three main types of grant representation. Grants may be general or in limited form. The type of grant will depend on the nature of the estate. This chapter should not be studied in isolation and must be read in conjunction with Chapters 12, 13 and 15.

14.2   Key points

a)   A will appointing executor(s) who are prepared to act leads to Grant of Probate.

b)   If no executors are appointed by the will (or the appointment fails) a Grant of Letters of Administration with the will annexed will be issued, generally to principal beneficiaries.

c)   If there is a total intestacy a Grant of Letters of Administration will be issued, generally to those entitled to the property ie a Grant of Simple Administration.

d)   *Grant may be general or limited*

   i)   General is not limited.

   ii)   Limited means limited in time or property under s113 Supreme Court Act 1981 eg:

   •   grant de bonis non administratis;

   •   Settled Land Act grant;

   •   grant durante minor aetate;

   •   grant of administration during mental or physical incapacity;

   •   grant to collect in the deceased's goods;

   •   grant of administration pending suit.

e) Note the practice of recognition of grants in Northern Ireland and confirmations made in Scotland.

f) Resealing of grants is process whereby Commonwealth country grants are recognised.

14.3 Key cases and statutes

* *Bolton, In the Goods of* [1899] P 186
  Grant of ad colligenda may be made where powers are needed to deal with assets

* *Galbraith, In the Goods of* [1951] P 422
  A grant de bonis non may be issued where a previous grant has been revoked

* Administration of Estates Act 1925, s22(1) – grant to special representatives for settled land purposes

* Non-Contentious Probate Rules 1987

* Supreme Court Act 1981, s113 – the power of the court to make limited grants

* Supreme Court Act 1981, s117 – administration pending suit

* Supreme Court Act 1981, s118 – grants for the benefit and use of a minor

* Supreme Court Act 1981, s119 – letters of administration with the will annexed

14.4 Questions and suggested solutions

QUESTION ONE

a) What is the practical importance of the rule that probate, when granted, relates back to the death of the testator?

b) Advise on the obtaining of representation in the following cases.

  i) David has left a will which reads, 'My solicitors, Hunt, Marsh and Co, are to pay my debts and hand over the balance of my estate to my sister Jane.' The firm of Hunt, Marsh & Co consisted of eight partners at the date of the will; six of them had died before David's death, the other two had retired and been replaced by other partners.

  ii) James has died intestate, leaving a widow, Lucy, a daughter, Hilda (his only child), and an estate worth £100,000 net, including a freehold house which, by the will of his father, who died in 1972, was devised to James in fee simple, subject to an annual payment of £5,000 to James' mother, who is still alive.

University of London LLB Examination
(for External Students) Succession June 1983 Q7

General Comment

This is a long question, so timing is of the essence. The first part simply requires an explanation of the doctrine of relation back. The second part is more complex and requires some careful thought.

Skeleton Solution

a) Position of executor – position of administrator – relation back.

b) i) Implied appointment of executors – appointment of a firm.

 ii) Settled Land Act 1925 grant – grant of Simple Administration – minor.

Suggested Solution

a) Where an executor is appointed to administer an estate the grant of probate he receives merely confirms his position and authority because probate merely confirms his appointment and is not the source of it. Consequently all the deceased's property vests in the executor on death and the executor is in a position to administer it and to protect it from that time by taking legal action, if necessary. The only necessity for having the grant is if the executor needs to prove his title in court: see *Chetty* v *Chetty* [1916] 1 AC 603.

The position of an administrator is different from that of an executor in that the grant of administration confers authority on the administrator and is his source of appointment. Until the grant is made, the administrator has no power to administer the estate or to issue any legal proceedings on behalf of the estate: see *Chetty* v *Chetty* and *Ingall* v *Moran* [1944] KB 160. Some time may lapse between the death and the grant and to ensure that this hiatus does not affect the administration of the estate the doctrine of relation back has been adopted by the courts in order to protect the estate from wrongful injury in this period. Under this doctrine the letters of administration relate back to the death of the deceased so as to enable the administrator to recover goods which have been wrongly seized or converted and to bring actions for trespass, negligence etc, where necessary: see *Foster* v *Bates* (1843) 12 M & W 226. The doctrine is only to protect the deceased's estate and it is not designed for any other purpose. Thus, in *Fred Long & Son Ltd* v *Burgess* [1950] 1 KB 115 it was held that it could not be used to bring life into a tenancy which had been lawfully determined by the deceased's landlords while it was vested in the President of the Family Division. As Asquith LJ said 'the doctrine of relation back cannot breathe new life into a corpse'.

b) i) In this case there has been an implied appointment of Hunt, Marsh & Co as executors in David's will. An implied appointment, sometimes called an executor according to the tenor, arises when the will shows an intention that a person should act as executor without expressly nominating him as executor. Thus, in *In the Goods of Cook* [1902] P 115 a direction to a person to pay all the testator's just debts was regarded as an implied appointment while in *In the*

Goods of Adamson (1875) LR 3 P & D 253, it was said that if any of the essential duties of an executor were cast upon a person he might be regarded as an executor according to tenor. Therefore, directions to collect the assets of the deceased to pay his funeral expenses and debts or discharge the legacies would be sufficient for this purpose. In the present case the solicitors have been asked to pay the testator's debts and effectively pay the rest of the estate to his sister Jane. This is a good appointment according to tenor.

David appears to have appointed the firm of Hunt, Marsh & Co as his executors in this case rather than any individual members of the firm. As a general rule the appointment as executor of a partnership firm is not permitted and where a clause in a will is so phrased the court construes it as appointing the individual partners as executors: see *In the Goods of Fernie* (1849) 6 NC 657; *Re Horgan* [1971] P 50. According to *Re Horgan* such a clause is to be construed as an appointment of the firm in the person of the partner or partners at the date of the testator's death and if there are more than four partners, then a grant will not be made to more than four in respect of the same part of the estate of the deceased: see s114 Supreme Court Act 1981. Therefore it will be up to the partners at the date of David's death to decide which of their number will take the appointment. In *Re Horgan* Latey J expressed some reservations about his conclusions on these matters and therefore, if the partners are in doubt they would be well advised to make an application to the court.

ii) By his will James' father left James a freehold house subject to an annual payment of £5,000 to James' mother, who is still alive. In my view it is reasonable to suppose that the annual payment is charged on the house thus bringing it within s1(1)(v) of the Settled Land Act 1925 and, accordingly, this property is to be regarded as settled land. As the settlement is continuing after James' death s22 of the Administration of Estates Act 1925 applies and in the circumstances James is deemed to have appointed the trustees of the settlement as his special executors. A grant will be made to these trustees which will be limited to the settled land. It is not indicated who the trustees are in this case and if there is any doubt in the matter then s30 of the Settled Land Act should be consulted.

As regards the remainder of James' estate a grant of letters of administration simpliciter will be necessary as he died intestate. The order of priority for obtaining a grant in such circumstances is dictated by r22 of the Non-Contentious Probate Rules 1987. The surviving spouse, namely Lucy, has the best right to the grant, followed by Hilda. If the estate is sufficiently large so that Lucy has a life interest in half the residue under the intestacy rules, or if Hilda, being entitled to a share on intestacy, is a minor then under s114(2) Supreme Court Act 1981 the grant will have to be made to either a trust corporation or two individuals. Should there be a life interest and Hilda is an adult she will probably be appointed along with Lucy. But, if Hilda is a minor the court may under s114(2) appoint Lucy as sole administrator or, alternatively, appoint James' mother to act with Lucy under r21.

QUESTION TWO

a) Victor was appointed sole executor of the will of Henry who died three months ago. Victor has not yet proved the will. Rich, who died in 1978, appointed Henry and George to be his executors and Henry proved Rich's will, power being reserved to George. The estate of Rich has not been fully administered, and Victor, though willing to act as Henry's executor, does not wish to deal with Rich's estate.

Advise Victor.

b) Brown died intestate leaving a widow Eileen and a brother Harry. Brown's death was caused by an overdose of drugs given by Eileen, who has since been convicted of the manslaughter of Brown. Brown's estate consists of personalty, worth £40,000 after payment of debts, and the fee simple estate in Greenacre Farm, worth £60,000, which was given to him by his uncle's will charged with the payment of £1,000 a year to Brown's aunt, who died three days after Brown. Edward, the executor of the will of Brown's uncle is still alive.

Advise who should apply for a grant, or grants of representation.

University of London LLB Examination
(for External Students) Succession June 1984 Q7

General Comment

The first part of this question requires a basic application of the chain of representation. The second part is more difficult and requires the application of a number of rules, including forfeiture.

Skeleton Solution

a) Chain of representation – Victor must accept both executorships or refuse both – if refuses has no status to deal – Henry's estate: may apply for grant administration; or George may apply for probate – Rich's will: break the chain of representation; Victor would be Henry's executor only.

b) Intestacy – grant of letters of administration – NCPR 1987 – spouse committed manslaughter – court may pass over s116 Supreme Court Act 1981 – note: Forfeiture Act 1982; Settled Land Act 1925 grant.

Suggested Solution

a) Under s7(1) Administration of Estates Act 1925, an executor of a sale or last surviving executor of a testator is the executor of that testator. Executor here means proving executor – ie one who has obtained probate.

Henry was Rich's sole proving executor. If Victor obtains probate of Henry's will, he will automatically become executor of Rich's estate, whether he likes it or not. So he must either accept both executorships, or refuse them both.

If he refuses them both, then he may have no status to deal with Henry's assets. He may, having refused probate, have the right to apply for letters of administration of Henry's estate with will annexed, under r20 of the Non-Contentious Probate Rules 1987. This depends on the terms of Henry's will. If he is not a trustee of the residuary estate, or a beneficiary, he will have no such right.

Another possibility is that George may now be persuaded to apply for probate of Rich's will. He will obtain a grant of double probate. This will breach the claim of representation. Victor is no longer the executor of Rich's last surviving executor, so by obtaining probate of Henry's will, he becomes only Henry's executor, and not Rich's.

b) To deal with the assets other than the farm Brown has died intestate. That must, therefore, be a grant of letters of administration.

Normally, the surviving spouse is entitled to the major part of the deceased's estate under the intestacy rules, and under r22 of the Non-Contentious Probate Rules, is the first person entitled to the grant. In this case, the spouse has been convicted of Brown's manslaughter. A sane person who commits manslaughter is, as a matter of public policy, debarred from taking under his victim's intestacy. This includes a person who is convicted of manslaughter by reason of diminished responsibility. He is not then entitled to a grant of letters of administration. This would mean that Harry, as the only other statutory next of kin, would succeed to Brown's property, and could obtain a grant as brother of the deceased. (This assumes that Harry has left no issue or parents, who have a prior right to the property and to a grant.)

If Eileen were insane, then she would not be debarred from succeeding to Brown's property. Her insanity, however, would be a ground for the court to pass over her as an administrator, and direct that the grant should issue to such other person as it thinks expedient, possibly Harry: s116 Supreme Court Act 1981.

If Eileen were sane, as she has been convicted of manslaughter rather than murder, she can apply to the court under the Forfeiture Act 1982. This Act empowers a court to relieve an applicant in part from the rule of public policy, and to allow the applicant to take some of the property to which he would have succeeded but for the rule.

If this relief is given, then, presumably, Eileen could apply for a grant of letters of administration unless the court thought it fit to pass over her.

Greenacre farm was settled under the Settled Land Act 1925 by the terms of the uncle's will. Section 1 of the 1925 Act provides that land is settled if charged voluntarily with payment of a sum of money for life. The land was still settled at Brown's death, but ceased to be settled three days after his death, when the annuitant died.

Where the deceased was tenant for life of settled land, and the land remains settled land at his death, then a grant linked to the settled land must be made to the deceased's special personal representatives. As Brown died intestate, the grant will be of letters of administration limited to settled land. The first persons with the right to apply are the persons who are trustees of the settlement at the time of their application for the grant.

If there are no trustees of the settlement, then the ordinary personal representative of the deceased can obtain a grant. Thus, assuming Harry is Brown's administrator as regards his general estate, he may, if he wishes, obtain a grant of letters of administration expressly including the settled land. However, as he is not a trustee of the settlement, he is not bound to act in regard to the settled land, and could as regards the settled land while still remaining an administrator of the other assets.

(Settled Land Act 1925, s23.)

If George does not, or cannot, obtain a grant expressly including the settled land, then he will obtain a grant of letters of administration expressly excluding settled land.

QUESTION THREE

a) Contrast the position of an executor with that of an administrator with particular reference to their respective powers to act before obtaining a formal grant of probate or letters of administration.

b) Sid has recently died leaving a will which, inter alia, bequeaths £10,000 to Terry, a freehold house worth £50,000 to Victor, and the matrimonial home and the residue of his considerable estate to his wife Wilma. Eric, who was appointed sole executor, predeceased him. The estate includes a block of shares worth £10,000 which Terry would like to take in lieu of his legacy.

Advise:

i) who is entitled to the grant to the estate;

ii) whether Terry can take the shares and, if so, how this would be effected;

iii) how the title to the freehold house would be passed to Victor.

University of London LLB Examination
(for External Students) Succession June 1992 Q7

General Comment

This is not an untypical probate question, set by the University of London when probate was still part of the syllabus. The first part requires an appreciation of the differences between executors and administrators, whilst the second part focuses on the grant under the NCPR 1987, valuation and the transfer of property.

Skeleton Solution

a) General statement of personal representative's powers – executor: derives power from will – administrator: derives power from letters of administration.

b) i) Effect of executor predeceasing testator – order of entitlement to grant.

   ii) Possibility of post-death variation of will – the mechanics of the variation.

   iii) Assent – memo on grant – mention stamp duty.

Suggested Solution

a) Personal representatives have very wide statutory powers for the collection, management and distribution of the deceased's assets and discharge of his liabilities. In theory an executor can exercise any of these powers at any time after the deceased's death as his authority is derived from the will which takes effect on death – the grant of probate merely confirms that authority. In practice, however, he will be unable to exercise many of these powers before obtaining a grant since the persons or authorities in control of the deceased's assets will usually refuse to transfer them without the production of a grant (unless the asset falls within one of the categories of property for which no grant is required). If he does exercise his powers in any substantial way (recognising debts due to the deceased and giving receipts for them; disposing of the deceased's personal chattels) he will have intermeddled with the estate in such a way as to indicate his acceptance of the office of executor and any subsequent attempt to renounce probate without fail.

By contrast an administrator's authority is derived from the grant of Letters of Administration to him. He is consequently unable to exercise any of the powers of a personal representative until the grant has been issued. If he intermeddles in the estate in the meantime he cannot, unlike an executor, be prevented from renouncing his right to the grant but he may incur liability as an executor de son tort.

An executor may issue proceedings before the grant pursuant to any cause of action vested in him on the deceased's death and may continue those proceedings until the court requires him to prove his title by production of the grant. If the grant has not been obtained by that stage the court will usually be prepared to stay the proceedings for a reasonable time to await production of the grant. An administrator cannot however issue proceedings until the grant is obtained as the deceased's rights of action do not vest in him until then. This is well illustrated by the case of *Ingall* v *Moran* [1944] KB 160. The deceased was killed by a negligent driver. The legislation then in force required any action to be commenced within a year of death. The deceased's father, claiming as administrator, began an action within this time but did not take out a grant until 14 months after his son's death. The action was dismissed: the father had no authority to bring an action prior to grant.

Certain acts are not regarded as intermeddling, for example acts of humanity and necessity, such as arranging the deceased's funeral and accepting the funeral account, securing the property and carrying out any urgent repairs.

Notwithstanding the above, in practice, the personal representatives (be they executors or administrators) will usually need to produce their grant before they can dispose of or otherwise deal with the deceased's assets in order to prove their title to do so. Thus an executor will have to produce the grant before judgment is entered in his favour; a purchaser will normally insist on seeing the grant before completing his purchase from a personal representative; a beneficiary in whose favour personal representatives have assented a legal estate in land is entitled to have a memorandum of that assent endorsed on the grant.

b) i) The office of executor is as a general rule personal to the executor appointed by the testator and cannot be assigned or transferred: s5 Administration of Estates Act (AEA) 1925. Thus if the executor dies after the testator but before taking out a grant of probate his rights in respect of the executorship die with him and do not pass to his personal representatives. In this case the executor has predeceased the testator and it will, therefore, be necessary to apply for Letters of Administration with the will annexed. By s119 Supreme Court Act 1981 priority to this grant is governed by the order set out in r20 Non-Contentious Probate Rules 1987. This rule provides that the persons entitled to the grant in respect of the deceased's will will be determined in accordance with the following rule of priority:

a) the executor;

b) any residuary legatee or devisee holding in trust for any person;

c) any other residuary legatee or devisee or, where the residue is not wholly disposed of by the will, any person entitled to share in the undisposed of residue.

Thus here Wilma will be entitled to obtain the grant.

The person applying for the grant must establish his title to it in the oath to lead the grant. He must clear off all persons with a higher entitlement in the priority order by renunciation or citation and swear to the manner of their disposal in his oath.

ii) A will may be varied or treated for inheritance tax purposes as having been effected by the deceased, rather than as transfers for value by the beneficiaries redirecting their interests, provided the variation complies with the provisions of s142 Inheritance Tax Act 1984. This section provides that where within the period of two years after a person's death:

a) any of the dispositions (under a will or the intestacy rules) of the property comprised in his estate immediately before his death are varied; or

b) the benefit conferred by any of those dispositions is disclaimed by an instrument in writing made by the persons or any of the persons who benefit or would benefit under the dispositions, the variation shall be deemed to have been effected by the deceased and inheritance tax assessed on that basis.

In the case of a variation it shall not be deemed to have been one made by the deceased unless written notice to that effect is given to the Board of the Inland Revenue within six months after the date of the instrument by the persons making the instrument. If the variation results in additional tax being payable the personal representatives must also give such notice (which may be embodied in the variation itself or in a separate document).

A variation may be made of any property comprised in a person's estate for inheritance tax purposes immediately before his death.

Thus here if Wilma agrees to the variation Terry may take the shares instead of his £10,000. A Deed of Variation would be drawn up and executed by Terry and Wilma and (if the variation increases the inheritance tax payable) the executor(s). It is good practice to annex the deed (or a certified copy) to the original grant of probate. At the very least a memorandum of the existence of such a deed should be endorsed on the original grant.

iii) Although personal representatives can transfer the legal title in land to a beneficiary by a conveyance by deed (and in one instance not relevant here must do so) it is more usually done by way of assent in the form prescribed by s36 AEA 1925. This enables the personal representative to transfer the legal title to the beneficiary by a simple written deed, signed by the personal representatives naming the person in whose favour it is given. There is no statutory requirement for a witness to the personal representatives' signatures although in practice one is usually supplied. No stamp duty is payable. Title to the freehold house will thus be passed to Victor by means of an assent which will be executed in his favour by the administrator of Sid's will. Victor will also require an office copy of the grant and should insist that a memorandum of the assent be endorsed on the grant.

Chapter 15

Revocation of Grant

15.1   Introduction

15.2   Key points

15.3   Key cases and statutes

15.4   Question and suggested solution

15.1 Introduction

Once made the court still has the power to revoke a grant. It is important to understand the reasons for the revocation and the effects of such a revocation.

15.2 Key points

a) If a Registrar is satisfied that a Grant should be revoked, he may make an order accordingly.

b) For example, fraud, another valid will, physical inability of PR, deceased not dead inter alia.

c) Protection for transactions made in good faith by purchasers and PRs before revocation of grant.

    i)   Section 27 Administration Estates Act 1925.

    ii) Section 37 Administration Estates Act 1925.

    iii) Section 39 Administration Estates Act 1925.

15.3 Key cases and statutes

* *Bloch, In the Estate of* (1959) The Times 2 July
PR must have acted in good faith to take advantage of s27 of the Administration of Estates Act 1925

* *Cope, In the Estate of* [1954] 1 WLR 608
Revocation where the grantee commits a serious breach of duty

* *Galbraith, In the Goods of* [1951] P 422
Revocation where the grantee is incapable of acting

- *Loveday, In the Goods of* [1900] P 154
  Revocation where the grantee has left the country permanently

- *Moore, In the Goods of* (1845) 3 NC 601
  Revocation will be granted where the grant was made as a result of a false statement

- *Priestman* v *Thomas* (1884) 32 WR 842
  A grant may be revoked where it has been made to the wrong person

- *Thacker, In the Goods of* [1900] P 15
  Revocation where the grantee wishes to be relieved of his duties

- *Trimblestown* v *Trimblestown* (1830) 3 Hag Ecc 243
  Revocation will be granted where the grant contains a material irregularity

- Administration of Estates Act 1925, s27 – the PR's indemnity

- Administration of Estates Act 1925, s37 – validity of a conveyance is not effected by revocation of grant

- Administration of Estates Act 1925, s39 – protection for third parties who enter into a contract with the PR on revocation of grants

- Supreme Court Act 1981, s121(1) – power of the court to revoke a grant

15.4 Question and suggested solution

a) What precautions should a sensible personal representative take to protect himself before finally distributing the estate?

b) Denis, who died in 1986, was though to have died intestate. His only surviving relations were his nieces, Edith, Frances and Gertrude.

Edith obtained a Grant of Administration, sold and conveyed Denis' house to Paul for £200,000, paid all debts and duties and divided the remainder of the estate equally amongst Frances, Gertrude and herself.

A will made by Denis has now been discovered, appointing Steven his executor and giving the house to John and the rest of the estate to Henry. Gertrude has died without any assets; Edith bought a bungalow with her share of the estate but is now insolvent and is being made bankrupt.

Advise Steven as to his rights and duties.

University of London LLB Examination
(for External Students) Succession June 1989 Q8

General Comment

This is quite a simple question, the two parts covering a number of issues related to the way in which a personal representative should conduct himself in the distribution of the estate.

Skeleton Solution

a) Search and advertise – no distribution in first six months – guidance by court.

b) Revocation – Steven's duties as PR – Steven's rights – conveyance to Paul – recovery of assets – devastavit – Edith – recipient – distribute.

Suggested Solution

a) A PR is personally liable to both creditors and beneficiaries to the extent of assets passing through his hands save insofar as these are shown to have been duly administered.

He is protected against claims from creditors or beneficiaries of whom he has notice, if he advertises for creditors and claimants to send particulars of claims to him within a stated time (not less than two months) by notice in the London Gazette, and in local newspapers circulating in the district where any land owned by the deceased is, and by such other notices in special cases as the court would have directed in an administrative action. He must distribute after the time stated in the notice and, in the case of land, make the same searches as an independent purchaser of land would make: s27 Trustee Act 1925.

A PR should therefore advertise and search early in administration.

He should also avoid distributing within six months of a grant of first representation to avoid personal liability from claimants under Inheritance (Provision for Family and Dependants) Act 1975 and upon rectification of a will: AJA 1982.

Finally, a PR may apply to court by originating summons to determine any question or grant specific relief.

b) It is Steven's duty as Denis' appointed PR to identify correctly the beneficiaries entitled to share in the estate, to ascertain the nature and extent of their beneficial interest, and to distribute accordingly.

His first step must be to apply to court for revocation of grant to Edith on the ground that it was made to the wrong person. A grant may be revoked in a number of cases, eg where the grant was made to the wrong person, where it was made as a result of a false statement, where it contains a material irregularity, where the grantee becomes incapable of acting, and where the grantee commits a serious breach of duty. Here, the grant was made to Edith in the belief that Denis died intestate, whereas the will found subsequently shows Denis appointed Steven: see *Priestman* v *Thomas* (1884) 32 WR 842. Steven's application will be under s121(1) Supreme Court Act 1981.

The beneficiaries under the will are John and Henry. Steven must identify them.

In order to distribute to John and Henry in accordance with the will, Steven must recover Denis' assets so far as he is able. The position as regards these is as follows.

The conveyance of Denis' property to Paul is valid and unaffected by the revocation: s37 AEA 1925 protects the 'purchaser by conveyance of an interest in real ... property.'

However, the beneficiaries have certain rights and remedies against Edith as PR and the recipients of their entitlement, Gertrude Frances and Edith.

A PR who fails to distribute to those property entitled commits devastavit (see *Re Diplock* [1948] Ch 465) and is personally liable to the beneficiary seeking to recover his loss.

However, John and Henry cannot sue on this ground for two reasons. Firstly, Edith is bankrupt and being made insolvent. Secondly, Edith is given a defence by s61 Trustee Act 1925 which gives a court a discretion to excuse a PR from personal liability for devistavit where that PR acted 'honestly and reasonably' and in all the circumstances 'ought fairly to be excused'.

John and Henry have a further remedy, which is a personal claim against those who received their entitlement wrongly namely Edith, Gertrude and Frances.

However, Edith is bankrupt and Gertrude died leaving no assets. We are not told Frances's financial position. If her share has been dissipated, then John and Henry will be unable to recover any of their entitlement. If she is solvent, they will be able to recover the amount which was paid to Frances on Denis's death.

Chapter 16

Vesting, Collection, Realisation of Assets

16.1   Introduction

16.2   Key points

16.3   Key cases and statute

16.4   Questions and suggested solutions

16.1 Introduction

This chapter deals with the first of the three stages involved in the administration of an estate – the vesting, the collection in of all the assets of the deceased and, of course, the realisation of those assets. This is an important process before the estate can be distributed.

16.2 Key points

a) Personalty and realty of deceased vests automatically in personal representatives ('PRs').

   i) Exceptions include settled land, joint tenancy.

   ii) Remain vested throughout administration.

   iii) Note doctrine of relation back.

Before a grant of administration, estate vests in Public Trustee: see s9 of the Administration of Estates Act (AEA) 1925, as substituted.

b) Causes of action against or belonging to deceased vest in PR likewise.

c) PRs under a duty 'to collect and get in the real and personal estate of the deceased': s25(a) AEA 1925.

d) If required by court, PRs must exhibit an inventory and account of the estate: s25(b) AEA 1925.

e) PRs have wide powers of sale and mortgage both statutory and common law.

f) A purchaser has statutory protection against an improper disposition by a PR:

   i) Sections 36(8) and 36(6) and 37 Administration Estates Act 1925.

   ii) Sections 204(1) Law Property Act 1925.

g) Generally, a PR has no authority to carry on the deceased's business.

  i) Exceptions: realisation and direction in will.

  ii) PR who does so without authority is personally liable for losses.

  iii) Indemnity.

h) Leases by which deceased was lessee devolve on PRs automatically.

  i) PR liable for rent due and breach of covenant to the extent of the deceased's assets.

  ii) PR who enters into possession is personally liable for same.

i) Powers of PR

  i) Sole PR has powers of joint PRs.

  ii) Where there are two or more PRs, powers are joint and several.

16.3 Key cases and statute

- *Anker-Petersen* v *Anker-Petersen and Others* [1991] LSG 1 May
  Application of s57 Trustee Act 1925

- *Baird* v *Baird* [1900] 2 WLR 1412
  Nominations are no different from other powers of appointment and thus do not need to be executed as wills

- *Beswick* v *Beswick* [1968] AC 58
  Contracts entered into before death are enforceable

- *Bridgett and Hayes' Contract, Re* [1928] Ch 163
  Where the deceased is the last tenant for life, the property will vest in his personal representatives

- *Crowther, Re* [1895] 2 Ch 56
  Another exception to the general rule is where there is a direction in the will to carry on the business

- *Dowse* v *Gorton* [1891] AC 190
  An exception to the rule in *Kirkman* v *Booth* (below) is where the business is carried on for the purposes of realisation of the estate

- *Foster* v *Bates* (1834) 12 M & W 226
  Doctrine of relation back

- *Kirkman* v *Booth* (1848) 11 Beav 273
  General rule is that the PRs have no authority to carry on the business of the testator

- *O'Grady* v *Wilmot* [1916] 2 AC 231
  Where personalty is appointed under a general power by the will, the personalty does not vest in the personal representatives

- *Powell* v *Evans* (1802) 5 Ves 839
  Unsecured debts should be demanded forthwith and if necessary legal proceedings
  should be commenced

- *Wankford* v *Wankford* (1704) 1 Salk 299
  An executor is entitled to do all the acts that are incidental to his office except those
  for which he needs a grant

- Administration of Estates Act 1925, s1 – the realty and personalty vests in the PRs

- Administration of Estates Act 1925, s9 – vesting in the case of intestacy

- Administration of Estates Act 1925, s25(a) – PRs under a duty to collect and get in
  the real and personal estate of the testator

- Administration of Estates Act 1925, s25(b) – PRs under a duty to provide a full
  inventory and account of the administration of the estate when required

16.4 Questions and suggested solutions

QUESTION ONE

See Chapter 19, Question 2(b).

QUESTION TWO

See Chapter 19, Question 3(b).

QUESTION THREE

a) 'Where trusts are declared in a will it may seem convenient to appoint the same
   persons to be both executors and trustees. In fact, however, the appointment of the
   same persons to perform both functions may give rise to problems and difficulties.'

   Explain and discuss.

b) Paul's residuary estate is given by his will to Andrew and Gerald on trust for sale
   and conversion, the beneficiaries under the trusts being Paul's wife, Louise, and
   his son Harold aged 12. The residue includes a wholesale electrical equipment
   business, and Andrew and Gerald have been asked by Louise to carry on that
   business.

   Advise Andrew and Gerald whether if they do so (i) they will be acting within
   their legal powers, (ii) they will run any personal risk.

   University of London LLB Examination
   (for External Students) Succession June 1986 Q9

General Comment

The first part of this question requires a standard discussion of the confusion regarding the duties of executors who are also trustees – the position can adequately be considered by looking at the three standard cases mentioned. The second part is a typical question on duties of a personal representative when dealing with the deceased's business.

Skeleton Solution

a) Compare authority of trustee and executor.

b) Circumstances when PR may carry on deceased's business and potential liability.

Suggested Solution

a) If the same persons are appointed to be both executors and trustees, the difficulty that arises is that it may be uncertain when, as regards any particular asset, they change from executors to be trustees.

The change has serious consequences. Their authority is different. Trustees have only joint authority, ie they must act together or the disposition by them is void. Executors have (with the exception of a conveyance of land) both joint and several authority, so that a disposition by one of two is valid. Thus, if A and B are appointed as executors and trustees, and A disposes of an asset, it is essential to know if A were acting as executor (valid) or trustee (void): *Attenborough* v *Solomon* [1913] AC 76.

If only A were appointed, as a sole executor he can give a good receipt for purchase moneys. A sole trustee for sale of land cannot.

If a sole or sole surviving executor dies, one must look either for a chain of executorship under s7 Administration of Estates Act 1925, or there must be a grant de bonis mon administratis in respect of the unadministered assets of the deceased. If, however, the executor had become a trustee by the time of his death, s18 Trustee Act 1925 will apply, and his personal representatives could execute the trust. Alternatively, they could merely appoint new trustees.

A trustee is protected by a six year limitation period; an executor by a twelve year period.

If the trustees were different persons from the executors, the capacity in which the asset was at any time held would be clear. A change of capacity could only be effected by an actual change in ownership.

If they are the same persons, there will be no change of ownership. So when will the change of capacity occur?

It seems probable that there is no change of capacity until they have made an assent in their own favour (*Attenborough* v *Solomon*), although this is not certain: *Re*

Cockburn's Will Trusts [1957] Ch 438. Even if an assent is essential, where an assent can be informal, it is not easy to tell whether or not an assent has been made. Unless s36(4) Administration of Estates Act 1925 applies, an assent can be oral, or inferred from the executors' conduct, or from lapse of time. An assent may be implied because the executors have fulfilled their duties as such, and the net residuary estate has been ascertained.

Section 36(4) applies to an assent relating to a legal estate in land, and states that the assent must be in writing, naming the person in whose favour it is named, and signed by the personal representatives. So as regards this particular type of asset only, there can be no doubt.

If the executors have not signed a written assent in their own favour, they still hold as executors: *Re King's Will Trusts* [1964] Ch 542.

b) Personal representatives may carry on the deceased's business with a view to its realisation as an asset of the estate. This is often necessary to preserve the goodwill, which on the sale of the business may be one of its most valuable assets. This only authorises them to carry it on for such period as is reasonable in order to sell it. There is a risk for the representatives, in that if they enter into any contracts (eg purchase of stock in trade), they will be personally liable on them. However, the payment made by them will rank as an administration expense, and so is payable from the deceased's assets before the deceased's creditors or the beneficiaries are paid.

The representatives may carry the business on for a longer period if the will authorises them to do so. There may be an express authority, although this will does not appear to contain one. There may be an implied authority, if the trust for sale confirmed in the will contains a power to postpone sale. In *Re Crowther* [1895] 2 Ch 56 it was held that a power to postpone carried with it by implication a power to carry on the business during the period of postponement.

If the authority exists, and the representatives incur personal liability on contracts, they have again a right of indemnity against the estate, but the right is limited. It is superior to the beneficiaries' claims against the estate, but is deferred to the claims of the deceased's own creditors. If the estate turns out to be insolvent, the right of indemnity will be useless. It is only if a creditor of the deceased has actively consented to the carrying on of the business that the personal representative's right of indemnity will take precedence over that creditor: *Dowse* v *Gorton* [1891] AC 190.

If there is no power to postpone sale, the personal representatives have no authority to carry on the business except for the purposes of administration. If they do carry it on without authority, they will be personally liable for any loss. The risk will be considerable, therefore, unless they obtain a promise of indemnity from Louise, or they obtain a court order authorising them to carry on the business.

Chapter 17

Payment of Debts and Liabilities

17.1 Introduction

17.2 Key points

17.3 Key cases and statutes

17.4 Questions and suggested solutions

17.1 Introduction

Having collected in and realised the estate of the testator, the next duty on the personal representative is to pay all the debts and liabilities of the estate. This must be done carefully in order to avoid any personal liability for losses to the estate. The distinction between solvent and insolvent estates should be noted. Only once all the debts are paid can the estate be properly distributed.

17.2 Key points

a) PRs have a duty to pay debts with due diligence: *Re Tankard* [1942] Ch 69.

b) Necessary but difficult to ascertain debts payable. Section 27 Trustee Act 1925 gives PRs protection against claims they had no notice of provided PRs advertise as required.

c) Funeral, testamentary and administration expenses.

d) Insolvent estates, ie where assets are insufficient to meet debts and liabilities.

   i) Order of payment of creditors is according to the Insolvency Act 1986 and Administration of Insolvent Estates of Deceased Persons Order 1986 (SI 1986/1999).

   ii) Order of priority as prescribed by s34(1) and Schedule 1 Part I AEA 1925:

- secured creditors;

- funeral testamentary and administration expenses;

- specially preferred debts;

- preferred debts;

- ordinary debts;

- deferred debts.

e) Solvent estates ie where assets are sufficient to meet debts and liabilities.

   i) Order of payment is governed by s34(3) and Schedule 1 Part II AEA 1925.

   ii) Order of payment, unless contrary intention is expressed in the will:

   - property undisposed of by will, subject to pecuniary legacy fund: *Re Lamb* [1929] 1 Ch 723;

   - property not specifically bequeathed or devised subject to pecuniary legacy fund: *Re Wilson* [1908] 1 Ch 839;

   - property specifically devised, bequeathed or appropriated for the payment of debts;

   - property of the deceased charged with the payment of debts: *Re Gordon* [1940] Ch 769; *Re Meldrum* [1952] Ch 208;

   - pecuniary legacy fund;

   - property specifically bequeathed or devised;

   - property appointed by will under a general power;

   - other property.

   iii) The above order is subject to contrary intention in the will: *Re Harland-Peck* [1941] Ch 182; *Re Kempthorne* [1930] 1 Ch 268;

   iv) Property changed with payment of money is primarily liable for that change: s35(1) Administration of Estates Act: *Re Birmingham* [1959] Ch 523.

f) The incidence of pecuniary legacies is governed by ss33(2) and 34(3) of the Administration of Estates Act.

17.3 Key cases and statutes

- *Diplock, Re* [1948] Ch 465
  Remedy of tracing

- *Green* v *Salmon* (1838) 8 Ad & E 348
  The PRs are entitled to an indemnity from the estate for funeral expenses

- *Harland-Peck, Re* [1941] Ch 182
  Variation of the statutory order

- *Lamb, Re* [1929] 1 Ch 723
  Definition of propery 'undisposed of by the will'

- *Meldrum, Re* [1952] Ch 208
  Variation of statutory order evidences by a clear intention of the testator

- *Rees* v *Hughes* [1946] KB 517
  PRs are under a duty to arrange for the funeral of the testator

- *Stevens, Re* [1898] 1 Ch 162
  The issue of loss to the estate is independent from the breach of duty

- *Tankard, Re* [1942] Ch 69
  The duty to pay debts can be modified by the will, but only as against the beneficiaries and not the creditors

- Administration of Estates Act 1925, ss33(2) and 34(3) – covers the incidence of pecuniary legacies

- Administration of Estates Act 1925, s34 – provides the order of payment of debts when dealing with a solvent estate

- Insolvency Act 1986 and the Administration of Insolvent Estates of Deceased Persons Order 1986 – provides the order of payment to creditors where the estate is insolvent

- Trustee Act 1925, s27 – provides guidance to the PRs for the purposes of ascertaining the debts payable to the estate

17.4 Questions and suggested solutions

QUESTION ONE

Jones, who died this year, by his will,

a) devised The Beeches and The Pines, two freehold houses to Brian;

b) bequeathed the Shares in 'Z' Ltd to Abigail 'subject to the payment thereof of all my debts';

c) gave the residue of his estate to Trustees on trust for Clarence and David in equal shares.

Clarence died a week before Jones, but the other beneficiaries are still alive.

Jones' estate consists of,

i) The Beeches and The Pines, two freehold houses each worth £80,000 both of which were mortgaged by a single mortgage to Max to secure a debt for £140,000,

ii) shares in 'Z' Ltd worth £40,000 and,

iii) other personalty worth £30,000.

In addition to the mortgage debt, Jones owed other debts amounting to £50,000.

Advise how the debts should be borne as between the persons interested in the estate.

University of London LLB Examination
(for External Students) Succesion June 1989 Q7

General Comment

It is important to identify very early on if the estate is solvent or insolvent. The answer to this question depends entirely on the state of the assets. The application of s35 Administration of Estates Act 1925 and the order of payment from Sch 1, Part II is thereafter a mechanical task.

Skeleton Solution

Insolvent or solvent estate? – Clarence's predeceasing therefore lapse – beneficiaries – creditors – secured debt: s35 AEA 1925 – unsecured debts – order of payment: will; AEA 1925 Sch 1, Part II – distribution to B and D.

Suggested Solution

Cr	£	D	£
personalty	30,000	mortgage	140,000
houses	160,000	other debts	50,000
shares	40,000		190,000
		available to distribute	40,000
	230,000		230,000

Jones' estate is solvent. As the above table shows, there are sufficient assets to meet all his debts and liabilities. The issue is how the incidence of these will affect his dispositions.

Clarence predeceased Jones. The general rule in such an event is that the gifts to the predeceasing beneficiary lapses ie fails. However the effect of s33 Wills Act 1837 as amended is that where a testator leaves a gift to his child who predeceased him leaving issue then, subject to contrary intention in the will, the gift will not lapse but will go to the issue. If therefore Clarence is Jones' son and leaves children, they will take his share in the residue. Otherwise, his gift will lapse.

It is assumed for this question that Clarence is not Jones' son. The only beneficiaries are David and Abigail.

There is a secured creditor, Max, and other unsecured creditors.

Property charged with the payment of money bears the charge, subject to contrary intention: s35 AEA 1925. The rights of the chargee are not affected by s35 which regulates the incidence of the charge as between the beneficiaries. The two houses devised to Brian are subject to one mortgage and there is therefore no question of the debt on one exceeding its value, and the undischarged balance being payable out of general residue: see *Re Holt, Holt & Holt* (1916) 115 LT 73. Because both are left to one beneficiary, it is irrelevant whether or not both properties are primarily liable for the charge.

The operation of s35 is subject to contrary intention 'by will, deed or other document'. Such contrary intention must clearly specify the charge either expressly (s35(2)(b)) or by implication: *Re Valpy* [1906] 1 Ch 531. Jones' direction to pay 'all my debts' out of his shares in Z Ltd is not sufficient to negative the section's operation.

The net value of the properties after payment of Max's mortgage is £20,000.

As to the unsecured creditors, a will may direct the order in which assets are to be applied for the payment of debts, and such a direction overrides the statutory order.

Jones' direction to pay his debts out of Z Ltd shares, coupled with his disposal of the residue without directing the payment of debts therefrom, infers that his direction is meant to relieve the residue from debts insofar as the shares can do: see *Re Gordon* [1940] Ch 769 and *Re Meldrum* [1952] Ch 208. His direction therefore makes the shares in Z Ltd the primary fund for paying debts and varies the statutory order.

The shares are worth £40,000, the debts £50,000. All the proceeds of the sale of the shares will therefore go towards paying debts. Abigail will not receive any money by virtue of Jones' bequest.

As to the last £10,000 of debts, the statutory order in AEA 1925 Sch 1 Part II will apply.

a) Property undisposed of by will, subject to pecuniary legacy fund.

b) Residue subject to pecuniary legacy fund.

c) Property specifically given for debts.

d) Property specifically charged with the payment of debts.

e) Pecuniary legacy fund.

f) Property specifically devised or bequeathed rateably according to its value.

g) Property appointed under a general power.

Clarence's lapsed share of the residue, £10,000 falls into the first two categories. Where there is such an overlap, an asset is deemed to fall within the higher category: *Re Kempthorne, Charles v Kempthorne* [1930] 1 Ch 268. Thus the lapsed share is deemed to fall within category (a) above.

On this order, the remaining £10,000 debts will be paid out of the lapsed share of residue. This clears the debt and the remaining assets can be distributed.

Brian will take the £20,000 remaining from the proceeds of sale of the properties.

David will take the residue which comprises his share of £10,000.

QUESTION TWO

a) 'In *Re Kempthorne* (1930) the Court of Appeal ... brought debts into line with legacies ... I can see no real difference between debts and legacies and I think that legacies ought to be brought into line with debts.' per Lawrence LJ in *Re Worthington* (1933).

Discuss.

b) Martin died this year. His will contained the following dispositions.

'i) All my shares in Moonrock Limited (the family company) to my sister Alice subject to the payment thereout of all my just debts.

ii) My freehold property The Maltings to my brother Bert.

iii) The residue of my estate to my trustees on trust for my nephews Henry and Oliver in equal shares absolutely.'

Oliver died a week before Martin. All the other beneficiaries named survive Martin.

The family company shares are believed to be worth £80,000. The remainder of the personalty is worth £40,000. The Maltings is valued at £250,000. Two years ago Martin executed a legal mortgage secured on the Maltings in the sum of £130,000. In addition there are general debts of £70,000.

Advise Ernest, the executor, as to who should bear the burden of the debts.

University of London LLB Examination
(for External Students) Succession June 1991 Q8

General Comment

This is a difficult two-part question. The first part is easier as it requires the discussion of the difficulties identified in the case law. The arguments from *Re Kempthorne* and *Re Worthington* answer the question. The second part is more complex, dealing with the difference in treatment of secured and unsecured debts.

Skeleton Solution

a) Statutory order for payment of debts – does it apply to legacies? – contrast express and statutory trust for sale – are legacies still payable primarily from personalty? – position for debts?

b) Secured debts s35 – contrary intention *Re Fegan* – unsecured debts: statutory order – category 4, intention to exonerate residue – undisposed of property, residuary property – only Bert will benefit, rest of estate taken to pay debts.

Suggested Solution

a) The whole area of the payment of debts and legacies is very confused with no real agreement between the various case law decisions. In 1925 the Administration of

Estates Act brought in new rules to regulate the incidence of debts in s34(3) and the First Schedule, but it is not clear whether these new rules apply to the incidence of legacies as well. The First Schedule sets out the statutory order of the application of the assets 'towards the discharge of the funeral, testamentary and administration expenses, debts and liabilities' of the deceased. In particular this order provides that undisposed of property is to be used for the payment of debts before the residuary estate. The statutory order applies unless it has been varied in the will. In *Re Kempthorne* [1930] 1 Ch 268 the deceased made a gift of 'all my leasehold property and all my personal estate and effects … subject to and after the payment of my funeral and testamentary expenses and debts'. There was a partial intestacy and thus property undisposed of as well as residuary property, but it was held that the debts had to be paid out of the estate as a whole before any division, as the statutory order had been varied by the wording in the will.

The real question is whether the statutory order applies at all to the payment of the pecuniary legacies under the will. In *Re Worthington* [1933] Ch 771 the testatrix bequeathed various pecuniary legacies and left her residuary estate divided between two persons, one of whom died before the testatrix. The question was whether the legacies, as well as the debts, should be paid primarily out of the undisposed of property. It was held that they should be. As there was an intestacy due to the undisposed of property, s33(2) applied which imposed a statutory trust for sale and directed payment of the debts and liabilities first and then the setting aside of a fund to pay the pecuniary legacies out of the undisposed of property. No distinction was to be made between realty and personalty. Thus *Re Worthington* supports treating debts and legacies alike as both were to be paid out of undisposed of property in accordance with the statutory order applicable to the payment of debts. In *Re Kempthorne* debts were to be paid out of residue as a whole before any division in accordance with the pre-1925 rules for the payment of legacies.

It is not clear what the position is if there is an express trust for sale imposed by the will and there is a partial failure of the residuary gift. In *Re Beaumont* [1950] Ch 462 it was held that the legacies were payable out of residue as a whole and not primarily out of the undisposed of property in accordance with the old rules for the payment of legacies and not following the statutory order for the payment of debts, but the later decision of *Re Midgely* [1955] Ch 576 did apply the statutory order for the payment of debts to the payment of legacies. It is suggested that the decision in *Re Worthington* should be applied also in cases when there is an express trust for sale as this would provide greater consistency in the law. In any event it is surely preferable that the same rules should be followed for both statutory and express trusts for sale. However in some cases the wording of the will may show that legacies and perhaps even debts should be paid before any division of the residue, as was the case in *Re Kempthorne*.

One further problem is whether debts and legacies should be paid primarily from the personal estate or from realty and personalty without distinction. No distinction was made in *Re Worthington* and it seems that for debts no distinction should be made. However there is considerable authority to indicate that legacies are still payable primarily out of residuary personalty. This was held in *Re Thompson* [1936] Ch 676 and *Re Rowe* [1941] Ch 343. If there is undisposed of property it seems that realty in that category will be taken before the residuary personalty for the payment of legacies as in *Re Martin* [1955] Ch 698.

In conclusion it is still not clear whether the same rules apply to the payment of legacies and debts. The new rules in the AEA 1925 for debts have sometimes been applied to the payment of legacies but not in all cases. It may be that the new rules will be applied to legacies only if there is a statutory trust for sale which brings in s33(2) and not otherwise, but although there is much authority to support this view, it seems most unsatisfactory.

b) The total debts, including the mortgage, amount to £200,000. The normal rule is that secured debts are payable out of the security itself as provided by s35 AEA 1925, but this rule may be varied by a contrary intention expressed in the will. It is specifically provided in s35 that a sufficient contrary intent is not shown by a general direction in the will to pay debts out of the residuary estate. If the will directs the payment of debts out of a specific fund, this will be sufficient to show a contrary intent under s35. Thus in *Re Fegan* [1928] 1 Ch 45 the testator directed the payment of debts out of a specific fund and left the proceeds of some insurance policies to his children. These policies were subject to a mortgage. It was held that there was a contrary intent to oust the general rule under s35 and that the mortgage should be discharged out of the specific fund, but that if the specific fund were inadequate to discharge the mortgage, the policies themselves would be liable for the remainder of the debt, as s35 would then apply. Here Martin has directed that his debts be paid out of the shares in Moonrock and, following *Re Fegan*, this direction will oust s35, so that Bert will be entitled to have the mortgage on The Maltings discharged out of the shares. Since the shares will not be enough to discharge all the mortgage, the balance will have to be paid out of The Maltings itself.

The order of application of assets for the payment of unsecured debts is governed by s34(3) and the First Schedule of the AEA 1925. Debts are payable primarily from undisposed of property subject to any contrary intention in the will. The gift to Oliver has lapsed as Oliver predeceased Martin and this property is undisposed of by the will. But Martin has directed that the shares in Moonrock are to be used for the payment of his debts. The gift of the shares appears to come within category 4 of the First Schedule unless there is a variation of the statutory order. A mere direction to pay debts out of a specified fund is not enough to vary the statutory order, there must also be an intention to exonerate the residuary estate from the payment of debts. In *Re Gordon* [1940] Ch 769 there was no variation when the testatrix gave a legacy subject to the payment of debts but made no disposition of the residuary estate. However the decisions in *Re Meldrum* [1952] Ch 208 and *Re James* [1947] Ch 256 suggest that there will be a variation when there is a direction to pay debts from a specific fund and a disposition of the residue with no direction to pay debts. Thus in this case the debts are payable primarily from the shares, then from the undisposed of property (category 1), then the residuary property (category 2) and finally the specific gift (category 6).

The total of the secured and unsecured debts amounts to £200,000, more than the value of the shares. It is suggested that the shares should be taken rateably to pay secured and unsecured debts and that the balance of the secured debt would be paid from The Maltings. The undisposed of property amounts to £20,000 which will all be taken to pay the unsecured debts and the residuary gift of £20,000 will also be needed to pay unsecured debts. The small remaining part of the unsecured debts will then be paid out of The Maltings. Thus Alice, Henry and Martin's next-of-kin will not benefit under the will as their prospective entitlements will be needed to pay debts. Bert will receive The Maltings but its net worth to him will be £170,000 after the discharge of debts.

QUESTION THREE

See Chapter 20, Question 5(a).

Chapter 18

Distribution of Assets

18.1   Introduction

18.2   Key points

18.3   Key cases and statutes

18.4   Questions and suggested solutions

18.1 Introduction

Having paid the debts and liabilities of the estate, the PRs are required to distribute the estate according to the provisions of the will. Clearly, this is only relevant where the estate is solvent.

18.2 Key points

a) Ascertaining the beneficiaries is necessary to distribute the estate.

   i)   Section 27 Trustee Act 1925 advertisements advised where difficult to ascertain.

   ii) Benjamin order by court advisable where beneficiary known but not located.

   iii) Inquiry for next of kin by the court.

b) Beneficiaries' rights before distribution.

   i)   PRs hold assets on a limited trust (see *Crowden* v *Aldridge* [1993] 3 All ER 603); and

   ii) beneficiaries have a chose in action.

c) Assents of personalty

   i)   May be oral or written.

   ii) Relates back to death.

d) Assents of land are governed by s36 Administration of Estates Act 1925.

   i)   Form governed by s36(4) must be in writing.

   ii) Assent vests legal estate in person to whom it is made.

   iii) Relates back to death.

e) Executors have power of appropriation: s41 Administration Estates Act 1925.

f) Executors have power to set off legacies against debts owed by the beneficiary.

g) Generally a personal representative holds assets as PR not a trustee but note special circumstances:

   i)   where beneficiary is an infant;

   ii) on intestacy;

   iii) where will expressly creates trusteeship.

h) Income and interest between death and distribution

   i)   Specific bequests and devises carry all accruing income though note statutory provisions as to future such gifts.

   ii) Immediate general legacy carries interest from time it is payable subject to exceptions.

   iii) Future general legacies do not carry income until they become payable.

   iv) Residuary gifts carry income and profit from death.

   v)   Future residuary bequests are the same subject to testator's contrary intention.

   vi) Deferred residuary bequest carries income from time it is payable.

   vii) Note rule in *Allhusen* v *Whittell* (1867) LR 4 Eq 295.

18.3 Key cases and statutes

* *Allhusen* v *Whittell* (1867) LR 4 Eq 295
  The residue can only be ascertained by treating legacies and debts as having been paid partly out of income and partly out of capital

* *Benjamin, Re* [1902] 1 Ch 723
  Application for an order where a beneficiary is known but cannot be traced

* *Commissioner of Stamp Duties* v *Livingston* [1965] AC 694
  The position of the beneficiary during administration is that he has a chose in action

* *Diplock, Re* [1948] Ch 465
  The PRs have a duty to distribute the assets to those entitled

* *West, Re* [1909] Ch 180
  The assent relates back to death giving the beneficiary the right to income and profits arising on the subject matter of the gift from death

* Administration of Estates Act 1925, s36(1) – governs assents to land

* Administration of Estates Act 1925, s36(4) – provides the formal requirements for an assent

- Administration of Estates Act 1925, s41 – power of the PRs to appropriate any part of the real or personal estate

- Administration of Estates Act 1925, s43(1) – PRs may permit the person entitled to land to take possession before making an assent

- Administration of Estates Act 1925, s44 – executor's year

- Trustee Act 1925, s27 – advertisements to ascertain the beneficiaries

18.4 Questions and suggested solutions

QUESTION ONE

Tim died in 1984 leaving a will by which he appointed his wife, Sally, and Green his executors and gave some jewels to his sister Mavis and the residue of his estate to Sally. Sally and Green proved the will, paid all duties and liabilities and told Mavis that she could have the jewels whenever she liked to collect them from Sally. Tim had contracted to buy the freehold estate in Whiteacre just before his death; and Whiteacre was conveyed to Sally and Green shortly afterwards. Green died in 1985. Sally has now died intestate. Mavis never collected the jewels; another sister of Tim's has taken them and refuses to give them up to Mavis. Sally's administrator wishes to sell Whiteacre.

Advise (a) Mavis, and (b) the administrator.

University of London LLB Examination
(for External Students) Succession June 1987 Q8(b)

General Comment

This is a typical question dealing with the requirements for the assent of personalty. However, there are several other issues covered, including s7 AEA 1925 and rr19 and 20 NCPR 1987.

Skeleton Solution

Requirements for an assent of personalty – Mavis's locus standi – NCPR 1987 – *Re King's Will Trusts.*

Suggested Solution

Mavis has an entitlement under Tim's will to the jewels thereby bequeathed. But this does not necessarily mean she has a proprietary right to these items and it depends on whether the executors, Sally and Green, assented them to Mavis.

In the case of land a written assent is required but with personalty an inferred assent may be implied from conduct. An instructive case is *Attenborough v Solomon* [1913] AC 76. Here it was held that when the executors had completed their executorship duties they could be regarded as having made an assent of certain plate to the beneficiaries thereof. Thus, following that case, it could be concluded that Green and Sally had inferred an assent of the beneficial interest in the jewels to themselves as trustees at the date they said she could collect them and thereafter Mavis had a beneficial proprietary interest in those jewels.

It must be stressed that even though Sally and Green have not passed the legal interest in the jewels to Mavis the effect of the assent is to convert Sally and Green from personal representatives into the trustees. Accordingly Mavis's entitlement to the jewels arises by virtue of a trust rather than by virtue of the will. It must be appreciated that at least in regard to personal estate there is no need to make any formal written assent on the transition from executorship to trusteeship. This is established by the cases of *Re Ponder* [1921] 2 Ch 59, *Re Cockburn's Will Trusts* [1957] Ch 438 and *Re Pitt* (1928) 44 TLR 371.

Accordingly this equitable title has given Mavis the locus standi to sue Tim's sister as third party recipient of trust property. The most appropriate action for Mavis to bring is a constructive trust claim against the sister based on the principle of *Bonney* v *Ridgard* (1784) 1 Cox Eq Cas 145 or *Nelson* v *Larholt* [1948] 1 KB 339.

Whether Sally as administrator has title to sell Whiteacre depends on the operation of the chain of representation under s7 AEA 1925. Under that section on the death of an executor his powers and duties can be transmitted to the executor of the deceased executor but this presupposes that the last surviving executor of Tim (Sally) has herself made a will appointing another executor. This is not the case here as the chain of representation is broken by intestacy. Therefore the only way in which the administrator could sell Whiteacre is by obtaining letters of administration cum testamento annexo et de bonis non administratis. For the administrator to do this he would have to also prove entitlement to a grant within r20 of the Non-Contentious Probate Rules 1987. As Sally is the ultimate residuary beneficiary her administrator may prove for a grant under r20 paragraph (iv) of these rules.

Having obtained a grant under r19 Sally's administrator would then be allowed to sell Whiteacre by relying on s39 of the Administration of Estates Act 1925 which enables a personal representative the powers of a trustee for sale of land.

Rule 20 paragraph (iv) will, however, be irrelevant if there has already been an assent to Sally as residuary beneficiary. In this case as the property is absolutely vested in Sally the administrator need only secure a grant of representation under r22 of the Non-Contentious Probate Rules which presumably has been done.

If this alternative view is taken of the above facts and an assent of Whiteacres can already be inferred to Sally as ultimate residuary beneficiary then the administrator would not need to take a grant of administration to the land under r20. However, such a construction may not be possible since the decision in *Re King's Will Trusts* [1964] Ch 542 which requires a formal assent in writing of land from an executor to himself in his separate capacity as beneficiary.

QUESTION TWO

What is the true status of a beneficiary under a will or intestacy during the administration of the deceased's estate?

University of London LLB Examination
(for External Students) Succession June 1988 Q7

General Comment

This is a frequently examined issue, and knowledge of five cases (mentioned in the solution) will answer the question.

Skeleton Solution

Nature of trust vested in PRs – beneficiaries' interest: a chose in action – discussion *Re Leigh*.

Suggested Solution

It has been suggested that interests must be either legal or equitable. This means that they operate and are effective in rem, ie they are legal and bind the whole world or that they are equitable and therefore operate in personam, ie they are personal rights only. It must be noted however that even legal rights were susceptible to being defeated, eg by a sale to a bona fide purchaser for value without notice of the earlier title in a market overt, eg *Reid* v *Commissioner of the Metropolitan Police* [1973] QB 551.

Prior to the distribution of the assets, ownership in them is vested in the personal representative(s). These assets are held upon a trust. However the trust is limited in its scope; it is to collect and preserve the estate which is the subject of the administration and to administer the assets according to the law and the terms of the will. Viscount Radd pointed out that there is no distinction in such a holding between legal and equitable interests. The whole of the property comes to him in a fiduciary capacity. Sir Robert Megarry VC made it clear in *Northern Developments Ltd* v *UDT Securities* [1976] 1 WLR 1230 that the reason for the non-distinction between the legal and equitable interests was based on historical factors. Courts of Equity called in aid equitable remedies only when such was necessary in order to enforce equitable interests. In the context of estates during administration the court could control the administrators without having recourse to the legal/equitable distinction. The beneficiaries are entitled to a chose in action which can be invoked for any purpose in or connected with the administration of the estate. This chose is transmissible by will (*Re Leigh's Estate* [1970] Ch 277) and it is assignable in the normal way.

Thus, it is quite clear that there may be a third right of property – a right of quasi-property referred to by Everton in an article ([1982] Com 118, 177). This is neither a legal right nor an equitable right but is somewhere in between. That such a right exists was, in part, recognised by Vinelott J in *Conservative Central Office* v *Burrell* [1980] 3 All ER 42.

However, the difficulties of a case like *Re Leigh* have not fully been appreciated. On the facts of the case the question arose whether these shares and the debt passed under the bequest. It was held by Buckley J that the testatrix was able to transfer his right to require her husband's estate to be duly administered to her executors and eventually to the legatee under her will. The assignment by the testatrix of her right to require her husband's estate to be properly administered could not fetter the new administrator of her husband's estate. However, it is difficult to see how, on the facts, a doctrine of ademption could operate if the shares, the subject-matter of the bequest, had been sold at any time before the testatrix's death in order to administer her husband's estate. It is also not clear what the position would be if the testatrix had also owned shares in the company in her own name both at the date of the will and the date of her death. Surely a question arises as to whether the gift would be valid on the certainty point.

Further, there is some doubt as to whether the rule applies to a beneficiary entitled to a specific legacy or devise: *IRC* v *Hawley* [1928] 1 KB 578. The case indicates that the court considered a specific legatee as having a beneficial interest in the legacy from death. But it can be submitted that specific legatees and devisees only have a chose in action as well.

Thus in conclusion one might point out that the true status of a beneficiary under a will or intestacy (*Lall* v *Lall* [1965] 1 WLR 1249) is that they are entitled to a transmissible chose in action which can be invoked for all purposes in or connected with the administration of the estate.

QUESTION THREE

a) Tom and Harold are executors in the estate of George. George owned a freehold property in North London of considerable value. Before his death, he had commenced a High Court action against a local hospital for a leg injury caused by uneven tarmac. Tom and Harold sold the property to X who disappeared shortly after completion and is believed to have emigrated to Kuala Lumpur. Tom and Harold have now exchanged contracts for the sale of the house with Z. Advise Tom, Harold and Z.

b) A died leaving inter alia a Rolls Royce car and a large pecuniary legacy to his brother, B. During administration it becomes clear that B owes A a substantial sum of money, an unsecured loan to purchase B's house. The administration is lengthy and B wishes to know if he is entitled to interest on the pecuniary legacy. When A died he did not own a Rolls Royce, but he did own a magnificent Bentley. Advise the PRs.

Written by the Editor

General Comment

This is a standard two-part question covering the vesting of freehold property and appropriation and set-off. It is important in these questions to consider the possible liabilities and rights of the personal representatives.

Skeleton Solution

a) Vesting of property – vesting of action – statutory protection of purchasers.

b) Appropriation – set off – income on legacy.

Suggested Solution

a) Freehold property vests in executors on the deceased's death by operation of law: s1(1) AEA 1925. G's house therefore vested in T and H on G's death. They then completed the sale of the house to X, following which they had no interest in the property. Despite this they purported to sell the house to Z. Z is advised that a purchaser in his position has the benefit of several statutory protections: ss36(6), 37 and 6(8) AEA 1925 and s204(1) LPA 1925. In these circumstances, s36(6) is relevant. This section provides that a purchaser can accept PR's written statement that they have made no previous assent or conveyance of the property as sufficient evidence of the same, provided there is no written memorandum of sale attached to the probate. However, the section only helps the purchaser such as Z where the previous conveyance is to a trustee or beneficiary; it will not keep him in circumstances such as these where there has been a previous disposition in favour of another person. Z is therefore advised that the PRs are in breach of contract as they are unable to do what they have contracted to do; ie convey the freehold to Z. Z should sue the PRs for the return of his deposit together with costs, any damages and interest thereon.

As to the action against the hospital, T and H are advised that the benefit of any right of action belonging to a deceased rests in his PRs. They may therefore continue the action.

b) There are three issues here.

Firstly, the testator left B a Rolls Royce but did not own one on his death. He did however own a Bentley. The PRs are advised that when it is expensive or difficult to sell assets to meet a legacy or buy property, then they may exercise their power of appropriation under s41 AEA 1925. If it is difficult or expensive for the PRs to sell the Bentley, they may appropriate it.

There are restrictions on the power and the PRs must pay attention to these. Firstly, appropriation may not prejudice a specific bequest or devise. So, if the Bentley has been devised, it will not be possible to appropriate it. Secondly, a beneficiary who is absolutely entitled must give his consent. Thirdly, PRs must employ a valuer to value the property it is proposed to appropriate. The relevant time is the time of appropriation not the date of death. Finally, it is subject to contrary intention in the will.

If the PRs do exercise the power of appropriation, then the Bentley will become a binding substitute for the gift of the Rolls.

The second issue is that B owed A money. The PRs are advised that executors have the power to set off money owed by a beneficiary to the testator against any legacy: *Re Rhodesia Goldfields Ltd* [1909] 1 Ch 239. They are therefore entitled to pay B the balance of the legacy after first deducting the amount of B's debt to A.

Finally, B wishes to know if he is entitled to interest on the pecuniary legacy. There are rules as to income and interest on gifts from death to distribution. The rule as to an immediate general legacy is that interest is payable from the date upon which it becomes payable. The will may fix this date. In default, interest will run from the end of one year after the testator's death. The current rate of interest is 5 per cent per annum.

QUESTION FOUR

Tom, a bachelor, has recently died. By his will he devised his house to Frank in fee simple; a legacy of £5,000 to George and 'the residue of the property after payment of all debts and liabilities' to Harry and Ian in equal shares. The house is worth £50,000 but is subject to a mortgage debt of £30,000. Tom's other assets are worth £40,000 but there are debts of £10,000 in addition to the mortgage debt. Shortly before his death he made a codicil which revoked the gift to Harry but made no other provision.

Advise the executors as to the distribution of the estate.

Would your answer differ if Frank produces a letter written to him by Tom saying 'I have left you my house in my will which free of the mortgage is worth £50,000'?

> University of London LLB Examination
> (for External Students) Succession June 1992 Q8

General Comment

This is a very specific question dealing with debts of the estate, both charged and unsecured. Knowledge of Sch 1, Part II of the AEA 1925 is crucial. The last part of the question re the letter is interesting and requires the application of s35(1) AEA 1925.

Skeleton Solution

Effect of charged debt – incidence of unsecured debts – contrary intention shown by letter?

Suggested Solution

Any debt already charged on the deceased's property at the time of his death must first be identified because any such debt is prima facie borne by the property on which it is charged: s35(1) Administration of Estates Act 1925 (AEA). Thus, if Frank accepts the gift of the house he will receive it subject to the mortgage.

The next question to consider is the payment of Frank's £10,000 debts. In the absence of a contrary intention on the part of the deceased (and we are not told here that there is such an intention) the deceased's assets will be applied for meeting the unsecured debts in the order set out in AEA Schedule 1, Part II, which is briefly as follows.

i)   Property undisposed of by will (subject to retention of pecuniary legacies fund).

ii) Property not specifically devised or bequeathed but included in a residuary gift (subject as in (i)).

iii) Property specifically appropriated or devised or bequeathed for the payment of debts.

iv) Property charged with, or devised or bequeathed subject to, a charge for the payment of debts.

v)   Pecuniary legacies fund.

vi) Property specifically devised or bequeathed, rateably according to value.

vii) Property appointed by will under a special power.

Thus here the debts would be paid out of the gift of residue and George's legacy would be unaffected.

However, it is possible to vary the statutory order by the terms of the will so that here the use of the words 'after payment of all debts and liabilities' would be regarded as a direction to pay the debts from the whole of the residuary property before dividing it into shares (although in this case because of the terms of the codicil the whole of the residue would go to Ian): *Re Kempthorne* [1930] 1 Ch 268.

Does the letter from Tom to Frank make any difference? Section 35(1) will not apply if the deceased has shown a contrary intention in his 'will, deed or document'. A contrary intention will be shown if the deceased has shown a clear intention that the beneficiary shall receive the property expressly free of the debt in question, in which event the debt will be treated in the same way as the unsecured debts. This will, obviously, have a substantial effect on the gift of residue to Ian since it will, in effect, wipe out the residue (£30,000 morgage + £10,000 other debts). Arguably, though, the letter is not clearly showing Tom's intention that Frank should take the house free of mortgage; the letter may be interpreted merely as a statement of fact as to the value of the house. Although s35 permits the establishing of a contrary intention on the part of the deceased to be evidenced by a document other than the will it is generally easier to establish if it is in the will itself. Attempts to use other documents have often failed because the deceased was not obviously directing his mind as to how the debt should be borne in the event of his death: see, for example, *Re Nicholson* [1923] WN 251; *Re Wakefield* [1943] 2 All ER 29; *Re Birmingham* [1959] Ch 523.

QUESTION FIVE

Andrew's will reads as follows.

'I give £10,000 to my eldest grandchild; my record collection to my wife, Beryl; my 5,000 shares in Esso Petroleum Limited to my daughter, Christine; and the residue of my estate to my son, Dorian.'

Christine had two children, aged 12 and 10, when Andrew died. Andrew owned 5,000 shares in Esso Petroleum Limited when he made the will but later he granted an option to his friend, Eric, to purchase the shares. Eric has given notice to the executors of Andrew's estate that he intends to exercise the option. It transpires that Eric was one of the witnesses to Andrew's will. The record collection was sold by Andrew a few weeks before his death and replaced by a collection of CDs containing substantially the same music.

The day before Andrew died, he told Dorian that he would cut him out of his will unless he stopped his excessive drinking. Dorian was so furious that he got into his car and drove at Andrew and Beryl intending to frighten them. Unfortunately, he failed to brake in time as he was less than sober. Andrew and Beryl were killed outright. Dorian was convicted of manslaughter and given a prison sentence of 3 years. Beryl died intestate and neither she nor Andrew have any relatives other than those mentioned above. Beryl was two years older than Andrew.

Advise on the distribution of Andrew's and Beryl's estates.

University of London LLB Examination
(for External Students) Succession June 1995 Q8

General Comment

This was a very well conceived question and thoroughly searching, but wholly fair. A mild criticism would be that the examiner did not indicate whether Andrew's will, as set down in the question, was meant to suggest that no executors' powers were included. Otherwise several intricate points emerged to challenge the best-prepared student.

Skeleton Solution

Specific bequests and their effect – construction of vested gift; requirement of receipt – whether asset adeemed or not – effect of option exercised after testator's death – grantee of option witnessing will – residuary beneficiary forfeiting gift – joint deaths in common accident: succession rule and exception.

Suggested Solution

By his will Andrew has made four different types of disposition:

i) the £10,000 'to my eldest grandchild' will be interpreted, under the class closing rules, as a pecuniary legacy to whomsoever answers that description at the date of Andrew's death, in the event the elder child of Christine;

ii) 'my record collection to my wife, Beryl', is a specific legacy which, on the facts, raises the question as to what happens when specific assets are replaced by substantially similar assets;

iii) 'my 5,000 shares in Esso Petroleum Ltd to my daughter Christine' is also a specific legacy, which has to be considered in the light of the option given to Eric;

iv) 'the residue of my estate to my son, Dorian' is a residuary gift, which will comprise all the remainder of Andrew's realty and personalty.

The sum of £10,000 will be treated as a vested gift for the benefit of Christine's elder child; as the recipient is a minor the child cannot give a valid receipt for it. Provided the will contains a receipt clause it will, however, be possible for the parent or guardian (Christine) of the child to give a valid receipt to Andrew's executors so as to discharge them from their administrative responsibilities. The child would itself have been able to give a receipt, if the will so allowed, on reaching the age of 16. If the child were to die under the age of 18, because the gift is vested, the £10,000 would pass through the child's estate.

The record collection which Andrew held at the time of his will was sold and replaced by the collection of compact discs containing substantially the same music. This will not cause an ademption. A will speaks from death so far as the property of the testator is concerned, unless there is a contrary intention shown in the will: see s24 Wills Act 1837; and see also the effect of *Re Tetsall* [1961] 1 WLR 938, and *Bothamley v Sherson* (1875) LR 20 Eq 304. Unless there is some evidence that Andrew intended only the record collection in his possession at the time of his will (which appears not to be the case) to go to Beryl, then Beryl will be entitled to the replacement collection. It would have been otherwise if the new collection was different in substance: that would have led to an ademption.

The option given to Eric to purchase the shares which, by Andrew's will, have been bequeathed to Christine raises the question whether the shares pass to Christine or, upon exercise of the option by Eric, to Eric? Is the gift to Christine adeemed?

Under the rule in *Lawes v Bennett* (1785) 1 Cox Eq Cas 167 where an option is exercised (even after the death of the testator) it is treated retrospectively as having been exercised at the date of the grant of the option with the result that the grantee takes the property concerned in priority to the legatee under the will. This extends as much to persons entitled to different types of personalty as it does to persons entitled to personalty and realty. So in *Re Carrington* [1932] 1 Ch 1 the testator bequeathed a holding of preference shares to A and left his residuary personalty to B. Subsequently, he granted an option to C to purchase the shares, the option to be exercised within one month of his death. The Court of Appeal held that the rule in *Lawes v Bennett* should apply so that when exercised the option became retroactive to the date of the grant so that B was entitled to the proceeds of sale.

The rule is subject to a contrary intention (see, for example, *Drant* v *Vause* (1842) 1 Y & CC 580), but that is not sufficiently evident on the facts of the problem here. Accordingly, prima facie the exercise of the option (when duly exercised) will cause the proceeds of sale of the Esso Petroleum shares to pass to the residuary beneficiary Dorian and the gift to Christine to be adeemed.

The fact that Eric is a witness to Andrew's will would mean that if he took a benefit *under* the will he would lose it: s15 Wills Act 1837. But Eric appears not to be taking a benefit under Andrew's will but exercising an option outside the will. Consequently he will not be deprived of the benefit.

Dorian's position as residuary beneficiary, and inheritor of the proceeds of sale of the option property, will be affected by his conviction for the manslaughter of his parents. It is a rule of public policy that a person shall not be allowed to benefit from his crime, whether by murder, manslaughter or any case of unlawful killing: see, for example *Re Giles* [1972] Ch 544 and *Re Callaway* [1956] Ch 559 (judgment of Vaisey J). Unless an order is made relieving the slayer from the effect of the rule, under the Forfeiture Act 1982, he cannot take under the will, or upon intestacy; nor can he make a successful family provision application.

Accordingly, Dorian loses his entitlement as residuary beneficiary. In consequence, the residue is undisposed of by the will of Andrew and falls into intestacy. In the events to be considered, when examining Beryl's estate, it becomes apparent that Beryl has not survived Andrew so that Andrew's intestate estate passes under s46 Administration of Estates Act 1925 to his surviving issue, Christine, Dorian being disqualified from inheriting (as stated above) equally with his sister as he would otherwise have been entitled to do.

In relation to Beryl's estate, she and her husband Andrew have been killed in a common accident with no evidence as to who died first. Under s184 Law of Property Act 1925 where two persons die in circumstances rendering it uncertain as to the order of deaths, known as commorientes, the younger is deemed to have survived the elder. On this basis Andrew has notionally survived Beryl. However, by s46(3) AEA 1925, where the elder of spouses dies intestate (as Beryl has done) the younger spouse is deemed not to have survived the elder.

As a result Beryl's estate does not pass into Andrew's estate and become adminis
as part of it; instead Beryl's estate by-passes Andrew and devolves upon his
the next category of persons entitled – in principle, Christine and Dorian in
on the statutory trusts of the AEA 1925. But, Dorian being disqual
inherits absolutely Beryl's estate.

Chapter 19

Remedies of Creditors and Beneficiaries

19.1 Introduction

19.2 Key points

19.3 Key cases and statutes

19.4 Questions and suggested solutions

19.1 Introduction

This chapter covers the remedies available for the creditors and beneficiaries against the personal representatives of the estate.

19.2 Key points

a) Persons interested may apply to court for an order of administration by the court: includes creditors and beneficiaries.

b) May bring an action for specific relief, in respect of a particular problem.

c) May bring an action against PR.

   i) A PR who breaches his duty commits devastavit.

   ii) PR is personally liable but has certain defences, for example:

   - s27 Trustee Act 1925;

   - s61 Trustee Act 1925;

   - s62 Trustee Act 1925;

   - acquiescence by creditor/beneficiary.

d) May bring an action against the person who has received the goods which were wrongly distributed.

   i) Personal action against recipient will be sufficient if recipient solvent, otherwise: see decision in *Gray* v *Richards Butler* (1996) The Times 23 July.

   Tracing action.

19.3 Key cases and statutes

- *Aldhouse, Re* [1955] 1 WLR 459
  If the advertisements under s27 Trustee Act 1925 are properly n
  representative is protected from personal liability to unpaid bene

- *Kay, Re* [1897] 2 Ch 518
  The personal representative must prove that he acted honestly and reasonably
  where he chooses to rely on s61 Trustee Act 1925

- *Marsden, Re* (1884) 26 Ch D 783
  The onus of proving acquiescence rests on the personal representative

- *Tankard, Re* [1942] Ch 69
  A devastavit may be committed by failing to pay debts and expenses with due
  diligence

- Administration of Justice Act 1985, s48 – allows the PR to rely on the opinion of a
  barrister regarding questions of meaning or interpretation arising out of a will

- Trustee Act 1925, s27 – guidance on advertising for creditors and beneficiaries

- Trustee Act 1925, s61 – excuses the personal representative for a devastavit where he
  acted honestly and reasonably and in all the circumstances ought fairly to be
  excused

- Trustee Act 1925, s62 – if the beneficiary or creditor instigated, requested or
  consented in writing to the breach, the personal representative will be protected
  from liability

19.4 Questions and suggested solutions

QUESTION ONE

Turner, by his will made in 1975, gave a legacy of £6,000 to Edna and the residue of
his estate to the children of Donald. After Turner's death a year ago, his executors
advertised under the Trustee Act for claims against the estate and subsequently paid all
the debts amounting to £40,000 of which they had notice. The executors knew that
Turner had guaranteed a loan to Brian from X Bank Ltd of £20,000 repayable on 1 May
1983, but made no provision for meeting any possible liability. Frank, a child of Donald,
had emigrated to Canada in 1950 and the executors divided the residue between
Graham and Harry, the remaining children of Donald. Graham has now died, insolvent
without assets.

Harry has invested his share of the residue in the purchase of a house.

A month ago, Luke, who never saw the executors' advertisement, proved to them that
Turner owed him £10,000. Brian has been declared bankrupt and the X Bank Ltd has

claimed £20,000 from the executors. Frank has recently returned to England and claims one-third of the residue.

Advise the executors.

University of London LLB Examination
(for External Students) Succession June 1983 Q9

General Comment

This is an excellent question testing the position of the executors vis-à-vis guarantees, unpaid debts and new beneficiaries.

Skeleton Solution

Turner's guarantee – missing beneficiary has reappeared – Turner's debt to Luke.

Suggested Solution

Three problems have arisen through the administration of Turner's estate: (1) the X Bank Ltd is claiming £20,000 under a guarantee given by Turner on a loan of that sum to Brian; (2) Frank who could not be found at the date of distribution, has reappeared and is claiming his share; and (3) Luke has just discovered the s27 advertisements and is seeking payment of his £10,000 debt owed by Turner.

As the executors knew that Turner had guaranteed the £20,000 loan given to Brian by X Bank Ltd they should have made some provision for it. Two courses are open to executors when possible future liabilities may arise. They may apply to the court for directions or, distribute without an order of the court. If the former course is adopted then the court's order will protect the executors from personal liability provided they have made a disclosure of all information and acted in accordance with the court order. Thus, in *Re King* [1907] 1 Ch 72 there was a possible future liability on some shares which had not been fully paid up and an order of the court that distribution be made to the beneficiaries exonerated the personal representatives from liability to the company. If the executors did not obtain an order then they are liable to X Bank Ltd to the extent of the assets they have distributed: see *Taylor* v *Taylor* (1870) LR 10 Eq 477. In the circumstances the executors could recover whatever they can from the beneficiaries to protect themselves against this liability arising. Assuming that the executors can claim against the beneficiaries, to recover anything from Graham's estate would be a waste of time and money as he died insolvent without assets. The executors could not recover the full £20,000 from Harry's share or a part of it from the residuary gift (unless the residue was small) because they are only entitled to recover from each beneficiary the sum he was properly liable to bear: see *Gillespie* v *Alexander* (1827) 3 Russ 130. The executors could raise some defences to X Bank Ltd's claim such as s61 Trustee Act, ie that they had acted honestly and reasonably or plene administravit, but if they did not seek the court's directions or set aside a sum to meet the liability, it is difficult to see how such a defence could succeed.

As regards the second problem, namely Frank's claim to a share of the residuary estate, the position was that the executors could not find Frank at the date of distribution. However, they advertised for claims against the estate under s27 Trustee Act. This provision covers both claims by creditors and beneficiaries: see *Re Aldhous* [1955] 1 WLR 459. However, such advertisements would not protect them against Frank's claim because the purpose of s27 is to ascertain persons who are unknown to the executors, it has no application to known persons who cannot be found even if they do not respond to the advertisement: see *Re Land Credit Company of Ireland* (1872) 21 WR 1351. In such circumstances the executors should have, after their enquiries amongst the family, applied to the court for leave to distribute under a 'Benjamin order'. This type of order would have allowed the executors to distribute on the footing set out in the order, for example, that Frank had died before Turner, unmarried and without issue. As this does not appear to have been done the position is that the residue after deduction of the outstanding debts. The options open to the executors in these circumstances are for them to plead either s61 Trustee Act or plene administravit in defence, which are unlikely to succeed or, alternatively, to try and recover from the overpaid beneficiaries what they can, excepting Graham's estate, which, as stated, is not worth suing.

The third problem is the £10,000 owed to Luke who has just come across the s27 advertisements. The executors will be personally liable for this debt if the s27 advertisements were incorrectly made of if they had distributed before the time limits set down for bringing in claims in the advertisement. However, if these advertisements were correctly made and observed, Luke will not have any personal claim against the executors (see s27(2)), his only remedy will be to recover his debt from those who have been overpaid or wrongly paid: see *Ministry of Health* v *Simpson* [1951] AC 251.

QUESTION TWO

a) Steven died this year, leaving a will which read 'The will of Steven Smith, I instruct my solicitors Bently and Clyde after discharging all liabilities of my estate to divide whatever remains between my nephews.'

   At the date of the will, there were two partners in Bently and Clyde; both died just after Smith and the practice is now carried on by two other solicitors. Smith left three nephews, aged 13, 15 and 20.

   Advise on the obtaining of a grant of representation to the estate of Steven Smith.

b) Gavin, who died in 1981, was thought to have died intestate. His only surviving relations were his nieces, Alice, Betty and Cara. Alice obtained a grant of administration, sold and conveyed Gavin's house to Richard for £80,000 paid all debts and duties and divided the remainder of the estate amongst Betty, Cara and herself.

A will made by Gavin has now been discovered appointing Ernest his executor and giving the house to Fred, and the rest of the estate to Gary. Cara has died without any assets. Betty bought a house with her share of the estate but is now insolvent and is being made bankrupt.

Advise Ernest as to his rights and duties.

University of London LLB Examination
(for External Students) Succession June 1985 Q9

General Comment

A mixed question covering the appointment of executors and in part (b) the rules on revocation of grant and the protection of personal representatives. This question also includes the examiner's favourite topic of tracing. None of the rules are particularly difficult and in spite of the length of the question should pose no problems.

Skeleton Solution

a) Who has been appointed an executor? – grant of letters of administration will be annexed – r20 NCPR 1987.

b) Revocation of grant – protection of purchasers – protection of personal representative who acted under revoked grant – recovery of assets from recipients – tracing.

Suggested Solution

a) If a testator purports to appoint a firm as his executor, the appointment is construed as an appointment of those persons who are partners in the firm at the date of death. The only two such partners are dead. The replacement partners are not treated as having been appointed. There are, therefore, no executors to obtain probate.

The appointment of the firm was not an express appointment. However, if a person is asked to carry out duties which are part of an executor's office, that is treated as an implied appointment. (*In the Goods of Cook* [1902] P 115 – a person directed to pay debts – held to be an implied appointment of the person as executor.)

As there is a will, but no executors, there must be a grant of 'letters of administration with will annexed'. Rule 20 of the Non-Contentious Probate Rules 1987 sets out in what priority people can apply for the grant. The first category that is relevant to these facts is category (iv) ie the ultimate residuary beneficiaries, ie the nephews. Only an adult can take a grant. There is only one adult nephew. In this case he cannot take a grant alone. Where there is a minority interest involved (ie the two other nephews) a grant of administration must be made to two administrators: s114(2) Supreme Court 1981.

Therefore, someone else must join in the application for the grant. Rule 23 of the 1987 Rules sets out the provisions for joining another person in the application for a grant. A suitable provision would seem to be r23(2)(b), which allows joinder of a person nominated by the guardian of an infant who would, but for his infancy, be entitled to a grant.

So a guardian of an infant nephew can appoint someone to apply for the grant with the adult nephew.

b) Ernest has been appointed as executor. He does not have to accept the appointment. He can renounce the right, by filing a form at the Registry.

If he does wish to act, he must apply for revocation on the grant of letters of administration, and for the grant of probate of the will to him. The fact that a will has been recovered is a ground for applying for revocation.

He must consider to what extent he can recover the assets. It is unlikely that he can recover the house from Richard. He is protected by s37 of Administration of Estates Act 1925. This provides that a conveyance made to a purchaser by a person to whom a grant has been made is valid notwithstanding the subsequent revocation of the grant. Richard must have been a purchaser for value in good faith. There is no reason here to doubt his good faith.

Ernest may consider an action against Alice herself. She, however, is protected by s27(1) of the Trustee Act 1925. This provides that a person making a payment or disposition in good faith under a grant is indemnified and protected, notwithstanding anything affecting the validity of the grant. This seems to apply to paying the debts, conveying to a purchaser, or distributing the assets to the 'beneficiaries'. This protection will not apply to any disposition made by Alice after she had reason to doubt the validity of the grant to her: *Guardian Trust and Executors Company of New Zealand Ltd* v *Public Trustee of New Zealand* [1942] AC 115.

The 'beneficiaries' who have been wrongly given the assets have no such protection. Ernest has the right, on behalf of the beneficiaries under the will, to claim refund from Alice, Betty and Cara of the property wrongfully distributed to them. It seems the action could succeed against Alice, who appears to be solvent. There is no point in pursuing the claim against Cara's estate, as there are no assets. An action against Betty for a refund may not be fully successful, as she is bankrupt, and there may not be sufficient assets to make full repayment.

Ernest also has the right to trace. This may be relevant in the case of Betty, as if he can identify any property as representing the assets wrongly received, he has first claim on that property, in preference to the other creditors.

The money cannot be traced, as it has not come into the hands of a bona fide purchaser for value without notice – ie the vendor of the house. He may also be able to trace into the house.

The right to the refund cannot be used until the prime remedy against Alice has been exhausted: *Re Diplock* [1948] Ch 465. But Alice seems to have a defence against any personal action against her based on her action as personal representative. She is only liable to refund the assets she wrongly took as 'beneficiary'.

Ernest should pursue whatever effective remedies he has to recover the assets, or a refund from those able to make one.

QUESTION THREE

a) 'The liability of a personal representative is normally limited to the value of the assets which have come into his hands, but exceptionally he may be liable to a greater extent.' Explain and comment.

b) Robert, who died in 1985, by his will made in 1970 bequeathed his shares in X Ltd in trust for such of the children of his sister Prudence as attained 21, and gave all the rest of his property to his brother Basil.

Prudence went with her husband and her child aged two to Australia in 1975 and no member of her family has heard anything of her or the child since 1980. Robert's executors wish to distribute the estate.

Advise them.

University of London LLB Examination
(for External Students) Succession June 1986 Q8

General Comment

A very good question that explores the potential rights/liabilities of personal representatives. There are few complexities to be concerned with and much of the question can be answered with the application of the basic rules.

Skeleton Solution

a) Explain representative liability, and the possible exceptions to it.

b) Section 27 Trustee Act 1925 and why it is unsatisfactory – a Benjamin Order.

Suggested Solution

a) A personal representative has a duty to pay the debts of the deceased with due diligence: *Re Tankard* [1942] Ch 69. However, the duty exists only to the extent that he has assets of the deceased under his control which are properly applicable for that purpose.

If there are no assets available for the payment of the debts, the personal representative is not under a duty to use his own assets to pay the debts.

Exceptionally, a personal representative may have to use his own assets to satisfy a creditor's claim. This will be because for some reason he has become *personally* liable, rather than liable in his representative capacity.

This could arise if he is carrying on the deceased's business, even if he is carrying it on with the authority, of the will. If he enters into a contract, say for the sale of the goods produced by the business or for purchase of stock, he is the contracting party and may be personally sued, and his own assets seized, if he fails to honour the contract. The only mitigation is that he may be entitled to an indemnity from the deceased's estate.

Personal liability can also arise if the personal representative succeeds to the deceased's leasehold. He is liable in his representative capacity for rent unpaid at the deceased's death, and for rent following due thereafter, before he arranges the lease. He is similarly due for breaches of covenant. This liability is limited to the assets he has had in his hands. However, if he actually enters into possession, he becomes personally liable as the new tenant of the landlord, and his own assets are at risk. However, he will again not be liable for rent falling due after he has assigned the lease.

Even though a personal representative is not personally liable, the protection is that the amount he has had in his hands provides the maximum amount of his liability. He could still be personally liable if he has improperly parted with those assets. Suppose, for example, he has £1,000 of the deceased's property under his control. Instead of paying a debt with the money, he distributes it to the beneficiary. The representative will be personally liable to the creditor to the maximum of £1,000 because he has had that amount in his hands. This situation should rarely arise, because of the protection of s27 Trustee Act 1925, but could arise, eg in the case of a contingent debt which unexpectedly becomes payable. In the case of a contingent debt, the personal representative would then have a right to be indemnified by the beneficiaries.

b) The gift in the will is a class gift. The executors know of the existence of one potential beneficiary. They have no idea of whether or not there are other children.

If they ignore the possibility of there being children who reach 21, and distribute all the property to Basil, they run the risk of committing a devastavit.

Section 27 Trustee Act 1925 might provide them with a defence against any children other than the one they know existed. Section 27 is usually thought of in the context of a defence against unpaid creditors, but it also protects a personal representative who has distributed the costs in ignorance of the existence of a beneficiary with a better claim: *Re Aldhous* [1955] 1 WLR 459. Section 27 provides that if a personal representative advertises for claimants against the estate (the advertisements are prescribed by s27), he may, after the expiration of the stated time for claims to be sent in, distribute to the persons entitled having regard only to the claim of which he has notice.

Section 27 is not going to be of great assistance in this case, as the executors do actually know of the existence of a child, and s27 cannot protect them in respect of that child.

The executors could apply to the court for directions. They cannot be liable for a devastavit if they distribute in accordance with these directions. After ordering appropriate searches, enquiries and advertisements for the missing beneficiaries, the court may give directions to the executors to distribute on the footing set out in the order. The order could direct distribution on the footing that Prudence is now dead, and that all her children have died without reaching the age of 21.

This would make distribution of the entire estate to Basil possible.

Chapter 20

Taxation

20.1 **Introduction**

20.2 **Key points**

20.2 **Key statutes**

20.3 **Questions and suggested solutions**

20.1 Introduction

This chapter deals with the taxation of estates on death. The most significant tax on death, inheritance tax, is considered fully. Of course, the tax thresholds will change from financial year to year so it is important to keep up to date. The principles and law are much more static.

20.2 Key points

a) *Inheritance tax*

  i) Introduction

   • Inheritance Tax Act (IHTA) 1984.

   • Charged on cumulative total of the persons 'transfers of value' in excess of nil rate band.

   • Death is deemed final transfer of value.

   • Tax is charged on: (i) assets of deceased on death; and (ii) lifetime gifts made within seven years.

   • Tax threshold: Current nil band £250,000.

2001/02	2002/03	Rate
£242,000	£250,000	Nil
More than £242,000	More than £250,000	40%

  ii) For the purposes of IHT there are three types of lifetime transfers.

   • Potentially exempt transfers (PETs): lifetime gifts not taxed if transferor survives gifts by seven years.

Years	0–3	3–4	4–5	5–6	6–7	7 and above
Rate	100%	80%	60%	40%	20%	0%

Note that gifts with reservation are deemed never to have been made and are therefore taxable. Definition: s102 Finance Act 1986. Note also the exceptions in s102.

- Chargeable transfers: gifts to discretionary trusts or to companies.

- Exempt transfers (see below).

Exempt transferees

1. Spouses – s18 IHTA 1984
   – note conditions.

2. Charities – s23 IHTA 1984
   – note conditions.

3. Gift for national purpose/public benefit – ss25, 26 IHTA 1984.

4. Political parties – s24 IHTA 1984
   – note definition.

5. Gifts to employee trusts.

6. Death on active service exemption (ie servicemen).

Limited lifetime gifts

1. Annual exemption – £3,000 – s19 IHTA 1984 – can be carried forward for one year only.

2. Small gifts – £250 – s20 IHTA 1984.

3. Gifts on marriage:

   Parents – £5,000 – s22 IHTA 1984;

   Grandparents or remote relatives – £2,500 – s22 IHTA 1984;

   Others – £1,000 – s22 IHTA 1984.

4. Normal expenditure out of income – s21 IHTA 1984.

5. Gifts for the maintenance of the family (ie spouse, ex spouse, maintenance of children).

iii) Reliefs

Business property – IHTA 1984, s103–114

1. *Conditions*:

   i) own business two years immediately before transfer;

   ii) NB retention of ownership qualification;

   iii) investment and property dealing businesses are excluded.

Agriculture property – IHTA 1984, s115–124A

1. *Conditions*: Either the transferor/ company controlled by him:

   i) occupied property for agricultural purpose for at lease seven years, or has been owned for seven years with others farming it.

   ii) owned property seven years ending with date of transfer and occupied by himself or another for agricultural purposes.

2. *Relief*:

 - 100% where transferor is sole proprietor, partner, controlled unquoted shares of trading company, unquoted shares in other company giving transferor more than 25% of votes.

 - 50% relief if minority holding in unquoted shares, quoted shares in trading company controlled immediately before transfer, land, building and machinery used by company.

3. Beneficiary who inherits business deemed owned it from date of death.

iv) Excepted estates

Qualify provided:

1. deceased domiciled in UK;

2. total gross value of estate (before deduction of debts and lifetime gifts specified below) does not exceed £180,000;

3. the estate consists only of property which has passed under D's will/intestacy/nomination, or beneficially by survivorship;

4. estate assets outside the UK do not exceed £30,000; and

5. any taxable lifetime transfers made within seven years of D's death consisted of cash, quoted shares/securities and did not exceed £50,000.

iii) NB retention of ownership qualification.

2. *Relief*:

 - 100% reduction if transferor had vacant possession or right to obtain it within 12 months of transfer.

 - 50% for other cases.

Non-qualifying estates:

1. where D made a PET as a chargeable transfer within seven years other than of cash or quoted shares/securities;

2. where D made a gift with a reservation of benefit which continued until death or ceased within seven years of death;

3. where D enjoyed an interest in possession in settled property at, or within, seven years of death.

v) Settlements:

Interest in possession – IHTA 1984, s49 et seq

Without interest in possession – IHTA 1984, s58 et seq

ie right to receive immediate income.

eg income accumulated or discretionary trust.

- if interest in possession changes, tax is charged.

- Every ten years, trust fund is taxed at 6% of its value after deducting nil-rate tax band.

- Accumulation and maintenance trusts – no charge to tax when person becomes entitled in possession.

b) Income tax – Income and Corporation Taxes Act 1988, s695 et seq

Principles governing income tax during period of administration.

i) Types of taxable income: interest on bank and building society accounts; dividends and interest from stock exchange/securities; profits from business; profit from any land let.

ii) Personal Representatives (PRs) constitute single continuing body of persons.

iii) All income generally taxable at basic rate. For PRs – basic rate of 25 per cent, no personal allowance/relief, no higher or lower rates.

iv) Net income is paid to beneficiaries. Note situations when payments are subject to deduction and paid gross.

c) Capital gains tax

i) Tax on the difference between price at which asset is acquired and value at which it is disposed of.

ii) Deemed to dispose of all assets on death.

iii) Where devolve on PRs, they acquire the assets at their value on date of death – but not liable for CGT.

iv) If PR sells asset at value higher than the value of the assets acquired at death – liable to 25 per cent tax on the gain (deducting all incidental expenses of sale). Note: annual exemption of £7,700 (2002/2003).

v) If PR distributes assets to beneficiaries, PR not liable for CGT. Note: s60 Taxation of Chargeable Gains Act 1992.

vi) Beneficiaries deemed to acquire assets at their market value at date of death (note: expenses incurred added to acquisition value of assets).

vii)Note: deeds of variation.

d) Tax planning

i) This is essential as considerable tax savings can be achieved, but the first objective is to ascertain the testator's wishes in distributing his estate.

ii) Pre-death planning can be made when advising a testator. For example, use of exemptions, ie exempt transferees, nil-rate tax band and use of reliefs on business and agricultural property. It is of no use if testator's spouse is given business property and £250,000 to his son, as the relief is wasted on the spouse who is exempted from tax.

iii) Post-death, various opportunities can be used.

- Section 142 Inheritance Tax Act 1984: sui juris beneficiary can vary/disclaim his interest in such a way that it is treated as having been effected by the deceased – limited to deceased's free estate. For capital gains tax: s62(6)–(10) Taxation of Chargeable Gains Act 1992.

- Section 4(2) Inheritance Tax Act 1984: spouses deemed to have died at same instance. But spouse's exemption is utilised as the estate of elder spouse passes to surviving spouse momentarily. Therefore, estate of elder spouse passes direct to the contingent beneficiaries free of inheritance tax – provided there is no survival clause in will.

- Discretionary trusts: s144 Inheritance Tax Act 1984 – where a discretionary trust is created giving the trustees widest power of appointment among a class of persons whom the testator wishes to benefit. If distribution is made within two years of death, no charge to inheritance tax. Note: there are other advantages of discretionary trusts.

20.3 Key statutes

- Inheritance Tax Act 1984 – provides the rules for taxes on death

- Taxation of Chargeable Gains Act 1992 – contains the main provisions on capital gains tax

20.4 Questions and suggested solutions

QUESTION ONE

On 1 May 2002 Arthur, who was a wealthy man, gave £3,000 to his friend Barbara. The following month he made a gift of £6,000 to his daughter Claire who was engaged to be married. The money was to assist Claire in the purchase of a flat. A few weeks before the marriage was due to take place David, Claire's fiancé, broke off the engagement, and the marriage did not take place. After the engagement was broken

Arthur gave Claire a valuable necklace to cheer her up and also paid her outstanding bill of £5,000 at Harrods.

In September Arthur settled property valued at £400,000 on discretionary trust for his children and grandchildren. He then granted to his son Edward a ten-year lease at market value of a freehold property, Whiteacre, which was worth £50,000. Arthur died suddenly in December 1991. In his will he gave £100,000 and the freehold reversion of Whiteacre to Edward and the rest of his property to his daughter.

Discuss.

> Adapted from University of London LLB Examination
> (for External Students) Revenue Law June 1989 Q7

General Comment

This is a simple question requiring a basic knowledge of a broad range of possible tax implications on a number of gifts.

Skeleton Solution

IHT – gift in consideration of marriage – PET implications: s22 – small gifts – discretionary settlement – IHT periodic charge and exit charge regime.

Suggested Solution

Arthur makes a series of gifts and transfers during the fiscal year 2001/02 up until his death in December 2001. Thus it must be considered, for inheritance tax (IHT) purposes, which of the given transactions will be seen as chargeable transfers and, of those, which are potentially exempt and which are chargeable immediately.

In order to be classed as a chargeable transfer, each transfer made by Arthur must be one of value (s2(1) Inheritance Tax Act (IHTA) 1984); ie, it must reduce the value of Arthur's estate: s3(1).

The outright gift of £3,000 to Barbara is a transfer of value and, if Arthur had made no other such transfers in 2001/02, would be exempt under s19 as the annual exemption for IHTA purposes. However, since Arthur makes further transfers in 2001/02 his s19 exemption is unlikely to be applied to this particular gift, because up until Arthur's death it is a potentially exempt transfer under s3A. Nevertheless, upon Arthur's death it will be treated as a chargeable transfer made in May 2001.

The gift to Arthur's daughter Claire would presumably, at the time of making the gift, constitute a gift in consideration of the marriage, up to the limit of £5,000 under s22. The remaining £1,000 would simply be a potentially exempt transfer (PET), as with the £3,000 given to Barbara. Thus if Arthur had died more than seven years after making these PETS no charge to IHT would have arisen.

However, since the marriage fails to take place, the marriage gift is likely to fall foul of s22: see *Re Park (Deceased) (No 2)* [1972] Ch 385. If this is so then the whole £6,000 will be a PET and become a chargeable transfer made in June 2001.

The valuable necklace given to Claire might be exempt under s20 as a small gift if its value does not exceed £250. If, however, it has a greater value it will again be a PET becoming a chargeable transfer upon Arthur's death. The payment of Claire's bill of £5,000 will also constitute a PET.

The discretionary trust worth £400,000 will be treated as a settlement by Arthur under s43. Since the trust is a discretionary one, it will be governed by ss58–85 for IHT so that on each ten-year anniversary of the commencement of the settlement there will be a periodic charge to tax at 30 per cent of the rate which would have been charged had the property been the subject of one single transfer. Any property leaving the trust under s65 between these ten-year periods will be charged in proportion to the time it remained in the trust from the date of the last periodic charge.

The grant of a lease at market value to Arthur's son Edward will have no effect for IHT purposes since it does not constitute a transfer of value under s2(1).

The £100,000 bequeathed to Edward in Arthur's will would come within s4(1) and thus be treated as though Arthur made a transfer of value of £100,000 immediately preceding his death. This will be added to all of Arthur's lifetime transfers which we will assume are all those made since 1 May 2001: namely £3,000 to Barbara, £6,000 plus a necklace and £5000 to Claire, and £400,000 settled in a discretionary trust. Edward's reversionary interest will be treated as being worth £50,000. £3,000 will be deducted from the total, being Arthur's s19 annual exemption, and the remainder will be chargeable to Inheritance Tax at a rate of 40 per cent. No tapering relief will be available since all the transfers were made in the year of death. However, the first £242,000 (£250,000 from 2002/03) of the chargeable transfers made by Arthur will not attract IHT. Of course, if Arthur made no lifetime gifts in the previous tax year, he would be entitled to carry that exemption forward for this tax year.

QUESTION TWO

Ian was an elderly widower. When Ian's wife died two years ago he gave his house, Oaklands, which was then valued at £200,000, to his son Harold. In June 2001 Ian gave his holiday flat in Spain, which was worth £70,000, to his other son, Jack. Unbeknown to Harold, in July 2001 Ian paid the credit card debts of £1,000 which had been incurred by Harold's son, Luke, who is a university student. Ian then bought a holiday in Wales for his sister-in-law which cost £1,000. Ian gave his daughter, Kathryn, three of his antique dining chairs as her birthday present in September 2001. These were part of a set of six chairs. Ian promised that he would give Kathryn the remaining three chairs later. Ian became seriously ill at the end of September 2001 and Harold, worried about his father living alone, invited Ian to move back into Oaklands to live with Harold and his family. Ian did this and remained there for two months. In March 2002 Ian was killed in a road accident. By then the value of Oaklands was £500,000. Ian's estate was valued at £350,000. Ian had failed to make a will.

Advise the administrators of Ian's estate on the inheritance tax position.

Adapted from University of London LLB Examination
(for External Students) Revenue Law June 1992 Q7

General Comment

This question deals with an intestacy and the tax implications arising out of a number of lifetime gifts. Detailed knowledge of the rules on lifetime transfers, including the reservation of benefits, is crucial.

Skeleton Solution

Gift of Oaklands to son: £200,000; PET, no reservation of benefit – June 2001: gift of flat to son; £70,000, PET – discharge of nephew's credit card bill £1,000: annual exemption applies – Wales holiday for sister-in-law £1,000: annual exemption – gift of antique chairs, part of set – promise of remainder of set – reservation of benefit? – death of Ian March 2002: estate valued £350,000, intestate; PETs chargeable – liability for payment of tax.

Suggested Solution

Note: All references are to the Inheritance Tax Act (IHTA) 1984 unless otherwise stated.

Ian's death in March 2002 will mean a charge to inheritance tax not only on the declared estate of £350,000 but also on certain additional amounts gifted by Ian during his life.

Lifetime transfers which, at the time the gift was made, have qualified as potentially exempt transfers (PETs) (s3A) remain exempt only if the donor has survived seven years from the date of the gift or transfer.

Ian has survived less than one year since the gifts were made, and therefore not only are the PETs brought into account in calculating the amount of inheritance tax (IHT) due but also there is no reduction in the rate of tax chargeable for survival of more than three years from the date of gift.

The lifetime transfers would be treated as follows:

a) The gift of Oaklands at £200,000 value would have qualified as a PET, as would the gift of the flat at a value of £70,000.

b) The discharge of the credit card bill and the payment made for a holiday in Wales total together £2,000, which is less than the annual exemption limit under s19(1). These would be ignored in any future calculations.

c) The gift of the antique chairs, not being a sale for full consideration, would be treated as a PET but valued at half the value of the complete set and not at the value of three individual items. Inheritance tax is based on the amount by which the donor's estate has been reduced.

On the death of Ian, his £350,000 is the starting point for the calculation of tax, which is charged at the death rate of 40 per cent: s7.

To this figure are added the values of the PETs as at the time the gifts were made, and not at their value at the date of death, giving a total estate chargeable to tax.

In calculating the amount of tax payable, the rate of tax at death (40 per cent) is applied to the PETs after deducting the nil rate band or tax-free band of estate amounting to £242,000 for tax year 2001/2002. If any other transfers were made by Ian in the previous seven years, these must also be brought back into the calculations.

Tax is then calculated on the value of the other estate at death, and the resulting tax represents, when added to the tax on the PETs, the total IHT payable.

Incidence of tax

The total tax payable on the estate and PETs is averaged over the total amounts chargeable to IHT, to provide an average rate of IHT which can be apportioned to each as an overall percentage rate of tax applicable to assets where it was necessary to apportion the tax for payment – for example to specific legatees or where property was gifted to a donee but the deceased retained a benefit from the gift.

However, such overall averaging is not appropriate for PETs since the tax payable by the donees is the amount of the recalculated tax which would otherwise have been payable during life but is now payable on death.

Responsibility for IHT

It is the duty of the personal representatives to deliver an Inland Revenue account within 12 months of Ian's month of death, ie by 31 March 2003. However, as interest on IHT is payable from six months after the month in which death occurs, ie from 30 September 2000, the making of a return as soon as possible is advisable. Tax relating to landed property can be payable in ten annual instalments, subject to a charge to interest on the tax outstanding.

The responsibility for payment of tax is primarily that of the personal representatives and is personal, extending to the assets owned beneficially by Ian at the time of his death and therefore limited in general to the assets received or taken over by the personal representatives. For PETs now subject to tax the donee is primarily responsible for payment of the IHT now due, failing payment of which after 12 months the personal representatives become liable. This would also be the case if tax was now due in a situation where a 'reservation of benefit' had been withheld by Ian on any gift made.

Reservation of benefit

In the case of the gift of Oaklands there is potentially a reservation of benefit which would have adverse consequences on the IHT payable on Ian's death. If reservation of benefit has occurred, tax is then payable on death at the full value of the property at the date of death and not, as in the case of it being a PET, at the value at the date of gift.

In normal circumstances, to avoid a reservation of benefit situation the donor has to be excluded from benefit at any time during the period beginning with the gift and ending with the death. The legislation uses the phrase (in s102 Finance Act 1986) 'virtually to the entire exclusion' of the donor. However, Sch 20 para 6 of the same Act provides relief on a change of circumstances of the donor resulting in the donor being unable to look after himself through old age or infirmity. This would be sufficient in Ian's case to avoid the reservation of benefit rules applying, since he also satisfies the 'relation' requirement of the section.

QUESTION THREE

Georgina was informed by her doctor last year that she was terminally ill. Although she had made some gifts in the previous years she had retained most of her wealth. During 2001 therefore she decided to make a series of gifts and settlements.

i) On the same day in April she gave £3,000 each to her two nephews who came to visit her;

ii) In May she settled shares valued at £300,000 on discretionary trusts for a wide range of beneficiaries including family and friends;

iii) Also in May she gave £10,000 to her favourite charity;

iv) In June she settled property on trust for her son for life remainder to his grandchildren if they should attain the age of 23;

v) She paid £1,000 fine for a VAT offence.

Georgina died on 1 January 2002.

Advise on the inheritance tax position.

> Adapted from University of London LLB Examination
> (for External Students) Revenue Law June 1994 Q7

General Comment

This question is yet another standard tax question examining the inheritance tax implications of lifetime gifts.

Skeleton Solution

Exempt and chargeable transfers – s2 – the charge on death – s4 – annual exempt amounts: s19 – transfer to discretionary trusts: not a s3A potentially exempt transfer (PET) – revision of tax charge on death: s7(2) – exemption for charity gift: s23 – interest in possession trust; treatment on creation; s3A – VAT fine – reduction of estate.

Suggested Solution

Note: All references are to the Inheritance Tax Act (IHTA) 1984 unless otherwise stated.

Inheritance tax (IHT) is charged on the value of assets comprising chargeable transfers. A chargeable transfer is other than an exempt transfer. Under s3A certain transfers of value are to be regarded as potentially exempt from IHT, but under s3A(4) only one potentially exempt transfer (PET) which is made 'seven years or more before the death of the transferor is an exempt transfer ...'. Hence all transfers of value made within seven years of death are within the charge to IHT.

In addition to the specified gifts mentioned in the facts of the question, reference is also made to Georgina having made some gifts in the previous years. Those which exceeded the annual exempt allowance, currently at £3,000, or were not otherwise exempt (ie falling within any of the exemptions of ss18–28), would be treated as chargeable transfers of value. The amount of such chargeable transfers of value would reduce the estate 'nil rate' figure (for 2001/2002) of £242,000 – Schedule 1 – available to reduce the charge on Georgina's estate. To the extent that these occurred more than seven years before her death they would be ignored when determining the amount by which the £242,000 had been reduced during her lifetime.

i) The exact date of the two gifts of £3,000 is not given but is assumed to be after 6 April for the purpose of the following.

The gifts of £3,000 to each of her two nephews would initially be considered for allocation of the annual exemption of £3,000 under s19. Because the £3,000 figure is exceeded the excess has to be dealt with for possible exemption under s19(3) and (3A). Under s19(3)(b) each gift would be partly exempt by the same amount of £1,500 since they were made on the same day. However, since they comprise gifts which would be potentially exempt transfers under s3A, they are initially not dealt with in allocating the annual exemption and are exempted at the time of transfer. Because other chargeable transfers are made later in the year which are not exempt, when Georgina dies these gifts of £3,000 will become fully chargeable: s19(3A)(b). It would have been beneficial to make the gifts separately – one before 6 April and one after – so that at least one would have gained the permanence of an annual exemption without it becoming chargeable on death.

ii) The settling of shares of £300,000 on discretionary trusts is a transfer of value but one which does not qualify for treatment as a PET under s3A. Only accumulation and maintenance settlements and those giving an interest in possession to the beneficiaries are within the PET regime – s49 treats the beneficiary of an IIP trust as beneficially entitled to the trust property which is consequently comprised in the beneficiary's estate and therefore within the s3A(2) exemption. However, there is no such beneficial interest for the beneficiaries of a discretionary trust and therefore the transfer of property which Georgina has made is not a PET. Tax would therefore be chargeable at the time of making the transfer. The £242,000 nil rate band would apply to part of the transfer, with tax at 20 per cent on the remainder.

Thereafter the discretionary trust trustees would be subject to the 'periodic charge' to inheritance tax under s58 et seq on each ten-year anniversary of the creation of the trust. However, at the date of Georgina's death the tax charge must include a revision of tax on all chargeable transfers made within the seven years prior to her death. This would include a recalculation of the 20 per cent lifetime rate to the 40 per cent rate on death in respect of the discretionary trust property: s7(2).

iii) A gift to charity which is absolute and unconditional, as appears to be the case in Georgina's gift to her favourite charity, is exempt from any charge to inheritance tax. That exemption does need to await the expiry of the PET seven-year period, but takes on the status of an exempt transfer, which keeps it beyond the scope of the main charging provision of s2 which catches only transfers of value other than exempt transfers.

iv) The creation of a trust for the duration of her son's life is an interest in possession trust and, as mentioned in (ii) above, a potentially exempt transfer. There is no charge to IHT immediately it is created and the trust is not subject to the periodic charge to which discretionary trusts are subject. However, the value of the property – the relevant value being that at the date of the creation of the trust – would be treated as still comprised in Georgina's estate at the date of her death and tax would be assessed accordingly, for payment by the trustees: s200(1)(b).

v) The payment by Georgina of £1,000 for a VAT offence represents monies paid out of her estate and therefore value which has passed out of her estate. Not being a recoverable amount there would be no addition made to her chargeable estate to increase it for this amount. Section 5 makes provision for the deduction of certain liabilities incurred before death, or other taxes arising on the transfers on death, but does not limit the deduction of liabilities already incurred and paid by the deceased.

QUESTION FOUR

EITHER

a) To what extent do you consider that the rules concerning the payment of debts of solvent estates need clarification and reform?

OR

b) Jim, a wealthy farmer and enthusiastic contributor of funds to the Conservative Party, comes to see you about making a will. He wishes to leave the bulk of his property between his wife and two children and a legacy to the Conservative Party. He asks you to explain *in outline* the operation of inheritance tax and to indicate how his will might be drafted in a tax efficient manner.

Advise him.

University of London LLB Examination
(for External Students) Succession June 1996 Q7

General Comment

This was an 'either/or' question. The two parts were unconnected, the 'either' question asking the candidate to consider whether the rules for payment of debts on solvent estates need clarification and reform. This is one of the most difficult subject areas of the law of succession and inviting an examination candidate to engage in a law-reform exercise is tough beyond measure! A fairer test of a candidate's ability in this area would have been a problem analysis question … but then every examiner has their own particular preferences!

The alternative 'or' question asked the candidate to explain the operation of inheritance tax and how a will might be drafted in a tax efficient manner. In principle, there is no objection to a question of this type, although it is hardly academic in its scope and must presume that the student has acquired a sufficient grasp of inheritance tax during the course to enable him/her to attempt an answer. Most students dislike answering questions 'in outline' because, rightly, they suspect they may not know how thickly or thinly to spread their knowledge.

Skeleton Solution

a) When an estate is solvent – statutory regulation – contrary intention in will – when implied variation – lapsed shares of residue – case law analysis.

b) Scope of inheritance tax – death charge – lifetime charge – nil rate band – exemptions and reliefs – spouse relief; agricultural relief – planning elements.

Suggested Solution

a) A deceased's estate is solvent if the assets are sufficient to discharge all funeral, testamentary and administration expenses, debts and liabilities. The beneficiaries under the will receive the net balance of the assets. Rules are necessary to ensure that the burden of the expenses, debts and liabilities are properly regulated because it is in each beneficiary's interest to claim that the burden should not fall on assets to which he or she is entitled.

For over 70 years, as with so much property legislation, the Administration of Estates Act (AEA) 1925 has regulated matters. Section 34(3) AEA 1925 provides for an order of application of assets set out in Pt II, Sch 1 of the Act, listing seven different types of property, the first two of which really hold the key: undisposed of residue (which thereby falls into partial intestacy), and disposed of residue. In both cases, the property is subject to the retention thereout of a fund to meet any pecuniary legacies given by the will.

The order makes no distinction between realty and personalty. All the real and personal property falling within a particular paragraph is therefore liable rateably for the expenses, debts and liabilities of the deceased's estate. There is sound logic in this and it makes for easier administration and application of assets.

Another key feature of the legislation is that the order is subject to any provisions contained in the will. This is as it should be: the testator should be able to direct the source from which the debts are to be paid. This, in practice, in a professionally drawn will, will be achieved by directing the executors to discharge the debts from residue unless the testator has particular reason to prefer that debts be paid from some other source, such as specifically devised, or bequeathed, assets.

Statutory regulation, therefore, assumes something of a fall-back position to cover those situations where a will fails to tackle the manner in which the debts of the deceased should be paid and, secondly, to regulate how any surplus debts should be paid in the event of a primary source directed by the will, such as residue, being inadequate for the purpose.

The present scheme raises a challenge when it has to be determined, as a question of construction, whether the testator has impliedly varied the statutory order. Most of the significant case law deals with lapsed shares of residue and requires a determination as to whether disposed residue, or undisposed residue, should bear the obligation. *Re Harland-Peck* [1941] Ch 182 is illustrative of one type of case; here the testator made certain gifts by her will and then provided that: 'subject to the payment of my funeral and testamentary expenses and debts … I devise and bequeath the residue of my property' to X and Y as tenants in common. Y died before T and his half-share lapsed and went to Z, who was T's next of kin entitled on her intestacy. The Court of Appeal held that the provision in the will varied the statutory order, so that debts were payable from residue as a whole, and not primarily from Y's lapsed share (the first paragraph of the statutory order).

The second type of case, illustrated by *Re Lamb* [1929] 1 Ch 723, is where the testator directs expenses and debts to be paid but does not specify out of what property they are to be paid. This is construed as a direction to pay them in the due course of administration, pursuant to the statutory order – that is, primarily out of any lapsed share of residue.

As Upjohn J said in *Re Meldrum* [1952] Ch 208, it is essentially a matter of construction of the will in each case whether the provisions of the statutory schedule of Pt II AEA 1925 apply, or whether they have been varied by the terms of the will. For instance, in *Re Meldrum* it was held that the statutory order had been varied so that property charged with the payment of debts (paragraph 4) bore the obligation in priority to disposed of residue (paragraph 2); by way of contrast, *Re Gordon* [1940] Ch 769 was a case where the statutory order was held applicable.

In conclusion, it can be asserted that the key to this difficult, complex area of the law of succession does not lie in clarification and reform of the present rules, which, over 70 years, have by and large yielded very few difficulties. No reform can detract from the essence, which is judicial flexibility in construing the terms of testators' wills. This is keenly illustrated by Upjohn J's dictum and the contrasting outcome of cases such as *Re Meldrum* and *Re Gordon*.

b) The advice to Jim, a wealthy farmer, about how his intentions can be carried into effect in a tax efficient manner must depend upon further information being supplied by him about the nature and extent of his assets.

On the information supplied it is possible, however, to explain the operation of inheritance tax and the manner in which it may be possible to effect tax avoidance (as opposed to tax evasion, which is unlawful) by legitimately minimising the impact of the tax.

Jim should be advised that inheritance tax, which is governed by the provisions of the Inheritance Tax Act (IHTA) 1984, effective from March 1986, is raised not only on transfers of assets at death, but also in relation to lifetime dispositions made by Jim less than seven years before his death and which are known as potentially exempt transfers (PETs). If indeed Jim is a wealthy man he may be able to afford giving away some of his assets to his family now: if he survives seven years from the date of the gift no tax will be paid on it, and if he survives between three and seven years from the date of the gift any tax attributable to it will be reduced by process known as 'tapering relief'.

In any event, Jim can be advised that the first £250,000 of a person's chargeable assets qualifies for the Nil Rate Band (NRB) of inheritance tax; this means that, aside from any available exemptions and reliefs, no tax is raised on the first £250,000 of Jim's assets.

Given Jim's position he could be advised to make use of the annual exemption (s19 IHTA 1984), which allows for transfers of value up to £3,000. If the full exemption is not utilised in one year, the unused balance may be carried forward to the next tax year. This means that a sum up to £3,000 could be deducted each year from the value of Jim's assets in calculating the tax on his estate.

Another lifetime exemption in any one tax year would be a gift not exceeding £250 to any one donee in total: s20 IHTA 1984. Jim could make use of this.

Of most significance is that Jim wishes to leave substantial assets to his wife, although the proportions between her and his children remain to be decided. The effect of dispositions made to Jim's wife will mean that the whole value of what is transferred is covered by the surviving spouse exemption: s18 IHTA 1984. This means that whatever Jim leaves to his wife, whether as a lifetime gift, or at death, and whether for a limited or absolute interest, will be an exempt transfer and no inheritance tax will be charged upon it. However, Jim's wife, on her death, will have to pay inheritance tax, in principle, on what she has received from him, unless, in the tax planning of her estate, she is able to reduce the impact of inheritance tax by available exemptions and reliefs.

Jim is a wealthy farmer. Agricultural property relief from inheritance tax (ss115–124A IHTA 1984, as amended by Finance Acts 1995 and 1996) therefore becomes a key feature. A reduction is available of either 100 per cent or 50 per cent in the 'agricultural value' of 'agricultural property'. Agricultural property is essentially agricultural land or pasture in the United Kingdom and the farm buildings used with such land; and agricultural value means the value of such property on the assumption it is subject to a perpetual covenant prohibiting its use otherwise than as agricultural property. Jim must have occupied the agricultural property throughout the two years prior to the transfer (that is, his death), or he must have owned the property throughout the seven years prior to his death. Provided Jim was the owner or tenant in possession the relief will be 100 per cent.

With regard to Jim's wish to make a legacy to the Conservative Party, he should be advised that transfers of value to exempt political parties are entitled to relief in the same way as transfers to charity. A political party qualifies for exemption if it had two members elected to the House of Commons at the last general election, or one member if the party's candidates obtained at least 150,000 votes.

The advice to Jim is that he can substantially arrange his affairs so as to virtually eliminate the prospect of inheritance tax having to be paid on his death. In principle, any lifetime dispositions, not otherwise exempt, would be added to his death estate to calculate liability, but given the following factors Jim's estate will escape tax:

1. availability of £250,000 nil rate band;

2. Jim's occupation as farmer – carrying relief at 100 per cent;

3. gifts on death to Jim's children up to the value of the nil rate band;

4. residue to Jim's wife, carrying the surviving spouse exemption.

As a precautionary measure Jim's will should be drafted so that his wife only inherits if she survives him by 30 days, thereby ensuring that control of his assets is retained within his estate in the event of her not so surviving him.

Law Update 2003 edition – due March 2003

An annual review of the most recent developments in specific legal subject areas, useful for law students at degree and professional levels, others with law elements in their courses and also practitioners seeking a quick update.

Published around March every year, the Law Update summarises the major legal developments during the course of the previous year. In conjunction with Old Bailey Press textbooks it gives the student a significant advantage when revising for examinations.

Contents
Administrative Law • Civil and Criminal Procedure • Commercial Law • Company Law • Conflict of Laws • Constitutional Law • Contract Law • Conveyancing • Criminal Law • Criminology • English and European Legal Systems • Equity and Trusts • European Union Law • Evidence • Family Law • Jurisprudence • Land Law • Law of International Trade • Public International Law • Revenue Law • Succession • Tort

For further information on contents or to place an order, please contact:

Mail Order
Old Bailey Press
at Holborn College
Woolwich Road
Charlton
London
SE7 8LN

Telephone No: 020 8317 6039
Fax No: 020 8317 6004
Website: www.oldbaileypress.co.uk

ISBN 1 85836 477 9
Soft cover 246 x 175 mm
450 pages approx
£10.95
Due March 2003

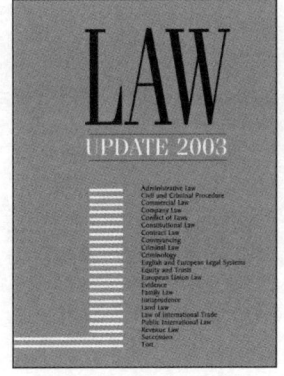

Unannotated Cracknell's Statutes for use in Examinations

New Editions of Cracknell's Statutes

£11.95 due 2002

Cracknell's Statutes provide a comprehensive series of essential statutory provisions for each subject. Amendments are consolidated, avoiding the need to cross-refer to amending legislation. Unannotated, they are suitable for use in examinations, and provide the precise wording of vital Acts of Parliament for the diligent student.

Commercial Law
ISBN: 1 85836 472 8

European Community Legislation
ISBN: 1 85836 470 1

Conflict of Laws
ISBN: 1 85836 473 6

Family Law
ISBN: 1 85836 471 X

Criminal Law
ISBN: 1 85836 474 4

Public International Law
ISBN: 1 85836 476 0

Employment Law
ISBN: 1 85836 475 2

For further information on contents or to place an order, please contact:

Mail Order
Old Bailey Press
at Holborn College
Woolwich Road
Charlton
London
SE7 8LN

Telephone No: 020 8317 6039
Fax No: 020 8317 6004
Website: www.oldbaileypress.co.uk

Suggested Solutions to Past Examination Questions 2000–2001

The Suggested Solutions series provides examples of full answers to the questions regularly set by examiners. Each suggested solution has been broken down into three stages: general comment, skeleton solution and suggested solution. The examination questions included within the text are taken from past examination papers set by the London University. The full opinion answers will undoubtedly assist you with your research and further your understanding and appreciation of the subject in question.

Only £6.95 Due December 2002

Constitutional Law
ISBN: 1 85836 478 7

Jurisprudence and Legal Theory
ISBN: 1 85836 484 1

Criminal Law
ISBN: 1 85836 479 5

Land Law
ISBN: 1 85836 481 7

English Legal System
ISBN: 1 85836 482 5

Law of Tort
ISBN: 1 85836 483 3

Elements of the Law of Contract
ISBN: 1 85836 480 9

For further information on contents or to place an order, please contact:

Mail Order
Old Bailey Press
at Holborn College
Woolwich Road
Charlton
London
SE7 8LN

Telephone No: 020 8317 6039
Fax No: 020 8317 6004
Website: www.oldbaileypress.co.uk

£138 000 00   KAMEL.

£10 000   AIR CLEANERS

KEITH   WORTH IT   EVERYBODY
M   SCRIPT BOUNA US.   150 PEOPLE

WROTE TO Q   RB MARKHAM

CAME TO SEE ME

SEND CHEQUE 138

WINDOW TOOK IT

6 MONTHS LATER

WINDOW WHAT DO   NOT KNOW

SUGGEST GIVE NOR + AD.

THEN NO

THEN CHERIE GIVE.KAM; BUS

NIGE MADE ROBTIC TO SET CHEQ
    BEAT UP WINDOW

WOULDN'T GIVE IT BACK

I ENDORSED CHEQUE OVER

ASKED BACK   SAID NO.

NIGEL WANTED STATELY HOME

Old Bailey Press

The Old Bailey Press integrated student law library is tailor-made to help you at every stage of your studies from the preliminaries of each subject through to the final examination. The series of Textbooks, Revision WorkBooks, 150 Leading Cases and Cracknell's Statutes are interrelated to provide you with a comprehensive set of study materials.

You can buy Old Bailey Press books from your University Bookshop, your local Bookshop, direct using this form, or you can order a free catalogue of our titles from the address shown overleaf.

The following subjects each have a Textbook, 150 Leading Cases/Casebook, Revision WorkBook and Cracknell's Statutes unless otherwise stated.

Administrative Law
Commercial Law
Company Law
Conflict of Laws
Constitutional Law
Conveyancing (Textbook and 150 Leading Cases)
Criminal Law
Criminology (Textbook and Sourcebook)
Employment Law (Textbook and Cracknell's Statutes)
English and European Legal Systems
Equity and Trusts
Evidence
Family Law
Jurisprudence: The Philosophy of Law (Textbook, Sourcebook and
    Revision WorkBook)
Land: The Law of Real Property
Law of International Trade
Law of the European Union
Legal Skills and System
    (Textbook)
Obligations: Contract Law
Obligations: The Law of Tort
Public International Law
Revenue Law (Textbook,
    Revision WorkBook and
    Cracknell's Statutes)
Succession

Mail order prices:	
Textbook	£14.95
150 Leading Cases	£11.95
Revision WorkBook	£9.95
Cracknell's Statutes	£11.95
Suggested Solutions 1998–1999	£6.95
Suggested Solutions 1999–2000	£6.95
Suggested Solutions 2000–2001	£6.95
Law Update 2002	£9.95
Law Update 2003	£10.95

Please note details and prices are subject to alteration.

To complete your order, please fill in the form below:

Module	Books required	Quantity	Price	Cost
		Postage		
		TOTAL		

For Europe, add 15% postage and packing (£20 maximum).
For the rest of the world, add 40% for airmail.

ORDERING

By telephone to Mail Order at 020 8317 6039, with your credit card to hand.

By fax to 020 8317 6004 (giving your credit card details).

Website: www.oldbaileypress.co.uk

By post to: Mail Order, Old Bailey Press at Holborn College, Woolwich Road, Charlton, London, SE7 8LN.

When ordering by post, please enclose full payment by cheque or banker's draft, or complete the credit card details below. You may also order a free catalogue of our complete range of titles from this address.

We aim to despatch your books within 3 working days of receiving your order.

Name

Address

Postcode   Telephone

Total value of order, including postage: £

I enclose a cheque/banker's draft for the above sum, or

charge my   ☐ Access/Mastercard   ☐ Visa   ☐ American Express
Card number

☐☐☐☐ ☐☐☐☐ ☐☐☐☐ ☐☐☐☐

Expiry date   ☐☐☐☐

Signature: ....Date: ....